**Asia and the Secular**

# Religion and Its Others

―――

Studies in Religion, Nonreligion and Secularity

Edited by
Stacey Gutkowski, Lois Lee and Johannes Quack

# Volume 10

# Asia and the Secular

---

Francophone Perspectives in a Global Age

Edited by
Pascal Bourdeaux, Eddy Dufourmont,
André Laliberté and Rémy Madinier

**DE GRUYTER**

ISBN 978-3-11-152360-6
e-ISBN (PDF) 978-3-11-073306-8
e-ISBN (EPUB) 978-3-11-073309-9
ISSN 2330-6262

**Library of Congress Control Number: 2022935668**

**Bibliographic information published by the Deutsche Nationalbibliothek**
The Deutsche Nationalbibliothek lists this publication in the Deutsche Nationalbibliografie; detailed bibliographic data are available on the internet at http://dnb.dnb.de.

© 2024 Walter de Gruyter GmbH, Berlin/Boston
This volume is text- and page-identical with the hardback published in 2022.

www.degruyter.com

# Table of Contents

André Laliberté, Pascal Bourdeaux, Eddy Dufourmont, and Rémy Madinier
**Asian Secularism from Words to Concepts and Practices** —— 1

André Laliberté
**Entangled Multiple Modernities and the Variety of Secular States** —— 19

Jean Baubérot
**Laicity, Secularism, Secularization(s): A Few Hypotheses** —— 43

Peter van der Veer
**Secularism in Asia** —— 61

Rémy Madinier
**Pancasila in Indonesia a "Religious Laicity" Under Attack?** —— 71

Michel Picard
**Religion, Secularization, and Counter-Secularization in Bali** —— 93

Pascal Bourdeaux
**States, Religions and Modernities for one Nation: Historicizing a Converging Secularization in Twentieth Century Vietnam** —— 115

Aminah Mohammad-Arif
**Indian Secularism: an Original Accommodation of Religious Plurality Endangered from Within?** —— 145

Eddy Dufourmont
**The Imperial "Civil Religion" and *seikyō bunri*: The Historical Process of Secularization in Modern Japan, from the Perspective of "Confucianism" (1868–1945)** —— 163

Ji Zhe
**Chinese Interpretations of French Secularism in the Early Twentieth Century** —— 187

Bénédicte Brac de la Perrière
**'Religion' as an Issue in Political Transition: Two Competing Secularities in Buddhist Burma (Myanmar)** —— 205

Marie-Dominique Even
**A Twisted Secularity. Anti-Religious Ideology *vs* Secularity and Secularization in Twentieth Century Mongolia** —— 229

**Index** —— 245

André Laliberté, Pascal Bourdeaux, Eddy Dufourmont, and Rémy Madinier

# Asian Secularism from Words to Concepts and Practices

**Abstract:** The introduction seeks to achieve three things. It first wants to outline that the emergence and the circulation of the concepts of the secular state and the *Etat laïc* in the different regions of Asia is contingent on the vicissitudes of complex historical evolutions. Then, we emphasize the structuring effects of language in the evolution of the theoretical debates on relations between states and religions in Western society and the consequences of exporting such legacy in Asia. Finally, we situate the contributions to this book as part of an ongoing effort to establish through a philological analysis the genealogy of Asian secular states in their variety.

## 1 Introduction

If the idea of the secular state was a central issue in the twentieth century, the twenty-first sees rising questioning over its relevance, especially in Asia. The first half of the past century saw the last phase of colonial domination, which came with new technologies of power and new forms of sacredness, both religious and secular, to impose this power. Among these technologies, the administrative practice of a secular state was seen as usurping the authority of the religious elites or governing through them. The 1960s represented the high tide of theories about the 'Death of God' (Vahanian 1961) and the high point about the secular state, seen then by its supporters as the hallmark of progress and the search for a new international order in the global context of decolonization and the cold war. Majorities of the population in Western liberal democracies and in socialist states perceived that as true. Likewise in post-colonial societies like India and Mexico, as well as in non-Western societies where Islam has been a major marker of identity before modernist revolutions, as the case of Turkey illustrated. In just three decades, however, these certainties have withered away, as many have written about the emergence of the new realities of de-secularization and the re-enchantment of the world.[1] The historical dimension of secularization

---

[1] Keyes, Hardacre and Kendall (1994) argue that modernization in modern Asian states coincided with a return of the religious; as for Berger (1999), one of the most articulate proponents of

and the secular state, long a central narrative defining the Western world, has become an issue of contentious politics in many modern societies, in the West and beyond. This has coincided with advances in the discipline of religious studies in the last few decades, which includes deeper knowledge of 'world religions', along with demands for a more objective understanding of secularism and *laïcité*.

## 2 The Contingent Concepts of the Secular State and the *Etat Laïc*

The focus on the secular state in Asia presented in this book aims to enrich with empirical evidence two debates that have recently generated significant scholarship. The first of these two debates seeks to address the issue of 'our secular age', as articulated by Charles Taylor (2007). In his book, he points to the social, political, and philosophical condition of our times, in which religious belief represents an 'option' rather than a hegemonic and structuring factor of social life in contemporary societies that have grown out of the Western Christian tradition. Many have responded to Taylor's own admission that his philosophical approach does not make claims about the universal applicability of his interpretation of the secular to all contemporary societies and have tackled the challenge of looking beyond the West to understand whether we can find resonance with this secular age in Asia, the Middle East, and Africa.[2] Our project hones in on one specific aspect of that problem, as we look at one key feature of that secular age, the secular state, from Turkey to Japan. The second debate, which in essence prolongs the first one, seeks to investigate whether there existed beyond the West, and before modernity, antecedents to the condition of secularity, understood as the differentiation of the sphere of the religious from other spheres of social life, or the distinction between religion and other systems of society.[3]

---

secularization theory, he radically changed his approach and analysed the contemporary visibility of the religious as a process of "desecularization". Others (see Willaime 2006) view in these recent evolutions a phase of "ultramodernity" in which the high level of secularization reached by our societies has opened the way for a more pluralistic and alternative reconfiguration of religion and religiosity.

**2** For good examples of this, see the texts assembled by Kuenkler, Madeley, and Shankar (2018).
**3** For concise statements about that research agenda, see Burchardt, Wohlrab-Sahr, and Middell (2015), Burchardt and Wohlrab-Sahr (2012, 2013, 2017). A large research team has been working since on this issue on a global scale.

Our projects focus on the antecedent to the secular state in Asia, a key aspect of these processes of differentiation and/or distinction of religion.

Two ideal-types immediately come to mind when thinking about modalities of relations between religion and state: The Anglo-Saxon varieties of secularism, and French *laïcité*. Bringing a different perspective from the francophone epistemic community serves the broader objective of understanding the plural reality of secular states. Looking into the ways other nation-states, in this case in Asia, have assimilated or not these two models can bring nuance to this opposition between them. As we think about the 'secular', we cannot help thinking through associated concepts and distinguish between 'secularization' as a social process, 'secularity' as the sociological distinction between a sphere of the religious from other spheres of society,[4] or 'secularism' as the political philosophy promoting the institution of the secular state, often identified in French under the name '*laïcité*'.[5] In what follows, we focus on the latter.

To understand this last concept, it may help to start with Alessandro Ferrari (2009)'s distinction between "legal *laïcité*", which is a matter of positive law, and "narrative *laïcité*" which is the by-product of a discourse about the nation. The first of these two approaches broadly refer to the "Law of 1905 on Separation between Church and State, which sets up the legal and political regulations of religious pluralism. It is international to the extent that some of its provisions (namely Article 4) were inspired by foreign examples (Scotland, the nascent United States), and the Law of 1905 has inspired other legislations around the world (Baubérot 2017: 3). This approach of "legal *laïcité*" provides a relatively flexible framework which over decades has adapted to the evolution of French society and which the various denominations have accepted. This flexibility is illustrated by the fact that, for historical reasons, two departments (Alsace and Moselle) continue to enjoy the exemption provided by their own "specific regime for religions (*régime spécifique des cultes*)", distinct from the rest of the French Republic. In contrast to this flexible regime of "legal *laïcité*", "narrative *laïcité*" stands out as constitutive element of a discourse about France that stresses instances of conflicts to serve its project of shaping a national identity. Its role is not the organization of relations between religions and the state in a specific context, but rather to design the contours of a Republican civil religion. For over a century,

---

4 A long tradition of German sociology has discussed this distinction and the research team led by Wohlrab-Sahr and Kleine explores secularity in a global perspective, going back before the colonial era.
5 This approach is also predominant in the Hispanophone world. A good example of the work on *Laicidad* is the three volumes under the direction of Ugarte and Capdevielle (2013), and the work of Blancarte (2019).

this "narrative *laïcité*" has crystallized tensions and disagreements, originally over Catholicism, and more recently over Islam (Baubérot 2009). Because of some claim to universality on this issue, these debates have spilled beyond the borders of France. It is this latent aspiration of "narrative *laïcité*" to establish some form of sacredness that differs from the Anglo-Saxon approach to secularism, rather than the more pragmatic approach of "legal *laïcité*". Baubérot presents these distinctions in the next chapter.

The complicated relation between the French state with its Muslim citizens, and earlier with Protestants and Jews, has inspired many of us to reflect on the fact that the experience of France can also serve as a warning of what can turn wrong if the secular state tries to impose a too rigid legal framework for people who want to practice their religion. It is important to recall not only the difference between the two approaches to *laïcité* suggested above, but also the more fundamental discrepancies between secularization and the condition of secularity that is its ideal-typical endpoint (understood here in a Weberian sense), on the one hand, and that of the secular state and the *Etat laïc*, whether as the expression of a legal system or as grand narrative. Although widely used in English, lexically speaking 'the secular state' points to a form of ideology or political doctrine as well as to a mode of social-political regulation, which can induce some confusion with the sociological concept of secularization. Secularization, which implies a differentiation of the religious sphere from the legal and political sphere, and when this distinction is completed, a condition of secularity where social interaction is autonomous from the influence of religion, scares those who subscribe to a totalitarian view of religion. In this book, we do not hold a firm view on whether this condition of secularity has been reached or not in many Asian societies, but we are aware that many social forces who are opposed to this condition of secularization oppose the secular state, whatever form it takes.

Some scholars have debated the theory of secularization itself, its relevance, and its limits. In 1994, José Casanova questioned in *Public religions in the modern world* the reality as well as the theoretical relevance of the privatization of religion, reducing mostly the secularization paradigm to the criteria of the institutional differentiation of religion. In 'Secularism and its critics', the authors brought together by Rajeev Bhargava (1998) raised the issue of the Western-centric origins of the concept while promoting an Indian variant of the secular state that is respectful of local conditions. Bertrand Badie (2009) used the comparative historical- sociological method to explain the difficulty faced by the Southern shore of the Mediterranean to adopt the secular model left in place in postcolonial times. More recently, Ahmet Kuru (2009) conceptualized the differences between passive and assertive models of the secular states to discuss the challenges faced by the United States, France, and Turkey.

Although Bhargava has engaged in a decade-long dialogue with Charles Taylor to compare models of secular states that are truly global in scope, there has been too few attempts to engage in a genuine comparative dialogue. Bhargava (2004) underlined that when conceptualizing secularization and secularity in the broader context of non-Western trajectories, we ought to be careful not to overlook the exclusions that mark the self-understanding of religions and must maintain a critical posture towards religiously condoned practices limiting freedom and having undemocratic consequences. These debates, by questioning the limitations of the concept of secularism and its universality, in relation to the political, have pointed to the importance of paying attention to the local, the vernacular, and to value the research produced by local intellectuals in their own language. As Casanova wrote in an essay (2006), "(...) a proper rethinking of secularization will require a critical examination of the diverse patterns of differentiation and fusion of the religious and the secular and their mutual constitution across all world religions". The edited volume by Berman, Bhargava, and Laliberté (2013) aimed to launch a research agenda with a large-scale comparison between secular states in Asia, Europe, and North America informed by historical sociological analyses. Van der Veer (2016) questioned the centrality of religious models or state formations in the analysis of relations between the sphere of the religious and the state in non-Western societies. He promoted an understanding of these societies in their own terms, even though translation and interpretation of these terms had to consider their relation to western scholarship. Commenting that Asian religions such as Buddhism, Daoism, Hinduism, have emerged through interaction, he wrote that comparative studies should show "awareness of the conceptual difficulties in entering 'other' life worlds" (Van der Veer 2016: 11). He presents the latest implication of his idea in this volume.

The question arises: how relevant is the paradigm of the secular state for societies that were not under the influence of a Christian conception of the religious? How does that relate to other meaning-producing systems such as Islam, Hinduism, Buddhism, Daoism, Confucianism, and other Asian traditions, that often explicitly reject the naming of religion and oppose to it 'spirituality', 'philosophy', 'tradition', or 'culture'? How did local elites—religious or not—responded to this paradigm at different times, as their states and societies changed? Building on the wider recognition of religion as an important component of modern societies and on the variations between secularizing processes among Western societies,[6] we have found inspiration with the framework of multiple modernities proposed by Shmuel Eisenstadt (2000, 2003) to move beyond the West. This approach explores the different ways in which religion interacts with modernity in different cultures and societies developing 'multiple institutional and ideological patterns', moving beyond a hegemonic model of modernity defined by Christianity, which Marcel Gauchet (1985) famously saw as the religion that prepares the 'way out of religion'.

This brings back the usefulness of the conceptual distinction between legal and narrative *laïcité* because such a distinction can help understand the dynamics of resistance to the secular state more broadly. For the few states that are closer in their practice to the "legal *laïcité*" or legal-formal secularism described above, people of faith need not feel threatened by public authorities when they practice their faith. However, very few of the states in Asia have adopted this approach, and some of those that did so face contestation: India is now facing a clear and present threat against this approach with the *Hindutva* movement in power since 2014; Japan had to face that issue from ultra-conservative politicians early on. There exist multiple causes behind this opposition to the secular state and the temptation of other states to move in that direction, such as the Islamic Republic of Pakistan and the Kingdom of Thailand. A question that arises is to what extent these positions of hostility to the secular state express the fear of secularization mentioned above, or a misreading of the secular state as a broad principle into the most extreme attempts to implement that. Hence, the experience of many important Asian states that have adopted an authoritarian form of "narrative *laïcité*" may have fed these attitudes. This refers to the nominally socialist states of China, Vietnam, North Korea, and Laos, and not long ago of Cambodia and Mongolia, which appear openly hostile to the religious practice of the faithful. To what extent the practice of these states has strengthened the pushback against all forms of secular states remains an open question.

---

[6] With respect to Europe, the essays brought together by Lagrée and Portier (2010), demonstrate the role of religion, "an essential component in the modern social regulation, provided that it adheres to the demo-liberal ethos" [our translation]. As recalled by Portier in the introduction to the volume, in several modern European democracies, religion is not absent from the public sphere (as indicated by Germany's *Partnerschaft*, Great Britain' establishment or Belgium's *pillarization*), unlike the French model of strict legal separation.

## 3 Theoretical Debates on Relations between States and Religions

We start with the observation that linguistic differences matter. Even in societies that have developed in the common original crucible defined by the Greco-Roman and Judaic culture, considerable differences have emerged over centuries, to the point where a shared terminology has come to mean different realities. The French term 'culte' offers a good example. The French state, in accordance with the liberal principle that it does not have the right to determine for individuals what constitutes a religion or not, therefore excludes the term 'religion', which implies such power of determination, in its legislation. Officials use instead the neutral term *'culte'*, which does not carry in French the negative connotation seen in the word 'cults'. The equivalent of the latter, *'sectes'*, does represent a controversial issue comparable to that of its English equivalent. If something got lost in the translation of 'cults' and *'cultes'*, one can only imagine the difficulty in applying the concepts of the 'religious' and the 'secular' in cultures where an absence of differentiation between spiritual and political authority precluded the need for the emergence of this abstract distinction in the first place.

The practice of secularism in France also differs from that of the Anglo-Saxons for another important reason. The long history of conflict between a dominant Catholic Church and the state has left a legacy of disputes that contrasts with the history of accommodation between the state and the variety of churches in the United Kingdom, Northern Europe, and in the United States. Before the emergence of the modern nation-state in the nineteenth century, empires, kingdoms, dukedoms, and other smaller entities variously reacted to the hegemony of the Catholic Church during and to the Reformation that challenged it. Throughout the Northern part of the continent, a variety of states expressed different approaches about what it means to be Christian, and they differed in the way they supported a plurality of convictions.

In the UK, there is no strict separation between religion and state. Ahmet Kuru argued in his comparative study of the United States, France, and Turkey that the plurality of denominations in America made secularism a better option for minority religions than granting preferential treatment to one. In France, the Catholic Church had more to lose in the eighteenth to early twentieth centuries because it did not have religious competitors. The French approach to *laïcité*, as suggested above, has reverberated in other countries of romance language, where Catholicism prevails as the religion of the majority. Although there exist differences throughout Latin America in state relations to religions, from the state control enforced in Cuba to state endorsement of Catholicism as state religion for Costa Rica, the Catholic Church stands as the unavoidable actor. The paths to modernity discussed by André Laliberté in this book stress the importance of religions as key political actors that shape the relations established between them and states.

This linguistic observation brings home another key issue that guides all the chapters in this volume: it is the historicity of each countries approach to secularism. With or without this absence of a pre-colonial binary differentiation between the religious and the political spheres of social life, most societies of Asia had to come to term with different European power's own institutionalization of this difference during the colonial encounter. The nation-states that sought to impose their rule in Asian societies, moreover, achieved that at different times, with consequences that varied accordingly. Between the first attacks against the Nguyễn Dynasty in 1858 to end the persecution of foreign Catholic missionaries and Ho Chi Minh's attendance to the French Socialist Party's congress in 1920, the relations between the French Republic and the Catholic Church had changed dramatically, with the passing of the 1905 law on the Separation of the Churches and the State (*Loi concernant la séparation des Églises et de l'État*). Hence, the French *laïcité*, as Jean Baubérot explains in his contribution, has taken a variety of shapes since the break with the ancient regime and will continue to do so. Likewise, the biases and the blinders of researchers have changed over decades as they look at religion and state in Asia.

Much comparative studies of the relations between religion and the state in these cases have referred to the three Abrahamic religions: Christianity, Islam, and Judaism. The research about Christianity and politics has focused on Western Europe (Portier 2010; Willaime 2006) or North America (Wald and Calhoun-Brown 2018) the post-Soviet and mainly Eastern Orthodox space (Ramet 1998), and Latin America (Levine 2012), much less on Africa (Ellis and ter Haar 1998), and too little about Asia (Heuzé and Selim 1998; Heng and Liew 2010), even though the third largest Catholic country on the planet, the Philippines, is in that continent, and Pentecostal churches expand dramatically in that part of the world. Likewise, most studies of radical Islam focus on the Middle East and North Africa (MENA), although the historical emergence of that movement and its demographic center of gravity resides further East, in the Indian subcontinent and in the Malay world.

The approach of multiple paths to modernity, which seeks to decenter the idea of a Western origin to its constitutive elements such as the secular state, the welfare state, and liberal democracy, reckons with the importance of the colonial encounter in its economic and political dimensions, with profound cultural consequences. At the intersection of the latter two, nationalism and the aspiration of establishing a strong state stands out. Peter van der Veer has long examined the issue of religion in a broad Asian context during the colonial encounter, considering the differences between Indic and Sinitic Asia. In this volume, he highlights the crucial connection between nationalism and the choices states have made when they choose their own modalities of relationships with religious authorities. The nationalist ideals, as articulated by people in their vernacular and nourished by their own traditions, have developed in a colonial context where the languages, the concepts, and the worldviews of the metropole exercised some influence. How much was it determinant? How much the British, Dutch, and French legacies differ? How much the pre-colonial shared legacy of Confucianism, Islam, and the Indic tradition transcended the colonial influences? Paying attention to comparative histories shall help answering these questions.

The second contribution of this book is to move beyond the area shaped by the monotheistic religions, to areas in which they have not yet erased pre-existing religions. Our empirical studies focus on an area influenced by the Hindu-Buddhist and Confucian traditions, and moreover in many cases some of them reckon with the impact of Islam before the colonial era, as well as the legacy of indigenous religious traditions such as Shamanism and Shintoism. The contributions to this volume look at whether the religions and traditions of Asia, with their immanent frame, can open possibilities for a third way between religious authority and that of the secular state. One could observe that even in a country such as Indonesia, where the monotheistic religions are majoritarian, they have spread over centuries in a society previously influenced by Hinduism and Buddhism, on top of previous religions, a sedimentation of religious traditions that gave Indonesian Islam and its politics their specific characteristics.

The coverage of Asia in this book includes countries with a wide range of historical experience: in terms of their experience with the colonial encounter, this includes ex-colonies such as India, Burma, Indonesia, and Vietnam; ex-colonial powers such as Japan; and states that have avoided direct Western colonial rule altogether such as China and Mongolia. These countries differ in their politics: from authoritarian Leninist China and Vietnam to liberal democratic Japan. It is striking that despite similarities in terms of religious diversity in most of these societies, the nature of political regimes appeared to have mattered more in the choice of approaches to *laïcité:* state corporatist control of a limited number of legalized religions in the authoritarian regimes vs. a more *laisser-faire* attitude in the liberal regimes.

Hence, religious diversity throughout East Asia, which sees indigenous religions such as Daoism in China and Taiwan, Shinto in Japan, and Shamanism in the Korean peninsula, co-exist with Buddhism, Christian minorities, and new religious movements, does not coincide with the approaches adopted by governments. The paired contrasts between China and Taiwan, between the two Koreas, or even between the two Vietnams before 1975, show contrasting attitudes in governments' attitudes towards religions despite shared cultural attributes such as a common language and esthetics. Likewise, colonial rule alone did not appear to have influenced decisively the choices of governments in their design for a secular state: the contrast between the trajectories of India and Pakistan since their independence comes to mind.

Most of the populations in the states that we discuss in this book adheres to polytheist religions, if we add up the populations of China, India, Japan, and Vietnam. Even in societies such as Burma/Myanmar and Mongolia where a majority professes Buddhism, the religious beliefs, which include the worship of different bodhisattva, arhats, and categories of spirits, and the ritual practices, differ from those of monotheistic religions. Some Asian countries can be grouped into clusters of societies where much of the population adheres to monotheistic religions, as in the Middle East and Southeast Asia. However, in the case of the latter, the monotheism of Islam (dominant in Malaysia and Indonesia) and Catholicism (which prevails in the Philippines), represents another episode in the long history of religious change in that part of the world where the legacies of Chinese religions, Buddhism, and Hinduism have submerged the indigenous original traditions.

The dominant perceptions for many years have opposed a deeply religious Southern Asia, influenced by Islam, Hinduism, and Buddhism, to a more secularized region of the world where the tradition of Confucianism has imposed over centuries a humanistic outlook to the civilizations of China and its immediate neighbors in Japan, Korea, and Vietnam. Each of the chapters in this book question this view, as they show the importance of religious issues in these societies. The resurgence of religion also affects countries of East Asia, as the multiple sources of conflicts over religion in China demonstrate. This includes the continued resistance of the Falungong to the Chinese Communist Party, the assaults on the rights of Uyghurs to practice Islam, the limitations to Chinese Christians' practice of their religions, and the attempts to promote as 'intangible heritage' to the UNESCO Buddhism, Daoism, and Chinese Traditional Medicine, decades after they have been attacked as 'feudal superstitions'.

An important scholarship has covered the nature and history of the different religious traditions in Asia. However, one issue remains slightly less explored in that scholarship: that of the secular state. Although the current governments of many Asian states like to insist on the specificity of their history to explain their approach to the secular state, ranging from its embrace in the most authoritarian form, as in China and Vietnam, or its rejection, as in Indonesia, the intellectual ferment that blossomed in the first half of the twentieth century suggests there were many possible trajectories each of these countries could have adopted as they sought to establish a modern state and as Asian intellectuals paid attention to the variety of Western approaches to the secular state adopted by different colonial powers.

The contributions to this volume tackle this issue. It is divided into two sections accordingly. On the one hand, it presents the type of questions that a focus on *laïcité* can bring: it discusses the different types of possible *laïcités*, multiple paths to the secular state shaped by the Asian dominant civilizations, and the consequences of colonial rule. The second part includes the contributions from ethnographies deeply embedded in local realities. They look at the extent to which the specific trajectories of the secular state or the debates that surround its establishment can validate the discussion in the previous section. The next section expands on the existing debate about the secular state and the *Etat laïc* and illustrates this by presenting the salient points discussed by each case studies presented in this volume.

# 4 A Genealogy of Asian Secular States through Language and Translations

A central issue for all the contributors to this volume and to all those who work on the relevance of the secular state is knowledge of national political histories, a context that determine the choices that governments have made. For many of them, such as India, Indonesia, Vietnam, Burma, and the states in the Middle East, this means paying attention to the colonial period, when European powers imposed new concepts on relation between religion and state through the enforcement of legal systems that superseded customary laws and undermined traditional authority, whether religious or political, or both. Paying attention to national debates also bring to light the experiences of China and Japan, which confronted colonial rule indirectly: In the case of China, via the privileges of extra-territoriality granted to citizens of Western powers and Japan, following outside pressures; in the case of Japan, in the response by the national bureaucracy to threats by British and American colonial powers. In each case, the colonial encounter meant superimposition of new norms of relations between political and religious authorities on societies in which these two sources of authorities were intertwined or differentiated to different degrees, if not fused together. In other words, paying attention to the effects of colonial rule recalls the necessity to better understand the specificities of pre-colonial societies.

The colonial encounter, by bringing together many different societies under the same legal-bureaucratic apparatus, meant attempts to homogenize conceptually heterogenous populations across continents unprecedented in scale because of their span over multiple continents. Colonial powers differed in their approach in Asia: The British rulers used the approach of *divide et impera* to manage the multiples components of their empire: Following the transfer of authority from the British East India Company to the British Crown after the 1857 Rebellion, they combined direct rule with protectorates established over princely states, which represented 23 percent of the Raj. The Dutch and French empires used a more direct form of rules, albeit they arrived there in stages, with the various trading posts of the Dutch East India Company coming under the direct administration of the Batavian Republic executive power in 1800 and the fractious Third French Republic bringing together five protectorates under the single entity of French Indochina in 1887. Mongolia stood out of the Western influence until the twentieth century: under the control of the Qing empire until 1911, it gained independence as the Bogd Khanate of Mongolia before falling into the influence of the Soviet Union in 1924 and experienced a different approach to the secular state.

The societies in which the European powers imposed their ideas about the way political power should interact with religion had often experienced centuries of what would become later known as religious diversity and meant then the existence of competing sources of religious authority. Between the Islamic and Indic worlds, Indonesia provides a good example of a secular state possible in a society where monotheistic religions of transcendence co-exist with religions of immanence so pervasive from India to Japan. Rémy Madinier argues that the Indonesian state, which governs the most populous Islamic community in the planet, has managed to pre-empt challenges from the most radical fringes of Islamic groups thanks to the state institutionalization of a religious framework, the national ideology of *Pancasila*, which makes good use of the resources of the country's Indo-Buddhic religious heritage. The religious engineering imposed by the state, up to a point, evokes the French approach to *laïcité*, which has imposed on religions conformity to a centralized model of governance, in exchange for legal recognition.

The chapter by Michel Picard presents another example of the Indonesian approach to the secular state: his case study demonstrates how much the Hindu tradition had to adapt to the new institutionalization of relation between state and *agama*. The doctrine of *Pancasila*, more than an attempt to solve a nonexisting conflict between religion and politics in the region, served the national construction. A local belief, the Balinese religion, had to emphasize its affiliation with Hinduism to obtain the status of recognized religion. The starting point of

Picard's comparative study is the paradigm of the invention of religions. He illustrates this by tracing the genealogy from indigenous religious tradition to the use of modern categories of religion, under the influence of orientalism and the project of nation-building. Terms from the Indian lexicon such as *agama* and *dharma* have been redefined historically and locally as they entered in contact with Islamic thought and modern political concepts. This chapter shows how the Balinese élites have tried to self-define their ritualized cultural and religious traditions in the modern context of a centralized state that has imposed on them official relations on a par with those that the majoritarian religion has established.

India represents an interesting case, as it has received its fair share of attention as a secular state (Bhargava 1998) decades ago, before the *Hindutva* movement emerged as a challenge. Amina Mohammad-Arif discusses in this volume the historical significance of this change. The only country where the Hindu tradition is predominant, this singularity has called into attention whether the plurality of that tradition had, until recently, predestined India to be secular. She contextualizes the emergence of secularism in contemporary India. She examines the prehistory of the term. Bearing in mind terminological issues, she then addresses the specificities of secularism in India using two parameters, the (non)interference of the state and citizenship. She concludes with an attempt to decipher the "nature" or type of this secularism by drawing on some of the "global theories" with which the present volume is concerned. In the process, she discusses how Hindu nationalists undermine secularism without being unconstitutional.

Japan represents an original case in East Asia. Many of its institutions represent adaptation to the local context of institutions developed during the Tang Dynasty in China. However, the attempt at a forced opening by Anglo-American led to a rapid appropriation by Japanese modernizing elites of the institutions that they believed necessary to achieve power. The adoption of secularism qua freedom of religion differed radically from the French model or any other European nation to the extent that it promoted the local tradition of Shinto as a de facto state religion superimposed on a regime of freedom of religion. The American occupation after the defeat of 1945 changed this situation but the tension between the new model of secular state and the return to the situation prevailing before the war remains. In Japan, the issue of *laïcité* does not reach dramatic consequences comparable to China, but nevertheless also constitute a key aspect of nation building. For conservative politicians in the ruling Liberal Democratic Party and for a vocal minority on the far right, a key objective remains the removal of provisions that enshrine secularism in the constitution, on the grounds that this was imposed by the US during their occupation after the war. Eddy Dufourmont traces the origins of these controversies before the war, in the crucial decades at the onset of the Meiji restoration that saw Japan laid down the foundations that would ensure it become in a few years a major power.

China has also enforced an extremely strict separation between religion and state. However, the road to that institutional arrangement has been a tortuous one, as explains Ji Zhe in this exploration of the debates around the French approach to the secular state in Republican China. He explains that the founders of the post-imperial regime neglected to pay attention to the key component of freedom of conscience, unfortunately for religious believers and free thinkers. The Republic of China, which relocated in Taipei after its defeat in 1949, would gradually open to this reality in Taiwan during the process of democratization and shows that the secular state qua freedom of conscience is possible in Sinitic societies. However, for much of the Chinese population, the only experience of the secular state they know represents a Chinese actualization of the most extreme version of what the anti-clerical and militant atheists in the French Communist Party could have dreamed about. Finally, the experience of China poses the greatest challenge. A sui generis case, it has influenced in its imperial past the immediate neighbors of Korea, Vietnam, and Japan. The colonial encounter, in the Treaty Ports at the margins of the continental Qing Empire, did not shape the regime of relations between state and religion. The change came through a slow pace of successive revolutions where the idea of secularism found rather shallow roots because in the absence of a deeply entrenched cognate concept of religion qua institution, the idea of secularism as separation between religion and state was problematic conceptually.

Another society culturally close to China, Vietnam, has directly experienced the approach of the French Republic to religion. The legacy of the colonial influence was complicated because the divisions in France over the separation between religion and state was reproduced in colonial Indochina, with proponents of Catholic missions in Asia and supporters of the secular ideology of development were at odds with each other about the content of what they believe was France's *"mission civilisatrice."* These debates unfolded in a society, like China, best characterized as religiously diverse, and one where the monarchy's authority had been intertwined with religious institutions for centuries. Pascal Bourdeaux situates the complexity of the contemporary Vietnamese religious policies as the concatenation of these multiple influences. He reveals that although colonial rule, and after its demise, the socialist regime, have sought to eliminate the older modes of interaction between religious and political authorities, they have not entirely succeeded. In his essay, Bourdeaux describes the many specificities of the Vietnamese situation, including the pre-colonial political-religious thought and their readaptation in colonial and postcolonial modernity. An important aspect of the Vietnamese approach to the secular state is its dual experiment with two distinctive modes during the two decades of political division in 1955–1975.

Bénédicte Brac de la Perrière goes beyond Taylor's query about how "secularism travels", and instead of questioning the relevance of this concept outside of the Western intellectual climate and the monotheistic religions from which it has emerged, she inverts the perspective. She argues that making sense of the Burmese religio-political situation must use as a starting point the local philosophical traditions of Indian monism and Buddhist non-dualist trends. She suggests that asking how the political and religious élites wish to define secularity reveals new perspectives on debates about sacred nationalism, and through this prism, about the nature of the state and the roles played by the military. It also sheds light on religious violence, religious and political pluralism, and what space Theravada Buddhist societies grant to secular actors and their worldly activities.

This situation contrasts with the case of Mongolia discussed by Marie-Dominique Even, where the anti-religious war waged on Buddhism by the communist regime in the 1930s hardly compares, she contends, with forms of secularization in liberal contexts, despite being generally referred to as such. During the Mongol empire, the Mongols experienced religious diversity, then religious monopoly when lay Mongol rulers invited Tantric Buddhist masters to convert their subjects and associate closely with the state. In 1911, breaking away from their Manchu suzerains, the Mongols fell back on the same model of dual governance, going a step further by enthroning as khan a high Buddhist reincarnation. Due to religion's pervasiveness in all social spheres and to the slow pace of modernization and education, Buddhism and Mongolia remained intrinsically linked. Nevertheless, separation of state and religion was proclaimed in the first constitution (1924) under pressure from its Soviet protector. A totalitarian turning point a few years later opened the way to the violent eradication of Buddhism and the spread of a more exclusive, compulsory, and all-encompassing faith in scientific atheism and communist utopia. A far cry from the freedom of conscience underlying the project of a secular state. Indeed, this basic element had to be mentioned in the legal texts but with no effect until the building of a state with the rule of law in 1990–1992. While separation between state and religious organizations and the freedom of belief are enshrined in the 1992 constitution, secularization of the minds and internal secularization of the Buddhist institution, frozen in time during communism, is an on-going process.

## 5 Conclusion

This volume contributes to the growing literature on the secular state by paying attention to the effects of the Chinese, Japanese, Malay, Indian, Turkic, Arabic, and European languages, on how post-colonial states thought about their development as secular states, such as Mongolia, or refused to go that way, as was the case with Indonesia. The attention to language will also put into stark relief, in the three East Asian case studies of China, Japan, and Vietnam, why it became so difficult for these states to institutionalize secular states in ways that are acceptable to the local population, as in Japan, or to international legal norms of freedom of conscience, as in China and Vietnam. Finally, the attention to language will also bring to light that even in countries shaped by English, local idioms have emerged with counter-discourses that question the principles of secularism in its liberal foundations.

## References

Badie, Bertrand. 2009. *Les deux États*. Paris: Fayard.
Baubérot, Jean. 2009. "L'évolution de la laïcité en France: entre deux religions civiles". *Diversité urbaine* 9 no. 1: 9–25.
Baubérot, Jean. 2017. *Histoire de la laïcité en France*. Paris: Presses Universitaires de France.
Bhargava, Rajeev, ed. 1998. *Secularism and its Critics*. Delhi: Oxford University Press.
Bhargava, Rajeev. 2004. "India's Model: Faith, Secularism, and Democracy". *Open Democracy* (November 3). https://beta.opendemocracy.net/en/article_2204jsp/ (Accessed December 17, 2021).
Bhargava, Rajeev. 2010. "The 'Secular Ideal' before Secularism: A Preliminary Sketch". In L. E. Cady and E. S. Hurd, eds., *Comparative Secularisms in a Global Age*, pp. 159–180. New York, NY: Palgrave Macmillan.
Blancarte, Roberto. 2019. *La república laica en México*. Mexico: XXI siglo veintiuno editores.
Bubandt, Nils and Martijn Van Beek, eds. 2012. *Varieties of Secularism in Asia, Anthropological Explorations of Religion, Politics and the Spiritual*. London: Routledge.
Burchardt, Marian and Monika Wohlrab-Sahr. 2012. "Multiple Secularities: Toward a Cultural Sociology of Secular Modernities". *Comparative Sociology* 11: 875–909.
Burchardt, Marian and Monika Wohlrab-Sahr. 2013. "Introduction: Multiple Secularities: Religion and Modernity in the Global Age". *International Sociology* (special issue) 28 no. 6 (November): 605–611.
Burchardt, Marian and Monika Wohlrab-Sahr. 2017. *Revisiting the Secular: Multiple Secularities and Pathways to Modernity*. Working Paper Series, Leipzig University, HCAS "Multiple Secularities Beyond the West, Beyond Modernities".
Burchardt, Marian, Monika Wohlrab-Sahr and Matthias Middell, eds. 2015. *Multiple Secularities Beyond the West: Religion and Modernity in the Global Age*. Berlin: De Gruyter.

Casanova, José. 1994. *Public Religions in the Modern World*. Chicago: University of Chicago Press.
Casanova, José. 2006. "Rethinking secularization. A global comparative perspective". *The Hedgehog Review* 6 (Spring & Summer): 7–22.
Eisenstadt, Schmuel Noah. 2000. "The Reconstruction of Religion Arenas in the Framework of Multiple Modernities". *Millenium* 29 no. 3: 591–612.
Eisenstadt, Schmuel. 2003. "Introduction: Comparative Studies and Sociological Theory from Comparative Studies to Civilizational Analysis: Autobiographical Notes". In Schmuel Eisenstadt, ed., *Comparative Civilizations and Multiple Modernities*, pp. 1–28. Leiden, NL: Brill.
Ferrari, Alessandro. 2009. "De la politique à la technique: laïcité narrative et laïcité du droit. Pour une comparaison France/Italie". In Brigitte Basdevant-Gaudemet and François Jankowiak, eds., *Le droit ecclésiastique de la fin du XVIIIe au milieu du XXe siècle en Europe*, pp. 333–345. Leuven, BE: Peeters.
Gauchet, Marcel. 1985. *Le désenchantement du monde: Une histoire politique de la religion*. Paris: Gallimard.
Ellis, Stephen and Gerrie ter Haar. 1998. "Religion and Politics in Sub-Saharan Africa". *Journal of Modern African Studies* 36 no. 2: 175–201.
Heng, Michael Siam Heng and Ten Chin Liew eds. 2010. *State and secularism: perspectives from Asia*. Hackensack, NJ: World Scientific.
Heuzé, Gérard and Monique Selim, eds. 1998. *Politique et religion dans l'Asie du Sud contemporaine*. Paris: Éditions Karthala.
Keyes, Charles F., Helen Hardacre and Laurel Kendall. 1994. *Asian Visions of Authority: Religion and the Modern States of East and Southeast Asia*. Honolulu, HI: University of Hawai'i Press.
Kuenkler, Mirjam, John Madeley, and Shylashri Shankar, eds. 2018. *A Secular Age beyond the West: Religion, Law and the State in Asia, the Middle East, and North Africa*. New York: Cambridge University Press.
Kuru, Ahmet T. 2009. *Secularism and State Policies toward Religion: The United States, France, and Turkey*. New York: Cambridge University Press.
Lagrée, Jacqueline and Philippe Portier, eds. 2010. *La Modernité contre la religion? Pour une nouvelle approche de la laïcité*. Rennes: Presses Universitaires de Rennes.
Levine, Daniel H. 2012. *Politics, Religion, and Society in Latin America*. Boulder, CO: Lynne Rienner Publishers.
Portier, Philippe. 2010. "L'essence religieuse de la modernité politique. Eléments pour un renouvellement de la théorie de la laïcité". In Jacqueline Lagrée et Philippe Portier, eds. *La modernité contre la religion? Pour une nouvelle approche de la laïcité*, pp. 7–26. Rennes: Presses universitaires de Rennes.
Ramet, Sabrina Petra. 1998. *Nihil Obstat: Religion, Politics, and Social Change in East-Central Europe and Russia*. Durham, NC: Duke University Press.
Taylor, Charles. 2007. *A Secular Age*. Boston, MA: Harvard University Press.
Ugarte, Pedro Salazar and Pauline Capdevielle, eds. 2013. *Para entender y pensar la laicidad*. México: UNAM.
Vahanian, Gabriel. 1961. *The Death of God: The Culture of Our Post-Christian Era*. New York, NY: G. Braziller.

van Der Veer, Peter. 2001. *Imperial Encounters, Religion and Modernity in India and Britain*. Princeton, NJ: Princeton University Press.
van Der Veer, Peter. 2013. *The Modern Spirit of Asia. The Spiritual and the Secular in China and India*. Princeton, NJ: Princeton University Press.
Wald, Kenneth D. and Allison Calhoun-Brown. 2018. *Religion and Politics in the United States*, eighth edition. Lanham, MD: Rowman and Littlefield.
Willaime, Jean-Paul. 2006. "La sécularisation: une exception européenne? Retour sur un concept et sa discussion en sociologie des religions". *Revue française de sociologie*, 47 no. 4: 755–783.

André Laliberté
# Entangled Multiple Modernities and the Variety of Secular States

**Abstract:** In this chapter I present the framework of multiple modernities, as developed by Eisenstadt, as a heuristic approach to appreciate the diversity of communities of shared meaning that large populations have developed about the influence should religions exercise or not in their societies and how political authority ought to manage that. I argue that a great analytical and political challenge is to resist the view that the idioms developed within each of the inter-subjective communities of Sinitic, Indic, Buddhist, and Indo-Malay modernities determine the choices societies have made about regimes of relations between religious and political authorities. I illustrate this point by drawing attention to the wide diversity of approaches to the ideal-types of secular states, states with a religious establishment, and states with multiple religious establishment, adopted within each of the four main approaches to modernity seen in Asia since the end of the colonial era.

# 1 Introduction

In this essay, I propose a critical appropriation of the multiple modernities theory that preserves its emancipatory potential for a global perspective on modernity and in particular, the institution of the secular state, understood as a state that guarantees the exercise of freedom of conscience.[1] This constructive critique of multiple modernities aims at the ongoing risk that the theory can lend legitimacy to cultural relativism.[2] For the early exponents of that theory, the Western world had established a precedent for modernity, but non-Western societies would modernize following their own patterns, determined by their respective cultural legacies. That theory originally appeared emancipatory in its rejection of Western hegemony, by suggesting that non-Western societies did not have to imitate the West to become modern. However, the rise at the global level of

---
[1] See the discussion of Roberto Blancarte, 2007.
[2] Therefore, this critique differs from that of Schmidt 2016, who advocated a critique based on political economy.

---
**André Laliberté** (University of Ottawa, GSRL)

https://doi.org/10.1515/9783110733068-002

nationalism and religious fundamentalism have led to the diminishing appeal of that theory, seen as an intellectual legitimation for their rise.[3] Some movements advocating these ideologies openly rejected modernity altogether while others, after changing its original meaning, used it to legitimate their own claims of uniqueness. The political hegemony or the rise to prominence of these ideologies has tragically obscured the fact that the values of modernity also matter for large segments of societies outside of the West.

The idea that societies with diverse cultures modernize each in their own way because their capabilities differ from each other does not predetermine their future path to modernity. Even if a fusion of horizon may appear distant, there is still a possibility of a convergence towards some key values, such as human rights, social justice, gender equality, respect for minorities, and, with respect to this chapter, freedom of conscience. In this essay, I propose that the theory of multiple modernities represents a useful tool to identify communities of inter-subjective meaning that can agree on the main terms of debates about the secular state, but that this cannot determine the choices made by social actors. To illustrate this, I will first use Eisenstadt's approach to multiple modernities and elaborate on the different paths to these modernities that one finds in Asia, starting with the main Sinitic, Indic, and Islamic paths, defined by the dominant worldviews in these societies. Then, I present a typology of the variety of secular states found in Asia, to demonstrate that there is no link between the multiple paths to modernity identified by Eisenstadt and the choices made to establish secular states or to adopt different approaches to religion.

## 2 Multiple Modernities as Emancipation and the Problem with Neo-traditionalist Ideologies

The idea of multiple 'modernities' refers to the specific concept of 'modernity' as it has developed in different civilizational area. The concept of 'modernity' refers to a specific temporality defined by material as well as cultural change. The concept has received criticism as a teleological perspective and as an ethno-centric view, on the ground that it has long posited emergence in Western Europe before

---

**3** This diminishing does not mean that the theory is ignored. The GSRL has organized in the Spring of 2019 a debate on the idea of multiple modernities with Jean-Paul Willaime and Philippe Portier. Furthermore, the research team with which I am associated in Leipzig, and which works on the issue of multiple secularities beyond the West, has explicitly made clear the linkage with the theory of multiple modernities. See Burchardt, Wohlrab-Sahr and Middel 2015.

becoming global in scope in the wake of colonialism. Earlier cultural analysis tended to look at the historical sequences from conflicts between church and state, to the rise of the nation-state, industrialization, liberal democracy, the welfare state, and market consumerism, a unique trajectory against which to measure other societies that have yet to arrive at that stage. The concept of 'multiple modernity' emerged from the obvious realization that such a sequential development cannot work in many societies where there is no church or its equivalent. Yet, as the recent history of Japan and the (re-) emergent giants of China and India reveal, most countries in Asia are establishing themselves as nation-states, welfare regimes, and a variety of capitalist market economies. They have arrived there through processes of self-determination resulting from the colonial encounter, either through direct colonial rule or in response to it, but also as result of tensions within each civilizational area between different social forces. Below, as I describe the different paths to modernity, I will outline the civilizational foundations out of which they have emerged and trace their own origins.

In this section, I have chosen to look at multiple modernities as ontology, that is, as the plurality of the historical trajectories travelled by societies that may share concerns for the global commons but also may interact and compete against each other in the world capitalist economy. The global convergence embraced by liberal philosophers faces rejection by their conservative counterparts, whether nationalist or religious, who believe in the irreconcilability of so-called national interests or in the impossibility of bridging theological and ideological differences without losing identity. I focus on the institution of the secular state, which constitutes the key issue in the disputes between those who believe in the possibility of reaching a global Rawlsian overlapping consensus on the secular state, and those who reject that option as against their idea of the national interest or even as a matter of evil. I understand the 'secular state' in this essay as one that protects freedom of conscience, that is, the idea that to believe or not is an option and not an obligation,[4] rather than more narrowly the institutional concept of separation between church and state,[5] or the state's principled distance from religion.[6] That being said, I do no count as secular states the People's Republic of China (PRC) and similar political regimes of state control of religion, which often violate freedom of conscience, even if they ostensibly claim a separation between religion and state.

---

[4] This position is closer to that of Taylor 2007.
[5] I refer here to the work of Kuru's comparison between the American, French, and Turkish models of secularism.
[6] This is the position of Bhargava 2013 on India's secularism.

The perspective of multiple modernities has received a fair amount of criticism because in its attempt to 'decenter' modernity, it has been at risk of legitimizing political projects that are illiberal and reject freedom of conscience outright as a foreign imposition. Originally conceived as a corrective to the Western-centric discourse on the origins of the secular state and related norms such as liberalism, democracy, and human rights, this perspective, as outlined by Eisenstadt (1999), questioned the teleology that attributed to Protestant Christianity the origins of modernity. Scholars brought together by Tu Wei-ming (1996) pointed to the East Asian 'economic miracle' and the nascent democracies of Taiwan and South Korea to vindicate the view that modernity could be rooted in other cultures. However, almost twenty years later, as China under its leader Xi Jinping rejects 'Western notions' such as constitutionalism and the rule of law and laud an authoritarian version of Confucianism, the appeal of multiple modernities has waned (Ringen 2018). Likewise, the rise to power of a vindictive movement promoting a Hindu revival critical of the secular state as a foreign import casts doubts about the meaning of non-Western modernity in India, the third largest economy in the world (Nag 2014). The same question had emerged before for Islam after the Iranian revolution, which saw both the Islamic revolution in that country and the export of Salafism by the Saudi Kingdom, promoting a muscular rebuttal to the secular state, then seen as a tool of Western hegemony (al-Azmeh 2009). These politically authoritarian and religiously intolerant assertions of non-Western modernity have understandably given a bad name to multiple modernities.

On the other hand, the retreat into the arrogant affirmation that the West leads the way in a universal modernity is becoming untenable, as China is about to overtake the United States and Western Europe in the leadership of the world economy, space exploration, artificial intelligence, and internet communication. The American claim to embody modernity appears even more dubious when considering the disproportionate influence that a vocal minority of climate-skeptic, anti-vaccination, and flat-earth believers exercise on the political system of the United States. Meanwhile, the increasingly popular illiberal political parties that oppose immigration in the name of protecting values such as secularism seriously undermines the soft power of Western Europe's modernity. These issues remind us that the problem that the concept of multiple modernities sought to address in the first place, the attitude that rejects the 'rest' as deficient in modernity, remains as present as ever. In this essay, I adopt the position that the secular state *qua* freedom of conscience, or the right to believe or not to believe, and change one's view on the matter, constitutes a universal right, but the practical political challenge remains to make this concept resonant with the *genus* of diverse cultures rather than an imposition resulting from outside political subordination.

Before salvaging whatever remains of the emancipatory potential of multiple modernities, it matters to recall what it reacted to in the first place. This perspective reacted to the self-serving perspective according to which Western modernity and the secular state were revolutionary and had universal validity because, among others, they put an end to the idea of the unquestioned authority of religious hierarchies in the affairs of society.[7] According to this narrative, the norm of the secular state has spread through colonialism in the Americas, then in Asia and Africa, making Western modernity global in scope. This reading of world history construes the rise of Islamic fundamentalism as resistance to modernity, and looks at the present travails experienced by India, as it faces the challenge of Hindu nationalism to its secular constitution, as an attempt to go backward and reject modernity. In relation to China, this approach positions that country as a late-comer, and when it recognizes the specificities of its modernity, it sees it, at best, as a derivative path to modernity, or at worst, as an unfinished, or even as an unrealized modernity. This reading of world history suggests that societies shaped by Islamic, Indic, and Chinese culture are laggard, or worst, that these cultures are inherently deficient and unlikely to experience a liberal form of modernity, as their religious and nationalist clamour seem to demonstrate, notwithstanding the importance of voices expressing the defence of liberal values in the same societies.

The perspective of multiple modernities reacted to this demeaning interpretation of non-Western history, by questioning the dominant, Euro-centric narrative. It started with the observation that Western modernity reveals a succession of crises in contexts of uncertainty, and the absence of a predetermined trajectory, only *ex post facto* justification of new political orders. There is no long march to secular modernity but a succession of crises, changes, and ruptures. Defined by opposition between sacred authority and secular power, enlightened despotism and popular sovereignty, state dirigisme and market economy, fascism and Stalinism, laissez-faire and welfare state, modernity includes all these elements, all in constant tension. The wide ranges of different societies between the liberal United States and the social democratic Sweden express this diversity within Western modernity. From Latin America to Central Europe and Oceania, it stretches a vast space, and its influence, because of colonialism, has been global in its reach. By its very nature as a succession of conflicts, therefore, contempo-

---

[7] I am aware that the post-colonial critique has challenged the discourse on Western modernity, but it pays little attention to religion and the secular state.

rary modernity can only be multiple, and the experience of the Western world alone cannot capture it in its entirety. The sociologist Schmuel Eisenstadt (2000a) coined the concept of multiple modernities to describe this reality better. Inspired by the sociology of Weber and his view of the Protestant reformation in the 'disenchantment of the world', he agreed that the separation between spiritual authority and political power constituted a key tension in the emergence of Western modernity. He also sees its consequences as resonating today, in the continuing tensions between religious movements and the variety of secular states within Western Europe and North America.

Eisenstadt furthermore took distance from mainstream theories with his argument that in societies where Christianity was not part of ancient history, the trajectories of modernity experienced in these various parts of the world were bound to be different. He picked from the philosopher Karl Jaspers the idea of axial religions and their influence in the shaping of different civilizations, and the idea of how the former have continued to affect the latter as they faced the challenge of Western civilizations (Eisenstadt 2000b). Hence, he looked at the traditions of Islam, Hinduism, Buddhism, and Confucianism, as sources of public morality and normative ideas. Most importantly, however, applying to these civilizations the same method he used for the West, he looked at each of these civilizations as a series of contradictions, conflicts, crises, and disagreements over the practical consequences of their central spiritual, ethical, and philosophical core traditions. In other words, for him and other promoters of this concept of multiple modernities, each of these civilizations had gone through its own process of change (Preyer 2013). Civilizations, spreading wide in time and space, have influenced each other, and all of them have been in contact with Western modernity. The global modernity that is unfolding before our eyes is not converging to an agreed upon script, according to this perspective. However, this indetermination does not mean that each approach to modernity will evolve towards irreconcilable horizons.

The multiple voices celebrating the resilience and the importance of the various spiritual traditions of the world outside of the West will continue to nourish political debates. They argue that these traditions are still shaping the nature of politics today. Whether it is the idea of the nation and its values, the views on the role of government in providing social services to the poor and the vulnerable, the acceptance of diversity, or the ends and means of society, they are influencing the public discourse, through the selective use of traditions by governments and their opponents. The impact of Western modernity, moreover, remains important as a major 'other' in relation to which each modernity interacts, often defensively. One striking characteristic of the present age that stands in contrast to the last century is that this interaction cannot be defined anymore by a process of catching up. Islamic, Indic, Chinese, and other forms of modernity, are defining themselves according to their own logic, sometimes against Western modernity, sometimes by borrowing from it. In sum, the concept of multiple modernities offers an important corrective to the idea of a hegemonic and unchallenged Western modernity asserting its supremacy over non-Western civilizations that stood by passively. It comes also with the risk that conservative and cultural essentialist voices will promote this diversity in limitative ways.

Going back to the issue of the secular state, I have underlined above that for Eisenstadt, the evolution towards this institutionalized coexistence between religion and politics, elevated as one of the principal elements of the Western program of modernity, was historically specific and culturally contingent (Eisenstadt 2003). It becomes easy to see then why many people in post-colonial societies see the secular state as a problematic issue of cultural imperialism, as it is construed in the culturally specific matrix of relations between church and state and meant to be applied in societies where this model often does not fit (Asad 2003). This may be less true for Latin America, where most societies have experienced the struggle between a hegemonic Catholic church and the state, but it is much clearer in societies where Islam, the Vedic tradition, or Chinese scriptures, have provided the foundations for the worldviews of societies from North Africa to Korea. Societies where there was no functional equivalent to churches saw through vastly different lenses the Western modernity that has emerged in the context of conflicts between the competing authorities of monarchs and churches in the West. In these societies, the state and religious authorities often had experienced entanglement and a variety of modes of differentiation for millennia that deserves further exploration.[8] In many of these societies, the state has tried to assert its authority over beliefs, promoted specific rituals and ethics. Each of the non-Western civilizations had developed over millennia different configurations of relations between the political and the spirituals sources of authority, long before Western secular states imposed on them their norms, directly through colonial rule, or indirectly through the appropriation of the same norms by nationalist intellectuals fighting for self-determination.[9]

---

[8] The discovery of these specific paths of social differentiation between religion and the other spheres of social life constituted the central core question examined by the more than twenty scholars assembled by Monika Wohlrab-Sahr and Christoph Kleine at the University of Leipzig.
[9] The case of Japan and Turkey comes to mind.

# 3 Sinitic, Indic, and other Paths to Modernity

Because this book's ambition is to investigate the entirety of the Asian continent, a geographical fantasy rather than a coherent whole, I shall now focus on the different paths to modernity in that part of the world. There is no such thing as an Asian modernity, but a constellation of different forms, each influenced by a core civilization. First, one can clearly distinguish a *Sinitic modernity*, in societies defined by China's cultural influence since millennia in Japan, Korea, and Vietnam.[10] In these contemporary East Asian societies, there are some striking elements of commonalities. The Chinese influence in East Asia is most obvious in the writing systems adopted in these countries, their architectural style, and their approach to statecraft. Their conception of nationhood evolves in all these four cases around the idea of a mythical, quasi-divine founding father of the Chinese, Japanese, Korean, and Vietnamese people. These societies have historically adopted Confucian ethics and a Chinese version of Mahayana Buddhism on top of their indigenous ritual, spiritual, moral, and ethical traditions. They have responded differently in their respective encounters with colonialism, China experiencing decay, division, and foreign invasion; Japan emulating Western imperialist powers by colonizing Korea and Taiwan, and invading China; and Vietnam falling under French colonial rule. In these contemporary East Asian societies, there are some striking elements of commonalities. One outcome of the Chinese influence is the similarities found in the languages of these four countries used to describe phenomena related to religion.[11]

The concept of a Sinitic modernity centered on China's evolution may raise issues when one considers that Japan has appropriated key elements of modernity and maintained full political sovereignty, economic prosperity, and military power a century before China, even becoming exporter of norms to the Korean peninsula and Taiwan through its own colonial empire and challenging Western imperialism in East Asia. When the Meiji bureaucracy adopted from Euro-American nations the instrument that would usher a Japanese path to modernity China seemed to fall behind its neighbor to the East because of its inner contradictions and its weaknesses on all indicators of comprehensive power on the political, economic, and military dimension. The shock brought by the colonial encounter following defeat in the Opium War, the calamity of the Taiping Rebellion, the fall of the Qing Dynasty, and the inability to institute a strong state be-

---

10 An idea captured a while ago by Vandermeersch 1986.
11 *Zongjiao* 宗教 in Mandarin, *shūkyō* 宗教 in Japanese, *jong-gyo* 종교 in Korean, and *tôn giáo* in Vietnamese.

fore 1949 have given the impression of a Chinese civilization unable to embark on a path to modernity. Yet, viewed in the perspective of the *longue durée*, this dramatic sequence of events obscures the fact that China since the Ming—if not before—had already embarked on its own path to modernity: A view that economist historians such as Bin Wong (1997) have promoted and, in relation to the theme explored in this book, an argument sketched by Jacques Gernet as he described the nature of intellectual cenacles in the late Ming Dynasty (Gernet 1994). The path to a Sinitic modernity from China has no doubt experienced enormous setbacks in the Ming-Qing transition and from the late Qing until the establishment of the PRC. Yet, even when Japan took the lead in East Asia and surpassed China in a path to modernity measured in terms of material power and influence, China continued to represent the center around which the countries influenced by Confucian culture looked to. The idea of Sinitic modernity makes sense again as China's future weigh increasingly more on Japan's fate.

One can also identify an *Indic civilizational space* found in societies from the Indian peninsula to the Malay Archipelago and most of the Indochinese peninsula, or all the societies shaped by the previous process of *Sanskritisation* identified by George Cœdès (Cowing 1968). Most societies of this region have adopted their writing system, their social system, their approach to statecraft, and their religions, from India. The sedimentation of diverse influences coming from outside the region over centuries, however, has led to differentiation between three different paths to modernity, defined by the substratum of pre-colonial political structures and religious influences. Within each of these paths, specific colonial encounters have led to a variety of modalities. First, one finds in India, Pakistan and Bangladesh, an *Indic modernity*, shaped by the ten centuries of interactions between Hindu traditions and Islam and the superposition of colonial rule during the British Raj. In India and Pakistan, the appeal of a secular state represented a break from the British model of an established religion because the framers of the constitutions in the two states understood in the years leading to independence the risks of identifying their new nations too closely to a religion. Both India and Pakistan could refer to the legacy of religious tolerance in pre-colonial Mughal India under Akbar, but the accommodation to religious diversity collapsed in Pakistan with Marshall Zia and faces a challenge under the BJP government in India that may put an end to the secular state in its current form.

One can identify in continental Southeast Asia and in the periphery of the former British Raj a *Buddhist modernity* where the Theravada school of Buddhism exerted an important influence in religious life, the social organization, and political legitimacy to monarchies prior to colonial rule. The modalities of relations between religious and political authorities changed and took different directions during and after the colonial encounter: Since the retreat of British and French colonial rule, the sangha has fought to establish its authority throughout the region. Only the Thai monarchy avoided colonial rule and saw continuity in the institutional entanglement between religious and political authority. The British absorbed the Kingdom of Kandy into its colony of Ceylon in 1817 and ended the Burmese Konbaung dynasty in 1885; once both colonies became independent Republics, the sangha fought to recover its influence. The monarchies of Laos and Cambodia outlasted French colonial rule in Indochina, but the sangha faced more serious challenges in asserting authority after the two countries became independent and went through war and political upheavals.[12] These different paths to a Buddhist modernity have presented a challenge to the notion of the secular state *qua* a regime of freedom of conscience.

Finally, an *Indo-Malay modernity* has developed in the archipelago that stretches from Malaysia to the Philippines.[13] In this case, the region as seen the concatenation of three cultural influences: the populations of the local thalassocracies have over centuries adopted on top of their indigenous traditions the teachings of Hinduism, Buddhism, and Islam transmitted by traders from South Asia and further to the West by Arab-speaking traders, before being subjected to the influence of Christianity by Spanish, Portuguese, Dutch, and British colonial rulers. An additional source of complexity in the region has been the migration of indentured laborers from China, who brought with them their traditional practices. The approach to the secular state in the Muslim majoritarian nations of Malaysia, Indonesia, and Brunei, and in the mostly Catholic Philippines and East Timor, differed from that of peninsular Southeast Asia and South Asia to the extent that the five states have struggled to accommodate religious diversity in their midst, as will be discussed below. The reference to Islam found in that part of the world does not echo the controversies in the Middle East, as the legacies of pre-Islamic periods remain present in the political terminology, as the reference to the Pancasila in Indonesia illustrates. The asymmetric religious diversity in the region's nation-states mirror that of the other two regions in the Indic civilizational space: While the discourse of a struggle between Hinduism and Islam shapes the contour of Indic modernity and the idea of Buddhism besieged appears often in the societies of Buddhist modernity, in the societies of the Indo-Malay modernity, it is the Abrahamic religions' worldview that frame political discourse.

---

12 The monarchy of independent Cambodia was interrupted between 1970 and 1993. The Laos monarchy ended in 1975.
13 Singaporeans may identify more with a Sinitic path to modernity.

So far, I have defined Sinitic modernity as an inter-subjective community that has constituted itself over millennia around the ethics of Confucianism, but also beliefs in supernatural and impersonal forces, collective foundational myths based on a godly ruler, and the religious influence of Mahayana Buddhism, which has spread in all parts of Asia where elites communicated with Chinese characters. I have also defined an *Indic modernity* defined by the conflict between the Vedic tradition that has sustained a social organization based on caste division and the development of Islam and other dissident religions that have provided succour to those excluded by the dominant social system. I have further distinguished a *Buddhist modernity* framed by Buddhism in peninsular Southeast Asia, Sri Lanka, and the Himalayas that bemoan the loss of influence of their tradition in the face of an imagined threat coming from religious modernities; and finally, a path to modernity shaped by the hegemony of monotheist religions that has superseded the Indian heritage in the Malay archipelagoes. This taxonomy points to religion as constitutive of each path to modernity. However, this may not work as well in the case of an *Islamic* modernity, as the vast discrepancies between societies such as Indonesia, Bangladesh, Turkey, and Uzbekistan, may suggest. The effects of language in defining the boundaries of inter-subjective meaning obviously matter as much as those provided in religious traditions.

More difficult and challenging to define would be the variety of *Central Asian* modernities: should language or religious affiliations define them? From Turkey to Xinjiang in China, as well as in the former Soviet Central Asian Republics, people speak mutually intelligible Turkic languages, although they write them in distinct forms pointing to the overlay of different influences: post-Ottoman in Republican Turkey and Xinjiang, and post-Russian in Central Asia, where the Cyrillic script remains in use. The same is true for the Persian-speaking states of Iran, Afghanistan, and Tajikistan. The former two states use Arabic-Persian script, and the impact of Islam has been especially strong. In the latter state, the use of the Cyrillic script goes along with a different trajectory for a lessened presence of Islam in public affairs (Thibault 2018). Mongolia, Tibet, Nepal, and Bhutan are all influenced historically in their statecraft by a form of Buddhism distinct from the Mahayana that prevails in East Asia and the dominant Theravada of Southeast Asia. They have in common with the Turkic-speaking and Persian-speaking states of the former Soviet Union a mode of social organization and economic activity defined by pastoralism and nomadism, as well as competing scripts that reveal the previous hegemonic powers ruling over them.[14]

The view of civilization adopted by the proponents of the multiple modernities theory is open-ended and opposite to the thesis of a 'clash of civilization' (Huntington 1996). The approach of Eisenstadt argues that civilizations are not monolithic blocs in opposition to each other, but that they constantly interact through the links of trade and cultural exchanges, although it does not engage with the approach of Fernand Braudel (1994), which pay attention to trade and material aspects of civilization alongside culture and religion. The greatest weakness of this approach, however, is the admission that multiple modernities will not converge into what the philosopher Hans-Georg Gadamer (1997: 302) called a fusion of horizons. As Katzenstein (2010: 17) argued, "modern societies are not converging on a common path". Each modernity will continue to change in response to transformations in the economic, social, political sphere on the global stage, but also in relation to the path dependency of its own historical trajectory of struggles, debates, and contradictions. This will be especially true in the realm of ideas. Although this idea suggests openness and resistance to hegemonic discourses, this also open the door to the cultural relativism and the rejection of universal standards in the name of civilizational grandeur. This issue appears clearly with respect to the secular state, an institution rejected by powerful political actors in many parts of Asia, in principle or in practice, or in both. However, the main point that I want to raise here is that the shared idioms within each of the modernities that I have outlined so far does not predetermine whether societies will establish robust institutions that uphold freedom of conscience. Below, I show that little fit exists between the countries that have adopted such institutions and the paths to modernity identified by Eisenstadt and his colleagues.

# 4 The Variety of Secular Constitutions in Asia

In this section, I propose to look at the extent to which the culturally differentiated paths to modernity have determined or not the formation of secular states in Asia. This observation requires the adoption of an operational definition of the secular state, no easy task when one keeps in mind the nuanced typologies that have drawn attention to fine distinctions between different forms of secular

---

**14** Mongols in the eponymous Republic have adopted the Cyrillic alphabet while those who live in China's Autonomous Region of Inner Mongolia use their own distinctive script.

states. Hence, Jean Baubérot, in this book, and in his previous work, alone, or with his colleague Micheline Milot, has devised detailed taxonomies meant to distinguish between different approaches to the secular states between countries, but also between forms of the *Etat laïc* at different junctures within French recent history and in Latin America (Baubérot 2015; Baubérot and Milot 2011). Ahmet Kuru 2009, in contrast, has proposed a simpler model of the secular state that distinguish between the passive form of separation between church and state practiced in the United States, and the more assertive form practiced in France, and in Turkey up until the time when Erdogan consolidated his power. While in the previous section I have pointed to clusters of Asian countries defined by the dominant religious tradition within their respective boundaries, a look at the institutions adopted by governments to regulate their interaction with religious actors reveals striking discrepancies within such clusters. Hence, if in the previous section I had alluded to a Sinitic modernity alongside Indic, Buddhist, and Indo-Malay ones, in this section I contrast the different approaches that states implement in accordance with their constitutions as enacted at the time of writing, through their laws, regulations, and politics. Hence, the typologies of states presented below differentiate between states that have regimes of separation between religion and state; states that have adopted a single national religion, with varying degree of tolerance for minority beliefs; and states that have developed multiple religious establishments.

A few distinctions about these concepts are in order. The regime of separation between religion and state is rarely, if ever, a reality. States that identified as such below have adopted legislations, enshrined constitutional principles, and amended them, in ways that limit state interference in religious affairs, but also ensure that religious involvement in politics is under conditions of non-discrimination against other religion or against people without religious affiliation or belief. These states would qualify as regimes of freedom of conscience, and they do not support the establishment of any religion. States with an established religion may have enshrined in their constitution freedom of conscience and/or freedom of religion, but the establishment of a religion points to privileges granted to one religion that the state denies to others. Multiple establishments refer to a variant of that principle, to the extent that more than one religion receives a form of legal recognition (Sullivan and Beaman 2013).

Religious establishment in its singular or in its plural form is not necessarily pluralist: it is a corporatist arrangement whereby the state licenses a religious group to manage the affairs of its believers, and sanctions dissidence as heresy or even as blasphemy. Regimes of religious establishment—whether in the singular or the plural—like secular states, implement their systems to different degrees. The security apparatus often helps established religions to enforce their authority. For example, police forces can harass and jail religious dissidents, even demolish their places of worship. Other regimes of religious establishment, while legalizing religious associations, do so for pragmatic reasons, such as ensuring that donation to charities is legitimate and that the wealthy do not use them as tax shelters. Finally, the degree of state hostility towards religion in general can vary in time, and depends on the religions targeted by governments, sometimes with the assent of the broader public.

## 4.1 Secular States

The democracies of South Korea and Taiwan are since the beginning of this century the only two states in the context of Sinitic modernity that can qualify as regimes of freedom of conscience.[15] Their government does not promote a religion, does not forbid others, and does not impose restriction on practicing, or even on proselytizing. Moreover, religions in these countries are important actors in the spheres of social welfare and culture. Before they adopted this approach, South Korea and Taiwan had more in common with regimes of multiple establishments that recognize a limited number of religions and would impose surveillance and restrictions on the others. One source of concerns in both countries is the power of minority religious organisations, in both cases socially conservative protestant churches, that organise their members and enlist other religions to join them to pressure governments into adopting restrictive policies against sexual minorities. The other five nations in Asia that count as secular states with freedom of conscience must deal with a major issue with greater political consequences: after they captured governments, religious organizations or political parties connected to them have sought public institutions to intervene on their behalf at the expense of religious minorities and non-believers.

Nepal and Mongolia stand out as two societies that embody a distinct path to modernity, a Buddhist variant of Indic modernity with the former, a unique central Asian path, in the case of the latter, towards a liberal and open regime.[16] These very recent democracies living in the shadow of demographic giants with hegemonic ambitions in their immediate environment, have managed to maintain state neutrality on religious matters. In the case of Nepal, this owes in good part to the multi-religious nature of that society. The country has endured a long civil war and the promotion of Hinduism or Buddhism would have been

---

15 On South Korea, see Baker 2013. On Taiwan, see Laliberté 2009.
16 For Nepal, see Letizia 2011. On Mongolia, see Even 2012.

likely to inflame passions again. In the case of Mongolia, the numerical predominance of Buddhism has not coincided with a proclamation of that tradition as a national religion. As observed in Japan, where people can relate to two different traditions at once, the simultaneous practice of Shamanism and other forms of ancient religions along Buddhism may explain this reticence to give the sangha too large an influence in Mongolia's affairs.

The secular institutions of India in the courts, the media, academia, and even in the entertainment industry, experience enormous pressure from a militant Hindu nationalist movement that has received considerable popular support because of its ability to instill fear over its claim that Muslims threaten India within the country, and outside, chiefly through Pakistan (Jaffrelot 2017). The 2015 general elections that brought the BJP to power by a landslide, and the 2019 that returned it, have critically undermined India's secular institutions. As it stood since 1947 as the most important secular state in South Asia, it represented an important source of support for the proponents of secularism in neighbouring countries and in the post-colonial world more broadly. The rise of Hindu nationalism over decades, however, has in turn reinforced the defensive appeal of Islamic and Buddhist fundamentalism in these societies. The hardening of religious identities in the Indian subcontinent dangerously threatens the Hindustani modality of an Indic path to modernity. A striking illustration of this trend is the project of Hindu nationalists to change the iconic representation of India for tourism promotion, the Taj Mahal, which stands as witness to the legacy of Mughal tolerance under the Emperor Akbar and as illustration of the Indian approach to the secular state. Its proposed replacement is the temple of Akshardham in Delhi, a Hindu monument without the same claim of multiple identities embodied by the famous mausoleum.

Japan represents, along with South Korea and Taiwan, another case of a Sinitic approach to modernity that appears entirely compatible with liberal freedom of conscience (Ravitch 2016). The ideal of the secular state remains cherished by much of the population, which interprets this principle as a strict separation between the religious and the political. Yet, as in New Delhi, politicians in the country remain bitterly divided about whether the secular state represents a graft imposed by a foreign power, or whether the constitutional separation between religion and state constitutes one of the fundamental institutions preventing a return to a conservative regime. These concerns are not entirely without basis. With the exceptions of 1993–1994 and 2009–2012, Japan has been ruled since 1955 by a conservative party whose most traditionalist elements would like to establish Shinto as a form of national culture, to grant it a status akin to that of a national religion. This approach would represent a setback for many Japanese citizens, as it would restore the situation that prevailed when a militarist movement that governed their country encouraged the worship of the head of state as a semi-God. Conversely, many partisans of the secular state object to the participation or the intervention in public life of the Soka Gakkai, a large lay Buddhist organization that sponsors the Komeito, a party participating in the ruling coalition in Tokyo. For them, this presence in government points to a betrayal of the secular state.

Including the Philippines in this category may seem counter-intuitive when one keeps in mind the pervasiveness of the Catholic Church in the country's public life (Pangalangan 2010). Yet, despite this sociological fact, the Philippines remains a secular state with a constitution inspired by that of its former American rulers. Although Catholicism is not an established religion according to the constitution, its episcopate's power has been significant at crucial historical juncture. This impact, however, has fluctuated, and on many occasions the state has ignored religious authority's remonstrance without paying the price. Moreover, the political position of the church is ambiguous: progressive at times, or reactionary at others, when seen through the lenses of political disputes. However, the common thread in both trends is a certain coherence of the Church doctrine, which does not fit with the dominant political cleavages. Hence, the church can be progressive on matters of economic justice, and conservative on issues of personal morality. During the last years of Marcos' personal dictatorship, the Church leadership provided guidance to the popular movement that opposed martial law. On the other hand, years later, it used all the influence it could muster to ensure that a referendum allowing divorce would be defeated, in conformity with Catholic doctrine.

Apart from the Philippines, Laos may be the only Southeast Asian state that could be qualified as secular, to the extent that it does not favor a religion in its constitution. In contrast to other socialist states in East and Southeast Asia, the Lao state does not limit recognition to just a few numbers of religions. On the other hand, it is hard not to see the limits of this secular state: the Lao Front for National Construction requires all religions to register with the government, and it reserves to itself the authority to oversee their activities. In sum, very few states in Asia qualify as secular states, and for many of those that do so, they face serious challenges in civil society by nationalist and conservative parties that seek to establish regimes with one established religion. No cultural path to modernity, whether Sinitic, Indic, or other, appears more likely than do others to favor the institutionalisation of a secular state. This clearly emerges when looking into the same cultural paths to modernity some vastly different approaches to freedom of conscience.

## 4.2 Regimes with One Established Religion

Although they appear different because their constitution promulgates that one religion deserves special recognition by the state, regimes with an established religion can be undistinguishable from secular states if their constitution enshrines freedom of conscience and protection of minorities as well. Hence, the Republic of Pakistan, established in 1947 as a homeland for the Muslims of the Indian subcontinent, affirmed at the time of its founding the rights of religious minorities.[17] The same is true for the Republic of Bangladesh, established in 1971 after secession from Pakistan on the grounds of linguistic differences rather than religious dispute. Bangladesh's constitution upholds Islam as the religion of the state, but it also proclaims that the country is secular (Rashiduzzaman 2018). The constitution of Malaysia represents a variation on that theme: it proclaims that while Islam is the religion of the Federation, "people can practice other religions in peace". One observes an analogous situation for most of the states where the constitution asserts that Buddhism represents the religion of the majority. The Thai constitution stipulates that the King must be a "Buddhist", but also that he is the "upholder of religions", or the protector of all religions, like his British counterpart. The constitution of Myanmar recognizes the special position of Buddhism as the faith of the majority, but it also recognizes Christianity, Islam, Hinduism, and animism. The approach of Sri Lanka is the most ambiguous among these states: it does not proclaim a state religion, but the constitution proclaims that the Republic should give "Buddhism the foremost place". In some cases, like Cambodia and Bhutan, where statistics reveal that most of the population identify as Buddhist, the idea of an established religion represents a less controversial issue, except for the non-believers.

States with religious establishment have proven very vulnerable to demagogue politicians using identity politics to reinforce their legitimacy. Hence, Pakistan has experienced an increasing influence of Islam in political life since independence (Mehdi 2013). The proclamation of the Islamic Republic by general Zia had served to mask the deficit of legitimacy after his *coup d'état* and the execution of former President Ali Bhutto. Ever since that decision, the country has had to contend with insurgencies by Islamist radical militants who have felt emboldened by this political shift. States with religious establishment have also proved vulnerable to pressures from groups that have felt encouraged to ask governments to more concretely implement the constitutional provisions suggesting that their religions deserve promotion. Bangladesh and Malaysia have gradually moved in that direction, as

---

[17] On the policy of its founder, Mohammed Ali Jinnah, see Ahmed 2005.

Islamist political parties have seen an increase in their popularity in recent elections.[18] In Thailand, Burma, and Sri Lanka, the 'religionisation' of politics has grown in importance as well, with the increasing stridency of clerics in recent years (Helbardt, Hellmann-Rajanayagam, and Korff 2013). Regimes with one established religion, for the most part, have evolved in the direction of greater involvement of religion in public life, at the expense of minorities. The idea that a symbolic recognition by the state would give the followers of majoritarian religion a sense of security has not worked that way: as the example above suggests, it had emboldened them to be even more assertive against minorities.

## 4.3 States with Multiple Establishments

On the surface, states with multiple establishments could appear as a compromise between states with one established religion and secular states that reconcile differences, but they could also amplify them. Most states that have gone that way, however, are authoritarian, and only a few of them are recently democratized ones. In one-party states, most of which embody a Sinitic path to modernity, the institutionalization of multiple religious establishments has protected a few religions at the expense of others. In China, for example, the CCP has categorised communal religions and popular beliefs such as divination, geomancy, and ancestor worship as 'feudal superstitions', and defined non-recognized heterodox religions as 'evil cults.' (Potter 2003, Goossaert 2006) It has mandated a State Administration for Religious Affairs to serve and to monitor the activities of national associations for the only five religions that the state recognizes: Daoism, Buddhism, Islam, Catholicism, and Protestant Christianity. Vietnam represents a variant of that approach: the Ministry of Home Affairs has instituted a Government Committee for Religious Affairs, and it gave a legal status to Buddhism, Islam, and the two branches of Christianity (Liên 2013). However, its approach appears slightly more liberal than China: it has extended recognition to two other new religious movements: the Hoa Hao and the Cao Dai. Conversely, North Korea, as the least amicable of the three nominally socialist states to religion, has given recognition to only four religions—shamanism, Chondoism, Buddhism, and Christianity—and it has imposed on them a much harsher regime of control.[19] Although these three states have in common elements of a Sinitic path

---

**18** For a study of Bangladesh, see Riaz 2010. For the case of Malaysia, see Mohammad 2010.
**19** There exists little written on this issue. For an exception, albeit a dated one, see Armstrong 2005.

to modernity because of a shared heritage of Confucianism, Mahayana Buddhism, and resistance to Western imperialism, they differ in significant ways from other states with which they share a language and a history of political entanglement. This is the case with Taiwan—officially known as the Republic of China—and with the Republic of Korea, the Southern half of the eponymous peninsula.

Indonesia is another major state that has instituted the principle of multiple establishments in its constitution, in a way that is unique in Asia.[20] While the three nominally socialist states mentioned above have grudgingly granted recognition to religions and favored the option of atheism, the Indonesian state goes in the opposite direction. The foundational state ideology of *Pancasila*, which refers to the belief in one God, requires of all citizens to identify with one religion. The Chinese Communist Party, the Communist Party of Vietnam, and the Workers' party of Korea all forbid membership in their organization to religious believers, and their ideology is premised on the idea of religion withering away under a socialist regime, not so the Indonesian regime. Its approach, which expected the allegiance of religious minorities in a majoritarian Muslim society, may have appeared as religiously plural at the onset, but during the authoritarian regime era, this meant that atheists faced persecution—suspected of sympathy with Communism and therefore of sedition—and they were treated as badly as adherents of non-recognized religions in socialist countries. With the process of democratic consolidation becoming entrenched in Indonesia, the multiple establishments promoted by the principle of *Pancasila* must contend with a new problem: pressures from extremist Islamist movements emboldened by the fact that Muslims represent an overwhelming majority of the population. This trend is worrisome for those who have taken pride in the fact that Indonesia, where live the largest Muslim community on the planet, embodied the idea of an Islamic democracy that celebrates religious diversity—if not entirely respect freedom of conscience, denied to non-religious people, whether religiously indifferent, agnostics, or atheists—or believers in non-theistic or polytheistic religions.

The stark contrast in East Asia between democratic-liberal secular states with freedom of conscience and totalitarian states that ambition control of religion has revealed that no single pattern of Sinitic modernity exists. The same is even truer for the notion of Indic modernity: there is little in common between pluralist and open secular states like India until the late 1990s and Indonesia today, on the one hand, and regimes of religious establishment from the Islamic

---

20 For a discussion about Islamic political thought in Indonesia, see Assyaukanie 2006.

Republic of Pakistan to the Buddhist monarchy of Thailand. In sum, although Chinese high culture has produced a taxonomy and symbols universally understandable to all societies in East Asia, this has not led to a common approach to the secular state as a constitutional principle. The same is true for each of the other three types of modernity based on the Indic, Buddhist, and Indo-Malay cultures. In all these communities of inter-subjective meaning, one finds both secular states neutral on religious matters and states with a religious establishment—whether in the singular or the plural. These observations leave the following puzzle: what factors could orient countries in each of the four cultural spheres towards adopting the feature of the secular state, and what prevented others in the same cultural sphere from doing so. The cumulative knowledge generated by the idiographic and configurative analyses offered in this book's case studies should start to shed light on these questions.

# 5 Conclusion

The institution of the secular state has represented in the West a major achievement of modernity, along with the more recent welfare state. Following a long succession of wars in Europe over the religion people should practice, it gradually established a separation between political power and religious authority that paved the way for freedom of conscience and thereby reinforced other freedoms and civil rights. That achievement has received almost universal support in all Western societies, regardless of people's political allegiance. For religious minorities, it represents a guarantee for their survival, for religious majorities, a recognition of their institution's legitimacy in the public sphere, and for non-believers, the legitimacy of their choice as individuals. For Asian societies, the modalities of secular states have resulted from a variety of different dynamics. In those that have experienced colonial rule, the legal and cultural institutions that implemented the secular state often came along other dimensions of domination. In those that experienced social revolution, crude version of state oversight of religion that neglected freedom of conscience became part of an authoritarian, at time totalitarian, attempt at social engineering. It is hardly surprising that in many of these cases the secular state has appeared as an alien graft or as an illegitimate imposition from above. However, the alternatives of a variety of neo-traditionalist modernities, whether the 'China dream', the 'Hindu Rashtra', or the 'Islamic State', or other forms of 'authenticity', repudiate individual emancipation and offer little in the way of constructing just societies jointly established by self-determined moral agents. These neo-traditionalist ideologies, in their claim to develop along paths trodden by their specific cultures, have proven to be very selective in the definition of what constitute them. The world needs a co-determination of global modernity out of the entanglement between its multiple paths rather than parallel and incommensurable multiple modernities.

# References

Ahmed, Akbar. 2005. *Jinnah, Pakistan and Islamic identity: the search for Saladin*. London: Routledge.
Al-Azmeh, Aziz. 2009. *Islams and Modernities*. London: Verso Book.
Armstrong, Charles K. 2005. "Familism, socialism and political religion in North Korea". *Totalitarian Movements and Political Religions* 6 no. 3: 383–394.
Asad, Talal. 2003. *Formations of the Secular: Christianity, Islam, Modernity*. Stanford, NJ: Stanford University Press.
Assyaukanie, Luthfi. 2009. *Islam and the secular state in Indonesia*. Singapore: Institute of Southeast Asian Studies.
Baker, Don. 2013. "Korea's Path of Secularisation". In Ranjan Ghosh, ed., *Making Sense of the Secular: Critical Perspectives from Europe to Asia*, pp. 182–193. London: Routledge.
Baubérot, Jean. 2015. *Les 7 laïcités françaises*. Paris: Maison des Sciences de l'Homme.
Baubérot, Jean and Micheline Milot. 2011. *Laïcités sans frontières*. Paris: Le Seuil.
Bhargava, Rajeev 2013. "Political Responses to Religious Diversity in Ancient and Modern India". *Studies on Indian Politics* 1 no. 1 (June): 21–41.
Blancarte, Roberto J. 2007. "Freedom of Conscience and the Secular State in Latin America". *Conscience* 28 no. 4: 34–37.
Braudel, Fernand. 1994. *A History of Civilizations, $15^{th}$–$18^{th}$ Century*, trans. Sian Reynolds. 3 vols, New York: Harper and Row.
Burchardt, Marian, Monika Wohlrab-Sahr and Matthias Middell, eds. 2015. *Multiple Secularities Beyond the West: Religion and Modernity in the Global Age*. Berlin: De Gruyter.
Coedès, George. 1948 (1968). *Les états hindouisés d'Indochine et d'Indonésie (The Indianized States of Southeast Asia*, edited by Walter F. Vella, translated by Susan Brown Cowing. Canberra, Australian National University Press).
Eisenstadt, Schmuel. 1999. "Multiple Modernities in an Age of Globalization". In Claudia Honegger, Stefan Hradil and Franz Traxler, eds., *Grenzenlose Gesellschaft?* pp. 37–50. Wiesbaden: Verlag für Sozialwissenschaften.
Eisenstadt, Schmuel Noah. 2000a. "Multiple Modernities". *Daedalus* 129: 1–29.
Eisenstadt, Schmuel Noah. 2000b. "The Reconstruction of Religion Arenas in the Framework of Multiple Modernities". *Millenium* 29 no. 3: 591–612.
Eisenstadt, Schmuel. 2003. "Introduction: Comparative Studies and Sociological Theory—From Comparative Studies to Civilizational Analysis: Autobiographical Notes". In Schmuel Eisenstadt, ed., *Comparative Civilizations and Multiple Modernities*, pp. 1–28. Leiden, NL: Brill.
Even, Marie-Dominique. 2012. "Ritual Efficacy or Spiritual Quest? Buddhism and Modernity in Post-Communist Mongolia". In Katia Buffetrille, ed., *Revisiting Rituals in a Tibetan Changing World*, pp. 241–272. Leiden/Boston: Brill.

Gadamer, Hans-Georg. 1997. *Truth and Method*. New York: Continuum.
Gernet, Jacques. 1994. *L'intelligence de la Chine: Le social et le mental*. Paris: Gallimard, Bibliothèque des histoires.
Goossaert, Vincent. 2006. "State and Religion in Modern China: Religious Policy and Scholarly Paradigms". https://halshs.archives-ouvertes.fr/halshs-00106187 (Accessed December 16, 2021).
Helbardt, Sascha, Dagmar Hellmann-Rajanayagam and Rüdiger Korff. 2013. "Religionisation of Politics in Sri Lanka, Thailand and Myanmar". *Politics, Religion & Ideology* 14 no. 1: 36–58.
Huntington, Samuel. 1996. *The Clash of Civilizations and the Remaking of World Order*. New York: Simon & Shuster.
Jaffrelot, Christophe. 2017. "India's Democracy at 70: Toward a Hindu State?" *Journal of Democracy* 28 no. 3: 52–63.
Katzenstein, Peter J. 2010. *Civilizations in World Politics: Plural and pluralist perspectives*. London: Routledge.
Kuru, Ahmet T. 2009. *Secularism and State Policies toward Religion: The United States, France, and Turkey*. New York: Cambridge University Press.
Laliberté, André. 2009. "The Regulation of Religious Affairs in Taiwan: From State Control to Laisser-faire?" *Journal of Current Chinese Affairs* 38 no. 2: 53–83.
Letizia, Chiarra. 2011. "Shaping secularism in Nepal". *European Bulletin of Himalayan Research* 39: 66–104.
Liên, Claire Trần Thị. 2013. "Communist state and religious policy in Vietnam: A historical perspective". *Hague Journal on the Rule of Law* 5 no. 2: 229–252.
Mehdi, Rubya. 2013. *The Islamization of the Law in Pakistan*. London: Routledge.
Mohamad, Maznah. 2010. "Making majority, undoing family: Law, religion and the Islamization of the state in Malaysia". *Economy and Society* 39 no. 3: 360–384.
Nag, Kingshuk. 2014. *The Saffron Tide: The Rise of the B.J.P.* New Delhi: Rupa/Rainlight Publication.
Pangalangan, Raul. 2010. "Religion and the secular state: National report for the Philippines". In Javier Martinez-Torron and W.C. Durham, eds., *Religion and the secular state: Interim national reports*, pp. 539–551. Provo, UT: The International Center for Law and Religion Studies.
Potter, Pittman. B. 2003. "Belief in control: Regulation of religion in China". *The China Quarterly* 174: 317–337.
Preyer, Gerhard. 2013. "The Perspective of Multiple Modernities on Shmuel N. Eisenstadt's Sociology". *Theory and Society: Journal of Political and Moral Theory* 30: 187–225.
Rashiduzzaman, Mohammad. 2018. "Bangladesh: Muslim Identity, Secularism, and the Politics of Nationalism". In Rolin Mainuddin, ed., *Religion and Politics in the Developing World: Explosive Interactions*, pp. 128–142. London: Routledge.
Ravitch, Frank S. 2017. "Secularism and Liberal Constitutionalism: Lessons from Japan". *Michigan State Law Review* no. 2: 149–161.
Riaz, Ali. 2010. "The politics of Islamization in Bangladesh". In Ali Riaz, ed., *Religion and Politics in South Asia*, pp. 59–84. London: Routledge.
Ringen, Stein. 2016. *The Perfect Dictatorship: China in the 21st Century*. Hong Kong: the Hong Kong University Press.

Schmidt, Volker. 2006. "Multiple Modernities or Varieties of Modernity?" *Current Sociology* 51 no. 4: 77–97.
Sullivan, Winnifred F. and Lori G. Beaman, eds. 2013. *Varieties of Religious Establishment*. Farnham, UK: Ashgate.
Taylor, Charles. 2007. *A Secular Age*. Cambridge, MA: Harvard University Press.
Thibault, Hélène. 2018. *Transforming Tajikistan: State-Building and Islam in Post-Soviet Central Asia*. London: Bloomsbury.
Tu Weiming, ed. 1996. *Confucian traditions in East Asian modernity*. Cambridge, MA: Harvard University Press.
Vandermeersch, Léon. 1986. *Le nouveau monde sinisé*. Paris: Presses universitaires de France.
Wong, R. Bin. 1997. *China Transformed: Historical Change and the Limits of European Experience*. Ithaca: Cornell University Press.

Jean Baubérot
# Laicity, Secularism, Secularization(s): A Few Hypotheses

**Abstract:** This chapter clarifies relation between laicity, secularism, and secularization within the framework of a comparative perspective between France and other countries, notably Asian states. To do this, it proposes a sociological approach to laicity that is not just an aspect of the sociological discourse on secularization. It seeks to construct a sociologically operative notion that overcome the problem raised the semantic proximity of the terms secularism and secularization. Using a typology of the different forms of laicities based on the four parameters of freedom of conscience, equality of citizenship, the way in which the separation is rendered concrete and state neutrality, it seeks to evaluate and compare the different forms of Asian laicity. It concludes with the two hypotheses that 1) secularization is still useful as an instrument of analysis even though the paradigm of secularization is questioned and 2) we are witnessing a societal exit out of the Enlightenment because its very success has engendered new problems that societies are dealing with.

## 1 Introduction

The term "secularism" is little used in France, while there is much talk about "laicity". It is therefore interesting to clarify relation between laicity, secularism, and secularization within the framework of a comparative perspective between France and other countries, notably Asian states. In international academic literature, France often appears as a radically secular State. Thus, Kuru (2009) contrasts "assertive secularism" in France (*laïcité*) and Turkey (*laiklik*) with the American case ("passive secularism"). For this author, "assertive secularism (is) opposed to the headscarf" and "passive secularism (is) in favor of it". However, Akan (2017) considers that "the exclusive focus on the headscarf (...) completely excludes (the) institutional differences from the comparative description of the political fields in France and Turkey". Other analysts have a more complex approach: Hurd (2004) notes that there are blind spots ("blindness to the limitations of secularism") in some studies on French laicity. Brugger (2009) proposes a typology of the various models of connections between state and religion

**Jean Baubérot** (Groupe Sociétés, Religions, Laïcités, CNRS/EPHE-PSL)

https://doi.org/10.1515/9783110733068-003

and he classifies French laicity under two divergent models: that of "moderate variant of the hostility between state and church", and that of "separation and consideration," which is softer than the American "strict separation." This approach is quite interesting because it reveals the complexity, the ambivalence of laicity in France. Furthermore, if there are aspects of "separation and consideration" in French laicity, then one can consider the "separation and consideration" of other countries and *a fortiori* the "strict separation" of some states in an overall examination of various laicities.

## 2 An Underestimation of the Political in the Theories of Secularization

Why propose a sociological approach to laicity that is not just an aspect of the sociological discourse on secularization? Without going back over the many criticisms of the secularization paradigm (see attempt at synthesis in Baubérot-Milot, 2011), I would like to mention that as early as 1980 F. Isambert (1980) blamed his partisans for "linking the economic and the cultural without realizing that a certain blank remained on the median plane of the exercise of power." Here, Isambert points out the unthought in the paradigm: its low level of consideration of the political, before studies on electoral behavior, and of the idea that the two dominant politico-economic models, the capitalist and the communist ones, would entail in the whole world an inevitable process of secularization.

At the beginning of the twenty-first century, this critique of a lack of consideration of the political has become widespread. Thus, for Koenig (2010), "theories (...) of secularization have ignored the State as an institutional framework for the links between politics and religion." The highlighting of differentiation, and above all the end of the belief in the decline and privatization of religion borne out of a global social dynamic, makes it impossible to underestimate the political regulation of various religious and convictional diversities. It is first and foremost to this regulation that a sociological perspective on laicity should pay attention.

Laicity is above all *a mode of socio-political organization*. In a given society, it is a major socio-political issue, in which situations of competition and alliance between different forces reveal themselves, in order to obtain the power to organize social life. It is materialized in public policies, legal systems, and ideological argumentations. It is therefore necessary to distance ourselves from the standard habitus of sociologists of religion and not privilege from the outset observations on religion (persistence of the religious, renewal of a "public" religiosity, etc.) even if these factors can be taken also into account.

Two other changes to the classic vision of the sociology of religion must be carried out. On the one hand, the myths and rituals characterized as "non-religious" must be considered, along with everything that can be connected to the problematic of civil religion. The sociologist of laicity will include the religious in a symbolic grouping that also includes what is socially considered to be non-religious. Then if, analytically speaking, laicity is a mode of organization of the political, on a social level it is also the object of various beliefs. Sociologists must then not only distance themselves from these secular beliefs but also take them up as objects of study, observing them, analyzing them as convictions of a symbolic order, which include analogies with beliefs commonly termed religious.

## 3 Laicity or Secularism?

In this distancing from social practices, why should we not adopt the term "secularism," which presents the advantage of being well-known in international academic literature? This usage is, of course, scientifically legitimate. Many debates have developed over the past few decades around the concept of secularism, which is at the intersection between the political and the religious (the notion of secularization is then located at the intersection between the religious and the cultural).

However, these debates are in part distorted by the semantic proximity of the terms secularism and secularization. As Krämer (2009) notes, "secularization and secularism are seldom distinguished within the political debate." Thus, in academic literature the adjective *secular* can often refer both the socio-cultural secularization and political secularism, or else to a kind of ambiguous mixture. This confusion makes the expression a bit fuzzy and makes certain amalgams possible. It facilitates preserving a routine use of the secularization paradigm, which remains a kind of background vulgate even when the contents inevitably change. Secularism then seems for some to be the political ideology of secularization. For others the notion of secularism is used without any real conceptual autonomy, which functions implicitly in connection with secularization, which remains an overall framework. And when one moves from synchrony to diachrony, secularism becomes… the process of secularization (the confusion just keeps going), whereas laicity becomes the process of laicization.

These confusions can lead to applying the critique of the secularization paradigm almost automatically to secularism, without considering the latter own characteristics. Secularism could then only function from within a secularized society and its 'destiny' would be necessarily bound to the avatars of secularization. These avatars play a role of course, but only in correlation with other factors. Thus, the type of democracy—or non-democracy—adopted (without reducing it to its Western-centric meanings) and its transformations shape secularism as much as transformations in secularization (and, one may add, as disillusion of sociologists of secularization regarding their subject!).

However, for the last fifteen years, international academic debates, which result in a sharper shape for 'secularism', have been developing. And the distancing of this term from the dominant social usages is for some researchers in the humanities and social sciences more readily understandable than for the term laicity. This must be considered as well. The use of each term therefore has its strengths and weaknesses. What matters is to construct a sociologically operative notion.

Both Laliberté and van de Veer (in this volume) use the concepts of secularism and of secularization independently. For Laliberté the primary criterion of secularism is the guarantee of freedom of conscience, that is, the right to believe or not to believe, and to change one's view on the matter. This is indeed an essential criterion (Plesner, 2008). But is it possible to make it the only criterion? Laliberté in the rest of his contribution must take into account the separation between state and religion. On the one hand, he does not view the communist countries of Asia as secular states. On the other hand, van der Veer includes these countries among secular states based on a reflection on secularism and Asian nationalism.

Since the 1960s at the time when sociologists of religion were articulating the paradigm of secularization, political scientists, and legal scholars, such as Smith (1963) or Galander (1965), elaborated the concept of secular state without any reference to this paradigm to analyse the links between state and religion in different countries. In their work, this concept is valid not only for the West, but also for other countries, such as Asian countries, like India.

According to them, this concept can be visualized as a triangle. The three angles constitute three series of relations—which are distinct but interrelated—between the state, religion, and the individual. This grouping makes it possible to define the secular state, keeping in mind that it is a measuring tool, an ideal type: for these authors, the state can be more or less secular, which in no way means for them that it is more or less secularized.

The three sides of the triangle represent three forms of socio-political relations:

- freedom of religion (and freedom in relation to religion: therefore, the freedom of conscience), regarding the relations between religion and the individual (I would add, within the framework of the state).

- citizenship without any religious condition, regarding the relations between the state and the individual.
- and finally, the separation of religion and State, regarding the relations between the state and religion.

Theorists of secularization, on the other hand, have made the secular state depend on a process of secularization. This is very clear in Berger initial analysis (1971). And yet, Weber in *The Protestant Ethic and the Spirit of Capitalism* had already separated the two perspectives by calling attention to the claims of freedom of conscience and separation of the Church and State, articulated by the radical Baptists of the sixteenth and seventeenth centuries in the name of "positive religious reasons."

# 4 A Non-Secular Secular State that Keeps the "Civil" and the "Religious" Separate

One figure mentioned by Weber is that of the pastor Roger Williams, the founder of the first secular state, Rhode Island, in British America of the middle of the seventeenth century. We can underline the importance of this historical fact for two reasons. On the one hand, it seems interesting from a theoretical perspective, with reference to the situation of *"religious societies"* or those that are so called today. On the other hand, most work on secularism that presents it as a component of secularization imperiously asserts that the secular state is a western creation dating back to the eighteenth century and the Enlightenment.

In his own way, Williams was "wildly religious", to use Berger's expression (2001): for him real faith is the only path. He was an evangelical, opposed to any ideal of secularization. However, according to him, in order to avoid generating religious conformism, the political freedom of religious practice was necessary. Williams' "dogmatism," Timothy Hall (1998) specifies, "was not inconsistent with the tolerance but rather the chief fount of it". It resulted in social experimentation, as the charismatic leader ended up founding Rhode Island.

Persecuted Christians of all persuasions and "blasphemers" found refuge in Rhode Island; they lived alongside the Indians whose "paganism" was respected. This final aspect is not to be overlooked: we can thus relativize the so-called Christian origin of secularism by also seeing it as a social construct that falls within a renunciation of the political imposition of Christianity to non-Christians. In addition, in a cultural universe that was saturated with religiosity, the pioneers of Rhode Island got rid of the institutional and financial links between religion and the state, gropingly constructing a "Wall of separation" between the civil and the religious (according to the formula invented by Williams himself and that Jefferson will take as his own).

This requires us to decide what falls within the scope of each of the two orders. Thus, despite the prescriptions of Paul the apostle ("Wives, submit yourselves to your own husbands"), the fact of perpetrating violence on a disobedient wife is not a part of the freedom of conscience, and neither are ritual human sacrifices. After sometimes animated debates, these practices become crimes that fall within the scope of public order. Thus political society gradually defines—through conflicts and negotiations—the borders between the civil and the religious and invents legal systematics to enforce them.

This progressive invention (which is of course not absolute) does not occur, in this historical case, in connection with a secularizing doctrine. It is the consequence of the political necessities of a situation of extreme pluralism, animated by a desire for tolerance connected to a religious ideal. And it also cannot be said that this social practice of secularism produced a massive secularization. In contrast, there is an affinity with the construction of a democracy-type society and the elaboration of individual rights. But this is not necessarily the case for all forms of secularism.

That being said, the political philosophy which, overall, provides the intellectual framework of secularism rather dates back to the end of the seventeenth century. In his theorization of the "limited State", but also influenced by a "travel book" where he found observations on tolerance in India (Klibansky 2006), John Locke also enacts a separation between what he considers to be civil and what is, to his mind, religious (Horton & Mendus 2004). He also establishes civil crimes that the state can impose restraints on, including when they involve actions proclaimed to be religious. Human sacrifices or sacred prostitution are cited as examples. However, although he himself advocated a "reasonable Christianity" (so, we might say, a rather secularized approach to religion), he does not at all limit freedom of conscience to that version of Christianity.

"Idolatry", "false or absurd" opinions are, he asserts, to its benefit. Contrary to what is often written, he does not exclude the Catholicism of "tolerance" because the example he gives of an "absurd opinion" that must be tolerated is the doctrine of transubstantiation. A key assertion, because the Eucharist (and the doctrine which is a representation of it) is then a practice considered to be both religious and eminently social. In contrast, Locke denies the right to submit to the pope as a power that excommunicated English royalty. He considers this submission to be a civil crime while others might consider it to be a religious obligation (Baubérot & Milot 2011).

Can we not find a few analogies with current-day situations, despite the existence of differences? Casanova (2006) notes that in the United States, "It is not clear where the secular ends and religion begins." It seems to me that this observation could be extended to the whole of the globalized world. Of course, on many points, that which is conceived as "civil" vs. "religious" has acquired a historical thickness and an international legal consistency which can—up to a certain point—make it seem like an obvious fact. But despite international conventions, discrepancies remain between countries and global socio-political development calls this into question, or even leads to modifications in legislature and jurisprudence.

Repeatedly, that which is "civil" for some can belong to the realm of the "religious" for others. This is why the three criteria established by Smith and adopted by Galander are not just quantitative measurement tools: their respective content and importance are still what is at stake in struggles and/or negotiations. From a humanities and social sciences perspective, the terms "religious" and "civil" must be completely de-substantialized. They take on meaning as part of a sociology of representations.

# 5 A Typology of Laicities

In this perspective, Micheline Milot and I (Milot 2008; Baubérot & Milot 2011) have added a fourth criterium to construct the laicity/secularism ideal type: the socio-political stakes that have to do with *neutrality* in relation to religion.

These four parameters for the analysis of laicity are therefore: the—freedom of conscience, equal (or unequal) citizenship, the way in which the separation is rendered concrete (or not) and, in addition, neutrality. These for criteria make it possible to decrypt, evaluate and compare different forms of laicity/secularism.

The link between these four parameters, and their dominant interpretation, is different depending on the types of laicity. One parameter can be privileged over others: in France, for over fifteen years, neutrality has been privileged over separation. And this seems to me to have strong links to the transformations of democracy in this country, the political reactions in the face of feelings on globalization, and then the terrorist threat. In the United States, over the *longue durée*, separation is most often emphasized over neutrality.

Furthermore, one interpretation may politically take precedence over other possibilities, and socially want to take on the value of the obvious: for example, the " Loi sur la laïcité" in Quebec (2019) extended the notion of neutrality to the dress code of public officials in positions of authority, whereas historically, it was more focused on behavior. And here, the strongest link seems to be the crisis of civic nationalism, which ties in with van der Veer's interference of the issues of nationalism and secularism, in this volume.

Based on this de-substantialization of laicity, it is therefore possible to elaborate a typology of laicity. Several are possible. A rather different one can be found in Baubérot&Milot (2011) built on Milot's typology (2008). I am proposing one, mainly elaborated from different cases of Euro-America, and which I will briefly confront with the analyses of Laliberté and van der Veer.

Six ideal-types can be distinguished:

### Anti-religious laicity

In this type of laicity, a civic/civil State religion tends to be explicit with its "dogmas" and its doctrinal corpus, which can discriminate against certain categories of individuals and groups. Religion is fought but entirely identifying with a logic of 'persecution' is not socially possible. A minimum number of compromises, transactions (ideologically considered provisional) exist in public policies. The freedom of conscience tends however to exclude freedom of religion —because it is considered an oppression of consciences—or at least to keep it strictly contained within the private sphere, reduced to the "intimate sphere." Citizenship equality is limited, because 'enlightened' citizens, those who have 'emancipated themselves from religious obscurantism' are seen to have a greater value than others. Separation is weak, and understood as an instrument for the state, which aims to reach a lessening of religious influence, perhaps even its ultimate suppression. Neutrality is not considered very legitimate: it would supposedly play into the persistence of a 'backward-looking' influence of religion.

### Regalian laicity

In this type of laicity, there are also "dogmas," in Rousseau's *Contrat Social* sense, that are considered necessary for social connection. They do not necessarily constitute a doctrinal totality but can induce certain differences in rights on limited points. Freedom of conscience exists within the limits imposed on the politico-religious culture(s) that the state considers legitimate. Access to civic equality therefore presupposes a certain acculturation to a civic/civil religion, which is more or less diffuse. Like the sovereignty of the state, separation is essentially understood to be beyond any ascendency of religious authority, and not like the independence of religions in relation to the state. This latter exercises a right of surveillance and can act against what it apprehends as a "threat." Neutrality is exercised within the cultural limits defined by the state.

## Identitarian Laicity
The state believes that it needs a legitimation afforded by a religion (often the historical religion), which gathers together one or more religious organizations, and with which it forges alliances and compromises. It has not managed to elaborate its own civil religion (or this civil religion needs the contribution of elements coming from "positive religions"), which differentiates this type of laicity from regalian laicity. Freedom of conscience, citizens' rights are, on certain points, even more strongly guaranteed if the individuals or groups are adepts or close associates of the identitarian religion. These rights can be limited if these citizens or groups distance themselves from it. Separation is relative: there is a reciprocal play of power/authority between the state and the religion that symbolizes national identity. Neutrality is weak because the main specific is indeed a distinct difference drawn between the identitarian believers, non identitarian believers and non-believers.

## Liberal Laicity
The state neither relies on nor combats religion. Freedom of conscience is strong but is legitimate first and foremost for individuals. They can then organize themselves into collectivities, with the logic that their association is considered to be a consequence of their individual freedom. Equality between citizens is also strong because it does not depend on religious considerations one way or the other. Separation is strict and generates indifference on the part of the state in relation to religions. Neutrality functions on a logic of abstention. However, "reasonable accommodation" linked to the freedom of conscience can make this type of laicity evolve towards a liberal multiculturalism and lead to politics of recognition.

## Collaborative Laicity
The state gives religion a certain social role. Freedom of conscience is recognized for individuals and religions as collective entities, with the possibility of a certain gradation depending on religions. Civic equality exists within the law; in fact, it can go hand in hand with certain inequalities, depending on religious affiliations. However, the more these inequalities exist, the closer one gets to identitarian laicity. Within the logic of the ideal type, it is religious phenomena or even convictions taken as a whole which are legitimated. Separation is relative because some degree of official coordination is necessary. Neutrality is relative because religion is seen as socially useful. Indifference in matters of religion is in fact devalued, but non-religious convictions can be analogically assimilated to religious organizations.

**Communitarian Laicity**
The state considers 'religious communities' as collective entities that help it keep individuals in line. Freedom of conscience is recognized for religious communities, not for individuals as such. Citizens' rights are dependent on the rights of their community. It is almost impossible not to adhere to one of them. The state is separate from the communities it oversees, but it can have special links to one or more of them. The communities have distinct rights. Neutrality is weak and can even be nonexistent when a quota system is implemented.

If liberal laicity is that in which the different parameters are the strongest, and that corresponds best to civil theories of political philosophy, it would be a mistake to reduce the field of laicity to liberal *laïcité* alone. First, liberal laicity can be the end result of other forms of laicity, and not historically first. Here again the term "laicity/*laïcité*" sheds a better light that that of "secularism." Indeed, "lay/*laïque*" is opposed to "cleric": to establish itself, laicity implies a certain anticlerical struggle, which can appear as an open struggle, but which can also present gentler characteristics, in particular by giving power to the non-religious persons (laypersons/*laïcs*) who have a political role at the very heart of national religious organizations (the case of Northern Europe, for example). Regalian laicity and, in another way, identitarian laicity can include an anticlerical aspect that liberal laicity does not have (or no longer has). Afterwards, within the context of liberal laicity, the idea that there is no more "clerical danger" can produce aspects of collaborative laicity. Thus, there is an internal coherence in the typology, which requires the inclusion of these six types of laicity.

# 6 A Hypothesis on Asian Laicity

Does this typology give too broad a definition to the concept of laicity/secularism? As I have indicated, such a typology aims to evaluate and compare. These types are ideal types and, as such, they do not exist in 'pure' form in empirical reality; rather they highlight certain specific features, as composite drawings do. A country can fall mainly within one type of laicity, while including components of other types (Baubérot 2010, 2015). In Asia as elsewhere, Asian states may therefore have characteristics of two or three types of laicity. Both Laliberté and van der Veer emphasize the importance of socio-historical changes that can lead to a permutation of the dominant laicity. Moreover, different social and political forces may clash in one single country, especially in the case of democracies, and seek to impose one type of laicity.

In addition, an evaluation of each type of laicity based on four parameters shows that there is no such thing as pure or absolute laicity. On the contrary, some types of laicity can be qualified as "minimalist laicity". Antireligious laicity on the one hand and communitarian laicity on the other are of course boarder line cases, on the edges of laicity. But I deem necessary to include them in the typology, otherwise empirical evidence of mixed types of laicity could not be accounted for. Van der Veer strongly relativizes the idea that Asian countries have not experimented, in their history, the confessionalization model. Traces of this model can be found today in some Asian states. Forms of theocracy can also coexist with legal elements of laicity, especially in states which have an established religion.

In my view, it should be possible to deduce the following classification from the analyses of Laliberté and van der Veer.

In communist countries, such as Vietnam, North Korea, and especially China, anti-religious laicity prevails (in Laos, it would be regalian laicity). However, they also feature elements of collaborative laicity (a limited number of religions are recognized) and of identitarian laicity (among the recognized religions, a distinction is made between national religions and religions perceived as "foreign"). In democratic countries, such as Taiwan, South Korea and Japan, liberal laicity dominates. In the first two countries, religious groups (such as conservative Protestants) seek nevertheless to impose a collaborative laicity, where their own norms shape public morality. This indicates that religion-state collaboration can sometimes work to the benefit of religion. Japan, on the other hand, a typical example of a nation-State built through confessionalization, is torn between liberal laicity, that has predominated since 1945, and elements of identitarian laicity, a religious nationalism. Nepal and Mongolia have some degree of liberal laicity combined with features of communitarian laicity, while in the Philippines, a regalian/collaborative laicity seems to prevail. Indonesia is, at present, a typical example of collaborative laicity as well as of its limits, with Muslim groups pushing towards for a more identitarian type. India has long been a mix of both liberal and communitarian laicity (see also Mohammad-Arif 2014), but Hindu fundamentalists would prefer to see the identitarian type dominate in India, as is already the case in Pakistan and, to a lesser extent, in Bangladesh. In all cases, it is possible to examine the various interrelations that different types of laicity have with different levels of secularization, as long as a mono-causal relation is not introduced between the two. Laliberté's observation that multiple forms of modernity do not correspond to different types of religion-state relations seems very significant. If secularization intervenes in the political process of laicization, conversely, political factors interfere with the process of secularization. Van der Veer rightly emphasizes the role of the constitution of the nation-states and the importance of nationalism. Can Confucianism be considered a secularizing element of Sinitic culture? I leave it to sinologists to decide this question. As for me, I note that the influence of Confucianism exists as much in countries where anti-religious laicity prevails as in countries where liberal laicity is dominant. Moreover, if countries with monotheistic traditions show a connection between secularization and the advent of a predominantly liberal laicity, the link is less obvious in countries where beliefs in impersonal and supernatural forces predominate.

Churches and other religious entities may think they have managed to limit secularization through a laicity with elements of collaborative laicity. But in general, this hope becomes a reality only when political factors or the need to defend against external threats induce a dynamic favorable to these groups, as in the cases of Taiwan and South Korea. And the results can be ambivalent due to resistance from civil society.

In some cases of identitarian laicity affinities with a secularized situation can facilitate "culturalization" and/or "nationalization" of the religious. However, this also promotes religious radicalism and the repression of dissenting beliefs, as in Pakistan. Emphasis on a politico-religious identity has made it possible to mask the deficit of political legitimacy. One can speak, for this state as well as for Thailand, Burma, and Sri Lanka of a 'religionization of politics' (Laliberté).

If communitarian laicity is globally linked to a low degree of secularization, the irony of history, as van der Veer notes, is that "the the secularist Muhammad Ali Jinnah became the Father of a Muslim nation while the deeply religious Mahatma Gandhi desired a secular state", one which included elements of liberal laicity and communitarian laicity. Political reasons played a role: Gandhi's purpose "was not only to confront the violence of the colonial state, but also to deal with the growing violence between the Hindu majority and the Muslim minority."

The regimes of laicity in communist countries —the regalian type and above all the anti-religious type— attempt to on individuals and groups a relative secularization (regalian laicity) or a complete secularization (anti-religious laicity). At the same time, on the societal level, secularization is often limited by forms of para-religious civil/civic religion ("Communist millenarianism have replaced the millenarian movements that were prevalent in China in the 1940s", writes van der Veer). In Eastern Europe, the political destabilization of these regimes can reveal that, for a large part, any secularizing social dynamic was blocked. Let us note here an interesting paradox: the more the laicity is anti-religious, the more researchers will question its reality. It is in this case that an authoritarian imposition of secularization on individuals and groups will be strongest.

All these are aspects that cannot be investigated if we reduce things to the overall concept of secularization alone. In addition, as I have noted above, when laicity is envisaged from a diachronic perspective, one can speak then of a process of *laicization*. In previous works on this subject (Baubérot 1998, 2007; Baubérot&Milot 2011) I have attempted to construct a typology of this process by distinguishing at first two, then three thresholds of laicization *(seuils de laïcisation)*.

I shall rapidly indicate other possible lines of inquiry. Generally, a sociological approach to laicity that takes account of the structuring into states grants importance to the fact that the states regulate religious realities that have a transnational dimension, complexifying the links between politics and religion. In addition, this approach is attentive to socio-political circulations and to socio-cultural translations (in a political cultural sense) between states and groups of states.

Thus, the critiques expressed by some (see Bhargava's work in particular) on the Western origin of secularism can be relativized by the fact that consideration (re-worked of course) of alterity, of different civilizations has played a role in the construction of secularism. We have observed this in the case of Rhode Island and Locke cites the example of the Indian doctrine of tolerance. The figure of Confucius (well-known thanks to the Jesuits and their writings) was valorized by Enlightenment philosophers as an important lever for contesting Christian society and indicating that other civilizations could legitimately be non-Christian. At a time when racialist theories dominated in biology, Jules Ferry took an interest in the Japanese school system when he wished to create a secular state school *(école publique laïque)* in France, and so on. "Civilizations spreading wide in time and space have influenced each other" (Laliberté), even if, for a few centuries, Western civilization claimed to dominate the world.

Of course, researchers must not be taken in by the context of their approach. In its innovative period, the secularization paradigm conjecturally underscored aspects, the re-use of which, like a routine vulgate, ended up being counterproductive (Baubérot&Milot 2011). In the same way, my insistence on the fact that the elaboration of secularism as a renunciation of Christianity (and/or a form of Christianity) that must be imposed politically is conjecturally determined. It is in the current socio-scientific context that such insistence appears heuristically interesting.

The final line of inquiry I propose regards the religious foreign policies of states that can be analyzed in terms of laicity/secularism (see Shakman-Hurd, 2008). International agreements can also impact laicity. In the countries belonging to the Council of Europe, there are even some guidelines of laicity/secularism on the level of supranational jurisdiction in which the European Court of Human Rights plays a role. However, not only does it leave the states plenty of room to maneuver, it must also sometimes consider other political clout. These are all paths we could take.

# 7 Secularization and the End of the Socio-Historic Period of the Enlightenment

To conclude, I will suggest two hypotheses on so-called secularization.

The first hypothesis will be rapidly presented. If the secularization paradigm is indeed dead, the notion of secularization, on the other hand, is still useful as an instrument of analysis. For example, we have just seen how the sociologist can "play" both with the notions of laicity/secularism and secularization. Casanova (1994) indicates that, given the three main propositions on religion expressed as part of the secularization paradigm (decline, privatization, and differentiation) it is the last, differentiation, which remains the most valid. Thus understood, the notion of secularization can often be linked with the notion of pluralism. At the point where the two overlap we can suggest the hypothesis of a triple accentuation of differentiation of the attitudes towards religion of various social actors. first, in each location in the globalized world, the religions on offer have multiplied, the deterritorialization of religion has increased. Then relations to religion have broadened and diversified to a point that the sociological usage of the terms orthodoxy and heterodoxy hardly seems pertinent anymore. Finally, a set of phenomena, that we try to account for by talking about mixes, *bricolages*, religious *métissage*, have expanded over the entire world.

The second hypothesis is more ambitious, and riskier. Several reflections have developed from Gauchet's (1985) thesis of a "(societal) move away from religion." Perhaps should we now wonder above all about a societal exit out of the Enlightenment, its secularization paradigm being in no doubt one of its last intellectual avatars. Let me be more specific, to immediately distinguish my sociohistorical hypothesis from certain conservative social discourses, and say that this process of societal "exit" is due neither to the fact that the Enlightenment is supposed to be the origin point of the totalitarian regimes of the twentieth century, nor to the fact that there is supposedly a "re-enchantment" of the world (as in the false stereotypical quotation from Malraux: "the twenty-first century will be religious or it will not be"). This process is connected to what we might qualify as a "crisis of success" (I have attempted to analyze this crisis of success through the lens of the transformations of medicine in France in Baubérot&Liogier 2010). The very success of the Enlightenment project engendered new problems that societies are now dealing with.

A cavalier view of history could stress structuring events. The Lisbon earthquake in 1755 on All Hallows, which caused the deaths of several thousand people in a profoundly catholic country and destroyed numerous churches, played an important role in the loss of sway of theodicy as a social belief. Voltaire and many others underlined the arbitrary aspect of the selection between victims and survivors. A debate between scholars attempted to explain the quake based on natural causes and consequently wondered if it would not be possible to prevent further catastrophes through the development of knowledge. Condorcet, then Kant were among those who took part. To the worry in the face of what had seemed unforeseeable, a new confidence in the capacity of mankind to master "nature" through knowledge was opposed, and it continued to grow during the nineteenth century.

Hence, a double discourse on progress. First, the representation of progress as a conjunction of various progresses: scientific progress engenders technical progress, which itself is transformed by the progress of public and political action into social progress, a progress in well-being. An eminently moral progress which legitimated a certain amount of collateral damage (see for example Foucault, 1973, on the development of medical knowledge). Then, the idea is that Europe (which then expands to the West) is the torch bearer of progress. It is of course recognized that Asian civilizations are older than European ones. But these civilizations got cold. Colonization, unfair treaties, imperialism will find a civilizational justification in this. Martin (2014) insists on the "birth of the sub-human at the heart of the Enlightenment." This seems pertinent if we reason more dialectically than he does by recalling the "*cosmopolitanism*" of the Enlightenment.

Various secularization processes have manifested and enchanted themselves through this double narration.

Even though these processes continued, the 1930s constitute the beginning of a disenchantment caused by an a posteriori reflection on another structuring event, not a natural catastrophe this time but a catastrophe all the same, consequence of "human" scientific and technical progress: the terrible massacre (and new phenomena such as the effects of asphyxiating gases) of the First World War of 1914–1918.

Then Auschwitz but also Hiroshima become new structuring events, which do not just put totalitarian barbarousness into play, but also the warrior policy of a democratic, and imperialistic, country.

However, these three events have most often given rise, not to a frontal critique of the narrative of progress but rather (very schematically), to an opposition between a bad military progress and a good, peaceful progress, a harmful military nuclear involvement, and a civil, harmless nuclear involvement.

Alas, two other structuring events make it currently impossible to sustain such a dissociation. After the first, Chernobyl, the demonstration was still incomplete, because we could pretend it manifested the deficiencies of the Soviet model. The second seems more significant and we can advance the hypothesis that—given its recent date on 11 March 2011 and the consequences still not under control and expected to last into the long term—we still have in a way not really measured. I'm referring of course to Fukushima.

We here find an event with multidimensional and important significations for this book: Japan is the country in Asia that, while resisting colonization victoriously, adopted and reinvented the Western model in its own way, and achieved most precociously a kind of synthesis of it. It did so in such a way that, despite a military defeat, it has surpassed most of the Western countries. If ever there were a safe country for thermonuclear power plants, a country where the most sophisticated technological precautions had been implemented, it was Japan.

Sociologists who are still more or less dependent (even in a critical way) on the paradigm of secularization perform analyses that are based on the idea that the course of History is linear; what if it looked more like a spiral? When they perceive that secularization grew out of the Enlightenment, they should ask themselves whether a socio-historical period, whose beginning can be symbolized by the Lisbon earthquake, has not come to an end in the ruins of Fukushima. This brings up again with a new emphasis the question of laicity/secularism. It is, in any case, a possible subject to address in a further collective reflection.

# References

Baubérot, Jean. 1998. "Two Threshold of Laicization". In R. Bhargava ed., *Secularism and its Critics*, pp. 94–136. New Delhi: Oxford University Press.

Baubérot, Jean. 2007. (5ᵉ éd. 2020), *Les Laïcités dans le Monde*. Paris: PUF.

Baubérot, Jean. 2010. "The Evolution of Secularism in France: Between Two Civil Religions". In L. E. Cady and E. Shakman Hurd, eds., *Comparative Secularisms in a Global Age*, pp. 57–68. New York: Palgrave Macmillan.

Baubérot, Jean. 2015. *Les 7 laïcités françaises. Le modèle français de laïcité n'existe pas*. Paris: FMSH éditions.

Baubérot, Jean and Raphaël Liogier. 2010. *Sacré Médecine. Histoire et devenir d'un sanctuaire de la Raison*. Paris: Entrelacs.

Baubérot, Jean and Micheline Milot. 2011. *Laïcités sans frontières*. Paris, Seuil.

Berger, Peter. 1971. *La religion dans la conscience moderne. Essai d'analyse culturelle*, (édit franç. de *The Sacred Canopy: Elements of a Sociological Theory of Religion*, New York, Doublebay, 1969). Paris: Le Centurion.

Berger, Peter, ed. 2001. *Le Réenchantement du monde*, (french transl. of *The Desecularization of the World*, Grand Rapids (MI): William B. Eerdmans, 1999). Paris: Bayard.

Brugger, Winfried. 2009. "From hostility through recognition to identification: state-church models and their relation to freedom of religion". In Hans Joas and Klaus Wiegandt, eds., *Secularization and the World religions*, pp. 160–180. Liverpool: Liverpool University Press.

Casanova, José. 1994. *Public Religion in the Modern World*. Chicago: University of Chicago Press.

Casanova, José. 2006. "Rethinking Secularization: A Global Comparative Perspective". *Hedgehog Review*, 6 (Spring/Summer): 11–22.

Foucault, Michel. 1973 [1963]. *The Birth of the Clinic: An Archeology of Medical perception*. Cambridge: Cambridge University Press.

Galander, Marc. 1965. "Secularism East and West". *Comparatives Studies in Society and History*, 7 no. 2: 133–159.

Hall, Timothy. 1998. *Separating Church and State. Roger Williams and Religious Liberty*. Urbana-Chicago: University of Illinois Press.

Horton, John and Suzan Mendus, eds. 2004. *John Locke. A Letter Concerning Toleration in Focus*. London/New York: Routledge.

Hurd, Elizabeth. 2004. "The Political Authority of Secularism in International Relations". *European Journal of International Relations*, 10 no. 2: 237–240.

Isambert, François. 1980. "Religion et politique. Discussions internationales". *ASSR*, N° 49/1: 77–81.

Klibansky, Raymond. 2006. "Préface". In Raymond Polin, ed., *John Locke, Lettre sur la tolerance*. Paris: PUF.

Koenig, Matthias. 2010. "Politique et religion dans les Etats-nations européens". In Jacqueline Lagrée and Philippe Portier, eds., *La Modernité contre la religion ? Pour une approche nouvelle de la laïcité*, pp. 237–255. Rennes. Presses Universitaires de Rennes.

Krämer, Gudrun. 2009. "Islam and Secularisation". In Hans Joas and Klaus Wiegandt, eds. *Secularization and the World religions*, pp. 108–121. Liverpool: Liverpool University Press.

Kuru, Ahmet. 2009. *Secularism and State Politics towards Religion. The United States, France and Turkey*. New York: Cambridge University Press.

Laliberté, André. 2014. "La circulation du modèle de séparation entre le politique et le religieux (*zhengjiao fenli*) adopté par le Japon, la Chine, la Corée et le Vietnam". *Colloque Sécularisations et Laïcités en Asie. Regards croisés sur ces phénomènes et leur approche*.

Martin, Xavier. 2014. *Naissance du sous-homme au cœur des Lumières. Les races, les femmes, le peuple*. Poitiers: Dominique Martin Morin éditeur.

Milot, Micheline. 2008. *La Laïcité*. Montréal: Novalis.

Mohammad-Arif, Aminah. 2014. "Le sécularisme à l'indienne: la réinvention d'un concept exogène". *Colloque Sécularisations et Laïcités en Asie. Regards croisés sur ces phénomènes et leur approche*.

Plesner, Ingvill. 2008. *Freedom of religion and belief – a quest for state neutrality?* Oslo: University of Oslo.

Shakman-Hurd, Elizabeth. 2008. *The Politics of Secularism in International Relations*. Princeton: Princeton University Press.

Smith, Donald E. 1963. *India as a Secular State*. Princeton: Princeton University Press.
Weber, Max. 2008 [1904–1905]. *L'éthique protestante et l'esprit du capitalisme suivi d'autres essais* (presentation and translation of J.-P. Grossein). Paris: Gallimard.

Peter van der Veer
# Secularism in Asia

**Abstract:** This chapter addresses two issues that do not seem to receive enough attention in the discussion of secularism. The first is the question of the secular as rational. This question is raised especially by Max Weber's work on Entzauberung. It relates to secular policies against magic or superstition, especially in communist states. The second issue is that of violence against religious minorities. The relation between minority and majority is crucial in all nation-states and secularism of the state seems an important factor in them. The chapter focuses on the comparison of secularism in India and China. In various ways, Asian intellectuals have sought to connect modern ideas about the location of religion in society and state with Asian traditions. In East Asia, this has led to various forms of repression of certain kinds of religion as superstitious impediments to progress. In South Asia, this is subsumed under a unifying impulse to create religious forms of nationalism. The imperative of modern nationalism is to nationalize religion. This leads to the understanding of some religions as belonging to the civilizational essence, while marginalizing other religions. The very existence of religious difference can be interpreted as a challenge to the unitary state and its developmental mission. Forms of secularism are essential in extending the protection of the state to religious minorities and to differences in beliefs and practices.

# 1 Introduction

In this contribution, I want to focus on Asian nationalisms, secular and religious. Asian states are modern and secular to the extent that they have legislatures, citizenship, territorial sovereignty, and forms of distancing between the state and religious institutions. They also have constitutions that declare religious freedom as a fundamental right. Secularity of the state belongs to a modern mission of development and progress that requires an adherence to scientific knowledge and planning. On the other hand, religious identities and institutions play a significant role in Asian societies. Religion is an important part of Asian nations and nationalism. The nation is a *project*, and never a finished one. Nationalism is the cultural politics that has the nation as its subject and its object. It derives its energy and motivating force from perceived threats to national

**Peter van der Veer** (Max Plank Institute)

https://doi.org/10.1515/9783110733068-004

unity from within and from outside. Nationalisms are secular to the extent that their primary reference point is "the people" and not "God". Xi Jinping is not a 'Son of Heaven' nor is Narendra Modi a 'dharmaraja'. Nationalists have to define who "the people" are and who do not belong to that category. In this definitional act, they may turn to religion, but they can also turn to ethnicity or language, or to a combination of these. The Chinese and Vietnamese communist nationalisms have not turned to religion, but primarily to ethnicity (Han or Kinh). Nevertheless, some religions like Daoism, Buddhism, or Hinduism are increasingly understood as closer to the ethnic essence of the national civilization than religions like Christianity and Islam that are seen as alien. The Indians have turned to Hinduism as a core of their nationalism, while, the Thai, the Burmese, and the Sri Lankans have turned to Buddhism. All of them have declared Islam as alien. The Pakistani, and increasingly the Malaysians and the Indonesians, on the contrary, have made Islam the core of their nationalisms and have distanced themselves from Christianity and Hinduism. None of this is stable. What matters is what can unify the majority of the nation. The ironies of history are such that the secularist Muhammad Ali Jinnah became the Father of a Muslim nation, while the deeply religious Mahatma Gandhi desired a secular state. These ironies show that there is nothing very fixed about 'the secular' or 'the religious' and that these terms have to be analyzed in their mutuality.

The nation-state frames the secular and the religious as well as their interactions. The secular and the religious have both to be interpreted from the perspective of socio-political organization (Baubérot, this volume). From a universal human rights perspective, particular practices in a nation-state, such as the curtailing of religious freedom, may be subjected to external criticism, but the sovereign power of the nation-state prevails. The global centrality of the nation-state is undiminished despite the tremendous increase of global connections in the past several decades. The spread of Covid-19 from China to the rest of the world has made this abundantly clear. Whatever the role of the World Health Organization may have been, national governments decided to close their borders and scramble for medical supplies to provide to their citizens. If there is anything that crosses boundaries, it is infectious diseases (McNeill 1976). Nevertheless, a global crisis was addressed by national policies. Even the supra-national European Union turned out to have no authority in coordinating the responses of their member states. What this health crisis also clarified was the immense gap in knowledge and understanding that still separates Asia from the rest of the world. In hindsight, it is hard to imagine how the threat of this virus could have been perceived as a problem limited to China, as if China is not an integral part of the world economy. The massive response by the Chinese authorities, however belated, and the similarly strict response by the Vietnamese authorities have been dismissed in the West as typical for societies in which the population blindly follows the instructions of the authorities.

One needs to go beyond residual orientalism by fully acknowledging that Asian societies are an integral part of the modern world. The nation-form of societies has been globalized. This implies that Asian nation-states are comparable to any other nation-states in the world system, without assuming that nation-states are identical to each other. There are multiple options in historical pathways that, once taken, have significant consequences for the nature of nation-states (see Akan 2017; Baubérot, Even, Laliberté in this volume). China did not have to become communist in the 1940s. India and Pakistan did not have to part ways and become enemies. In fact, even at the end of the 1930s such an outcome for China and India would have been hard to imagine. What connects Asia to the West is the formative period of imperialism, the colonial struggle, and the postcolonial predicament. The present shape of Asian nation-states has therefore to be interpreted not only in relation to the pre-colonial past, but also to imperial interactions that have shaped Asia and Europe (and the USA) in equal measure.

In what follows I want to address two issues that do not seem to receive enough attention in the discussion of secularism. The first is the question of the secular as rational. This question is raised especially by Max Weber's work on *Entzauberung*. It relates to secular policies against magic or superstition, especially in communist states, such as Vietnam and China (see Ji, Bourdeaux, Picard in this volume). The second issue is that of violence against religious minorities. The relation between minority and majority is crucial in all nation-states and secularism of the state seems an important factor in them.

Let me begin with the Weberian question of *Entzauberung* which is usually translated with disenchantment, a term that does not enough emphasize *Zauber* or magic. As I have argued at some length elsewhere, in India and China the concepts of the religious and secular need to be further connected with 'magic' and 'spirituality' (Van der Veer 2014). Together they form a syntagmatic chain of religion-magic-secularity-spirituality, which means that they do not possess stable meanings independently from one another and thus cannot be simply defined separately. They emerge historically together, imply one another, and function as nodes within a shifting field of power. This syntagmatic chain occupies a key position in nationalist imaginings of modernity. In Asia, the imperial encounter shapes these connected conceptions. The nineteenth-century Western distinction between religion and magic purports to 'purify' religion from a large category of beliefs and practices that are seen as contrary to scientific knowledge. Religion becomes in that way a source of morality (individual, national, universal) that is in no way competing with scientific progress or hindering it. Magic, then, is a rest-category that is supposed to disappear gradually from secular modernity thanks to literacy and general education. Most influentially, Max Weber argued in his comparative work on world religions that it was only ascetic Protestantism that had led to a complete elimination of magic and thus had laid the foundation of the modern world (Weber 1989: 114, 450; Lehmann 2009). Other religions had only achieved modern rationality in partial ways. From Victorian anthropology which saw magic as 'false science' to Weberian sociology magic signified an evolutionary phase that had to be left behind in attaining modernity. Scholars and missionaries either conceptualized the Asian traditions as superstitious and false, or proposed ways in which the magical should be separated from the truly religious or spiritual. In Asia, orientalist scholarship with these suppositions could connect to traditional indigenous critiques of certain beliefs and practices.

In China modern secularism fed on a deeply ingrained opposition between literate elites and illiterate, popular masses. One of the perceived tasks for modernizers in late nineteenth-century China was to remove traditional obstacles to progress. Religion as such was not to be eradicated except for those elements that were deemed superstition. In the second half of the twentieth century, the communist party continued this campaign against popular beliefs, despite its claim that it was the champion of the popular masses. In contemporary China, the opposition between officially approved religions and local forms of superstition gives authorities great leeway in controlling and repressing all kinds of religious expressions. This also characterizes the situation in Vietnam. In both China and Vietnam, the state shows sovereign power through arbitrariness in alternatively and intermittently repressing, controlling, or supporting religious manifestations (Wang 2020).

Chinese secularism in particular is a form of scientism and rationalism. Using a nineteenth-century enlightened and evolutionary perspective on history and society, it pitches scientific rationality against magical superstition. This secularist project is shared by intellectuals of all persuasions, including the nationalists and the Communists, but also by many Confucian reformist thinkers. While the secular stance of Chinese intellectuals resembles that of French intellectuals, it is part of a much global phenomenon. Casanova puts the role of intellectuals in a broad comparative perspective. In his view, "the study of modern secularism, as an ideology, as a generalized worldview, and as a social movement, and of its role as a crucial carrier of processes of secularization and as a catalyst for counter-secularization responses should be high on the agenda of a self-reflexive comparative historical sociology of secularization" (Casanova 2006: 17).

One also finds scientism and rationalism in India, but here it is inflected by anti-Brahmanical ideologies, especially in South India, where it is connected to rejections of the caste system (Binder 2020). Reformers did often attempt to purify religion from magical superstition but did not pose an opposition between religion and science. Instead, they argued that religion was rational and had scientific foundations, allowing it to be the basis of modern nationalism. Secularism in India emerges in the context of a supposedly secular colonial state that many Indians suspected to hide its Christian nature. Religion became a major element of anti-colonial mobilization while at the same time reinforcing the mutual antagonism of Hindu and Muslim communities. The Partition and its aftermath have not ended the use of religion for political mobilization. It continues to characterize politics in India, Pakistan, Bangladesh, Sri Lanka, and Myanmar.

The ways in which secularism and religion feed on each other is subject to much debate (Asad 1993; Goossaert & Palmer 2011). This is clearest in the ways in which Communist millenarianism have replace the millenarian movements that were prevalent in China in the 1940s (Dubois 2005). Rather than secularism wiping out religion it takes over some of its messages, or even rituals, while transforming the space of public religious activity in significant ways. In China, this process is under way already under the Kuomintang regime, and before (Nedostup 2009). In South Asia, we find that Hindus, Buddhists, and Muslims have made religion the core of national civilization. This is also true for secularists like Nehru and Gandhi. Both recognized that only a secular India would allow various minorities to live together, while acknowledging that India was at core Hindu. In the end, more than anything else, at the heart of secularism is the question how minorities are treated and how violence is prevented. This leads me to the second issue that is important in understanding secularism, which is that of political violence in the relation between religious majorities and minorities.

Majorities and minorities belong to a politics of numbers that only become possible with censuses and other tools of modern governance. They become the basis of electoral politics in modern democracies, but they are also significant in minority policies in communist societies, like China and Vietnam, that do not have electoral mobilization (see Picard, Madinier, Ji, Bourdeaux) in this volume). It is important for authorities to know how many members there are of a religious or ethnic community and whether they are located in geopolitically sensitive areas (Ngo 2016). An important question is how such communities related to one another before modern state formation (Bayly 1985). Nationalists often answer this historical question in civilizational terms of indigenous belonging or foreignness.

Casanova has recently argued that to understand the history of the modern secular nation-state one should examine the confessionalization of early modern European states: "Everywhere in early modern Europe one finds similar processes of state-led confessionalization. Northern Europe becomes homogenously Protestant, Southern Europe homogeneously Catholic and in between one finds three bi-confessional societies-Holland, Germany, and Switzerland-unable to eliminate the other religious half, having to coexist, and developing their own patterns of Protestant-Catholic confessionalization: confessional pillars in the case of Holland, confessional Länder in the case of Germany, and confessional cantons in the case of Switzerland" (Casanova 2018: 14 – 15). He views secularization as a process that begins with confessionalization leading to the formation of national identity. In his interpretation, the Reformation and the Counter-Reformation created the conditions for nationalism through state-controlled religious confessionalization, involving ethnic or religious "cleansing", where adherence to a national church was a prerequisite to full belonging.

Is the early-modern European history of religious warfare and cleansing relevant for our understanding of pre-colonial India and China? Scholars often answer this question in the negative by referring to doctrinal indifference as well as the insignificance of belief (as opposed) to ritual in Asian religions such as Hinduism, Daoism, and Buddhism (Watson 1993). These religions have come to be seen as essentially syncretistic and tolerant, which leads to the assumption that their contemporary intolerance is a product of modernity (Nandy 1995). However, as Casanova (following the historian Kiri Paramore) has pointed out, the confessionalization of the Japanese state and the cleansing of the Christian minority in the sixteenth century bears an interesting resemblance to European history. The Jesuits entered Japan in 1549, supported by the Portuguese. At the end of the sixteenth century, after the crucifixion of 26 priests and converts, Christianity was violently suppressed. Only pockets of surviving hidden Christians, similar to Marranos in Spain, remained in Japan, constantly fearing to be questioned about their beliefs. Japan's nationhood and its state control over religious belief emerged from the purging of Christianity (Paramore 2009). In the twentieth century, according to Helen Hardacre (1989) Shinto was transformed into State Shinto that was used to legitimate military expansion (see Dufourmont in this volume).

In China, outright religious warfare occurred regularly between the imperial state and millenarian movements. These movements often got their inspiration from Buddhist ideas about the end of an era (*kalpa*) and the coming of the Maitreya Buddha. Messages about the immorality and injustice of imperial rule were conveyed through spirit writing or spirit possession. We know about these movements mainly through imperial archives that often designated them as White Lotus Movements (Ter Haar 1992). This makes it difficult to interpret them, but it is perhaps not incorrect to see some resemblance with heretics and various dissenting Protestants in Europe, challenging the religious authority of the state.

The Taiping movement, significantly influenced by Christianity, and ethnically related to the Hakka outcasts, created a massive rebellion against the Qing between 1850 and 1864, which cost an estimated 20 million dead and caused an enormous migration of tens of millions of people to South-East Asia. Minorities like the Hmong-Miao and Hakka in Vietnam and Laos all originate from China and fled in this period. It is hard to overestimate the significance of this iconoclastic movement that destroyed sacred places in a large part of Southern China.

A big difference between China and Europe, obviously, is the singularity of the imperial state. The Chinese imperial formation has been able to prevent separate nation-formations that, in principle, would have been quite feasible on grounds of history, language, and religion. As long as the Mandate of Heaven and the institutions of the state were accepted, a large measure of doctrinal diversity was allowed. In that sense, one could perhaps argue that the Qing Empire practiced secularism with Confucian characteristics (Van der Veer 2016). To an extent the Communists (and before them the Nationalists) have inherited this form of secular state control, but the difference is that today China has a developmental state that targets a society with now almost one and a half billion population, two times the size of entire Europe that has 50 sovereign states. The Communist state has also inherited the results of the Qing expansion in the nineteenth century. The Qing acquired Tibet and Xinjiang only after their defeat of the Zungar Mongols in the eighteenth century. This is simultaneously the period of massive Han migration into South-West China (Yunnan, Sichuan). All these areas have known widespread ethno-religious resistance against the penetration of the Qing and later the Communists. It is precisely in the areas where ethnic nationalism aligns with religion (Tibetan Buddhism, Uyghur Islam) that separatism is a possibility. The Chinese case shows the significance of religious nationalism not only in the resistance against the Chinese state, but also in the recent attempts by the Chinese state to use so-called national religions (Chinese Buddhism and Daoism) against the expansion of so-called foreign religions, like Islam and Christianity.

Is there a precolonial Indian history of religious conflict and warfare, resulting in religious purification and ethnic cleansing, comparable to those elements of European history? The obvious case in the recent history of nation-state formation is the Partition, which caused the displacement of around 14 million people and the loss of hundreds of thousands of lives. That India had a history of religious warfare before the colonial period is widely accepted in Indian studies, but the interpretation of that warfare is bitterly disputed.

Hindu nationalists understand the history of iconoclasm as part of the Muslim conquest of India as the contemporary legitimation of the destruction of mosques and the re-claiming of Hindu sacred territory. The most famous case is that of the Babar mosque in Ayodhya, but there are similar disputed mosques in Varanasi or Mathura. In my own work on Ayodhya, I have tried to show that there is in fact substantial evidence of the support of Hindu temples by the Nawabs of Awadh, rulers of the area (Van der Veer 1988). However, such a more nuanced view of the relations between Muslim rulers and the Hindu population does not alter what comes into the history textbooks in Indian schools (Benei 2008).

The religious wars of early modern Europe have generally been interpreted as leading to forms of pacification, such as the Westphalian Peace treaty, which resulted in a system of international relations between nation-states. Casanova's emphasis on the process of confessionalization as a step towards the secular nation-state as well as Terpstra's historical account of religious purification and ethnic cleansing draws our attention to the study of violence and sovereignty (Terpstra 2015). Such a perspective may also be important for the study of Asia. Gandhi's non-violent political action was in my view a form of secularism in the sense that its purpose was not only to confront the violence of the colonial state, but also to deal with the growing violence between the Hindu majority and the Muslim minority. For this purpose, Indian secularism has to discuss the legacy of Muslim state formation in a Hindu majority society in a critical manner. There is clear historical evidence that Muslim states did not attempt to purify India from Hindu beliefs and practices. In fact, Muslim rulers often wanted to avail themselves of the indigenous, magical powers of the land. Sometimes this led to iconoclasm, the memory of which is a crucial element in Hindu nationalism, but in other times, it also entailed Muslim patronage for Hindu temples and ascetics. This history is not one of syncretism and tolerance, but of power and sovereignty, often implying religious warfare and iconoclasm. It did not lead to the formation of a number of confessional states, simply because Muslims remained a minority in an overwhelmingly Hindu society. The postcolonial state inherited the unified territory of British India, but the Partition resulted in confessionalization. Pakistan became a confessional homeland for Muslims and India as a secular Hindu nation-state is now in the process of transformation into a confessional Hindu state.

In China, recurrent clashes between millenarian movements and the imperial state did not result in confessional states. The Confucian mandate of heaven continued after the Manchus became the dominant force in a Han majority society. Secularism in China entails state control over religious expression and from time to time outright repression of divergent beliefs and practices. The legitimation of this control and repression is the prevention of religious conflict, and especially of a millenarian challenge to the state, as shown by the ruthless repression of the Falungong.

In conclusion, the Asian states have adopted forms of secularism from the Western colonial powers, but Asian nationalisms build on complex histories of ethno-religious relations and conflicts. In various ways, Asian intellectuals have sought to connect modern ideas about the location of religion in society and state with Asian traditions. In East Asia, this has led to various forms of repression of certain kinds of religion as superstitious impediments to progress. In South Asia, this reformist tendency is also noticeable, but it is subsumed under a unifying impulse to create religious forms of nationalism. The imperative of modern nationalism is to nationalize religion. In the number games of both democratic regimes and communist regimes, this leads to the understanding of some religions as belonging to the civilizational essence, while marginalizing other religions. The very existence of religious difference can be interpreted as a challenge to the unitary state and its developmental mission. Forms of secularism are essential in extending the protection of the state to religious minorities and to differences in beliefs and practices (see Laliberté in this volume).

# References

Asad, Talal. 1993. *Genealogies of Religion*. Baltimore: Johns Hopkins University.
Akan, Murat. 2017. *The Politics of Secularism: Religion, Diversity, and Institutional Change in France and Turkey*. New York: Columbia University Press.
Bayly, C.A. 1985. "The Pre-History of 'Communalism'? Religious Conflict in India, 1700–1860". *Modern Asian Studies*, 19 no. 2: 177–203.
Benei, Véronique. 2008. *Schooling Passions*. Palo Alto: Stanford University Press.
Binder Stefan. 2020. *Total Atheism. Secular Activism and the Politics of Difference in South India*. Oxford: Berghahn.
Casanova, José. 2006. "Secularization Revisited: A Reply to Talal Asad". In David Scott and Charles Hirschkind, eds., *Powers of the Secular Modern. Talal Asad and His Interlocutors*, pp. 12–30. Palo Alto: Stanford University Press.
Casanova, José. 2018. "Asian Catholicism, Interreligious Colonial Encounters and Dynamics of Secularism in Asia". In K. Dean and P. van der Veer, eds., *The Secular in South, East, and Southeast Asia*, pp. 13–34. Berlin: Palgrave MacMillan.
Dubois, Thomas. 2005. *The Sacred Village. Social Change and Religious Life in Rural North China*. Honolulu: University of Hawaii Press.
Goossaert, Vincent and David A. Palmer. 2011. *The Religious Question in Modern China*. Chicago: Chicago University Press.
Hardacre, Helen. 1989. *Shinto and the State, 1868–1988*. Princeton: Princeton University Press.
Lehmann, Hartmut. 2009. *Die Entzauberung der Welt. Studien zu Themen von Max Weber*. Göttingen: Wallstein.
McNeill, William. 1976. *Plagues and Peoples*. Garden City/New York: Doubleday/Anchor.

Nandy, Ashis. 1995. "An Anti-Secularist Manifesto", *India International Quarterly* 22 no. 1: 35–64.
Nedostup, Rebecca. 2009. *Superstitious Regimes: Religion and the Politics of Chinese Modernity*. Cambridge, MA: Harvard University Press.
Ngô, Tâm T. T. 2016. *The New Way: Protestantism and the Hmong in Vietnam*. Seattle: University of Washington Press.
Paramore, Kiri. 2009. *Ideology and Christianity in Japan*. London: Routledge.
Terpstra, Nicholas. 2015. *Religious Refugees in the Early Modern World*. Cambridge: Cambridge University Press.
Ter Haar, Barend. 1992. *The White Lotus Teachings in Chinese Religious History*. Leiden: Brill.
Van der Veer, Peter. 1988. *Gods on Earth*, London: Athlone.
Van der Veer, Peter. 2014. *The Modern Spirit of Asia. The Spiritual and the Secular in China and India*. Princeton: Princeton University Press.
Van der Veer, Peter. 2016. "Is Confucianism secular?". In Akeel Bilgrami, ed., *Secularism Beyond the West*, pp. 117–134. New York: Columbia University.
Wang, Xiaoxuan. 2020 *Maoism and Grassroots Religion. The Communist Revolution and the Reinvention of Religious Life in China*. New York: Oxford University Press.
Watson, James. 1993. "Rites or Beliefs: The Construction of a Unified Culture in Late Imperial China". In Lowell Dittmer and Samuel Kim, eds., *China's Quest for National Identity*. Ithaca: Cornell University Press: 80–103.
Weber, Max. 1989. *Die Wirtschaftsethik der Weltreligionen, Konfuzianismus und Taoismus. Schriften 1915–1920*, ed. by Hedwig Schmidt-Glinzer. Tübingen: Mohr-Siebeck.

Rémy Madinier
# Pancasila in Indonesia a "Religious Laicity" Under Attack?

**Abstract:** Unlike most Muslim-majority countries which, at the time of their independence, had to choose urgently and sometimes painfully between a secularized regime and the adoption of Islam as the state religion, Indonesia is one of the rare cases in which in-depth political debates were held on the relationship between religion and the state. If one were to attempt nonetheless to define the Indonesian approach to the place of religion within the state, one would be tempted to use an oxymoron: "religious laicity." Adopted at independence in 1945, the Indonesian official ideology enshrines as the first of its five principles (Pancasila) the "Belief in One Almighty God" (Ketuhanan yang Maha Esa) as the foundation of the Indonesian nation. This original formula, unprecedented in the history of religious policy of a modern state, is based on both spiritual inventiveness and a keen sense of political pragmatism. Pancasila was inspired by a plurality of spiritual references and founded a religious status quo still in force today in which Indonesia, home to the world's largest Muslim population, gave equal recognition to six religions (Islam, Protestantism, Catholicism, Hinduism, Buddhism and Confucianism), despite large demographic differences. Defended by religious minorities and enshrined by various political regimes since independence, Pancasila is, however, regularly challenged, in various ways, by militant Islam.

## 1 Introduction

Adopted at independence in 1945, the Indonesian official ideology enshrines as the first of its five principles (Pancasila) "the Belief in One Almighty God" (*Ketuhanan yang Maha Esa*) as the foundation of the Indonesian nation.[1] This orig-

---

[1] "Ketuhanan Yang Maha Esa" has been Translated into English in many different ways: "Divine Omnipotence" (Sidjabat 1965: 20); "The Being of Supreme Deity" (Kafrawi, 1956); "Oneness of God" (Kafrawi, 1956: 2). Until the end of the 80's the most frequent official translation was "Belief in God" (Yayasan Proklamasi: 1978) but, interestingly, "Belief in the One and Only God" seems the new official translation. As was rightly noted by Darmaputera (1988:153), "God" is Allah in Indonesian, a particular God of Islam and Christianity. "Tuhan" is "Lord" in English.

---

Rémy Madinier (CASE-CNRS-CRISEA)

https://doi.org/10.1515/9783110733068-005

inal formula, unprecedented in the history of religious policy of a modern state, is based both on spiritual inventiveness and a keen sense of political pragmatism. Pancasila was inspired by a plurality of spiritual references and founded a religious status quo still in force today in which Indonesia, home to the world's largest Muslim population, gave equal recognition to six religions (Islam, Protestantism, Catholicism, Hinduism and Confucianism), despite large demographic differences.[2]

When speaking about Indonesia's approach to religion, it is difficult to do so otherwise than in terms of what it is not. The status quo established at the birth of the state reposes on a delicate balance of forces which is still operative today. This equilibrium was founded on a process of detachment from two antonymic notions—an Islamic state (*Negara Islam*) and a secular state (*Negara Sekular*)—a process which has deep historical roots.

Concerning the detachment from secularism, these roots can be traced back, first and foremost to the Indonesian nationalist movement's desire to emancipate itself from the Dutch colonial legacy which was closely associated with secularism. Although the Dutch term (*secularisme*) was transposed into Indonesian as *sekularisme* it soon acquired such a pejorative connotation that it became common to refer to "religiously neutral" nationalism (*netral agama*) when referring to the political writings of Soekarno, the nation's founding father and the inspiration behind Pancasila (Noer 1973).[3]

---

The prefix "ke-" and the suffix "-an" means an abstract idea or a concept. So the correct way to translate "Ketuhanan" is "Lordship". The word *Maha* is from Sanskrit, meaning great, abundant, or mighty. *Esa* is also from Sanskrit and it means existence but in Malay and Indonesian it has taken on the meaning of "one". So a more literal translation of "Ketuhanan Yang Maha Esa" should be "(belief) in the great one Lordship".

**2** In the 2010 Indonesian census, 87.18% of Indonesians identified themselves as Muslims, (Sunnis comprised more than 99%, Shias 0,5% Ahmadis, 0,2%), 6,96% Protestants, 2,91% Catholics, 1.69% Hindus, 0.72% Buddhists, 0.05% Confucianists, 0.13% other, and 0.38% unstated or not asked.

**3** Jean Baubérot (2014) provided another argument against the use of the term "secular" when he pointed out that it would run the risk of distorting the debate due to its "semantic proximity to the terms secularize and secularization." Secularism seems for some to be the notion associated with secularization, drawn from political ideology. This is the case for many people in Indonesia as shown at the beginning of the 1970's by the very negative reactions to the proposal of *sekularisasi* by the prominent Muslim scholar Nurcholish Madjid. Madjid himself misused the term, since he was only calling on the Muslim community to pursue de-sacralization (*desakralisasi*), that is to say to avoid the sacralization of human institutions. At the time, he faced very harsh criticism. In 2005, a fatwa from the Indonesian Ulema Council condemning secularism showed to what extent using this term was still fraught with risk.

The notion of an Islamic state, on the other hand, was to the forefront of the Muslim nationalist movement's claims in the years before independence and was prevalent during the pre-war years. It was subsequently hijacked by *Darul Islam*, a regionalist rebellion which proclaimed an Islamic Indonesian state in 1949 and against which the Indonesian Republic was engaged in a constant struggle until the early 1960s. This rebellion forced a change upon Masyumi, a major political party whose goal was to establish a Muslim democracy and who had used the term *Negara Islam* during the independence struggle. Following the *Darul Islam* insurrection, however, it decided to remove references to *Negara Islam* from its manifestoes for fear of there being a confusion between the two.

In an attempt to avoid being confined to one of the categories ordinarily used to define the relations between the political and religious spheres, the Indonesian authorities insisted on pointing out that their country was "neither a secular nor a religious state." ("Bukan negara agama, bukan negara sekuler").[4] The president of Indonesia from 1999 to 2001, Abdurrahman Wahid, a respected cleric who presided for many years over the fortunes of the main traditionalist Muslim organisation, Nahdlatul Ulama, and who had a certain way with words, spoke of a *"negara bukan-bukan"*, a "neither-nor state" (Ridwan 2018).

If one were to attempt nonetheless to define the Indonesian approach to the place of religion within the state, one would be tempted to use an oxymoronic term: "religious laicity". The country is most decidedly religious, having placed a divine principle at the core of its foundations containing as it does one of the most religious populations in the world.[5]

As for the term "laicity", it is an accurate reflection of the remarkably ingenious way in which the state has developed its relations with religions. As was the case for France, the state approached the place of religion by setting out very precise rules. The difference between the two countries lies in the fact that where French law-makers favoured a principle of strict separation between the fields of spirituality and governance, their Indonesian counterparts on the

---

4 See for examples, the declaration made to this effect by the constitutional court judge, Patrialis Akbar, in 1964 or that in 2018 by Mahfud MD who had been the presiding judge of the same court between 2008 and 2013 and who is now a member of the Presidential working unit for the implementation of Pancasila as the state ideology.

5 A study by the Pew Foundation in September 2008 of 23 countries showed that 99% of Indonesians consider religion to be important in their lives, with 95% saying it was very important. These results placed Indonesia at the top of the list, far ahead of other Muslim countries such as Jordan, Pakistan, Nigeria, Egypt or Turkey. *The Pew Global Project Attitudes*, September 2008.

other hand wished to fully assume their cross-pollinating relationship and to give it a framework.

By pronouncing the principle of *"Ketuhanan yang Maha Esa"*, the nation's founding fathers gave the state the means to elaborate a "dialogic process of localisation of 'world religions' and globalisation of 'local religions'" (Picard and Madinier 2011: xi). Although it is not possible to speak strictly about a separation between the state's main religion and its institutions, one can nonetheless remark that the widespread use of very diverse references allowed the state to distance itself from Islam. The way in which it did so, however, has been and remains the subject of lively debate since independence.

## 2 The "Birth of Pancasila", a Subtle Blend of Diverse Spiritual Influences

Unlike most Muslim-majority countries that had to choose urgently and sometimes painfully at the time of their independence between a secularized regime and the adoption of Islam as the state religion, Indonesia is one of the rare cases in which in-depth political debates were held on the relationship between religion and the state (Boland, 1982). In most Muslim countries, debates on Islam and secularism ended with the victory of one over the other, either with the victory of Islam, such as in Pakistan, Iran, Saudi Arabia, and Malaysia, or the victory of secularism, such as in Egypt, Turkey and Tunisia. In Indonesia, the debates conducted during the last months of the Japanese occupation, over the course of a number of successive forums held between April and August 1945, led to the formulation of an ideology based on compromise, a Middle Path, taking into account the complexity of the country's spiritual legacy and its wide variety of religious and intellectual influences from elsewhere.

If one wants to have an idea of the diversity of references which nourished the collective debate and deliberation that took place between April and August 1945 and led to the adoption of Pancasila, one need only read Soekarno's famous speech of June 1, 1945, later called "the Birth of Pancasila."[6] In this speech, the founding father of the Republic of Indonesia proposed to adopt five founding principles gathered under the term Pancasila with reference to Mpu Prapanca (Nagarakertagama) and Mpu Tantular (Sutasoma), two great thinkers and poets who

---

[6] For a complete (French) translation and analysis of this speech as well as an examination of the extraordinary political destiny of what still remains today the official ideology of the Republic of Indonesia, see Bonneff et *al.*, 1980.

lived under the Hindu Kingdom of Majapahit during the reign of Hayam Wuruk (fourteenth century). He explained that independent Indonesia needed a *Weltanschauung* (in German) or what was called in Dutch a *philosophische grondslag* (philosophical grounds). He acknowledged the influence of Adolph Baars, a Dutch socialist thinker, and of Sun Yat Sen, the founder of the Republic of China (Soekarno had read Sun Yat Sen's work *San Min Chu I* [The Three People's Principles]), he quoted Ernest Renan, the French historian of national identity, and also Mahatma Gandhi (Ismail 1995: 32–35). In the course of his speech, Soekarno laid out "five principles"—*Pancasila* in Sanskrit—as the cornerstones of the new Indonesian state. These five principles were nationalism (*Kebangsaan*), internationalism or humanism (*Perikemanusiaan*), democracy by consensus (*Permyusawaratan*), social prosperity (*Kesejahteraan sosial*) and belief in one God (*Ketuhanan*). The founding father of Indonesia, in his long intellectual journey which led to the "ketuhanan" proposal, also met, and to some extent absorbed, the secularist ideas of Mustafa Kemal Attatürk (1881–1936), the founder of modern Turkey who was responsible for separating religion from the state. But in Soekarno's mind, however, religion and state could be united, and in this he was also influenced by the ideas formulated by modernist Islamic thinkers such as Muhammad Abduh and Jamal al-Din al Afghani, whom he discovered during his stay in Surabaya with H.O.S. Tjokroaminoto—a Muslim intellectual and at that time the leader of Sarekat Islam.

The announcement of the fifth principle, "belief in one God" was greeted with a sigh of relief by the Muslim representatives, as it ruled out the prospect of a completely secular state.[7] Independent Indonesia would, then, as Muhammad Yamin had proposed a few days earlier, be religious (*akan berketuhanan*). However, Soekarno, explaining the nature of religion in the new state, said:

"every Indonesian wants to be able to worship his faith in his own way. Christians according to the commands of Jesus, Muslims according to the Prophet Mohammad's, the Buddhists according to their Holy Books ... It is within this fifth principle, my friends, that all religions which exist in Indonesia at the moment will be able to find their place."

---

7 A few weeks later, the "belief in one God" became the first of *Pancasila's* principles.

## 3 The Reasons for the State's Detachment from Islam – an Old Javanese Vision of Religion

Islam, then, was simply referred to in the same vein as the country's other religions. No reference was made to a particular status which Muslims considered themselves entitled to demand given their numerical superiority in the country. In the Soekarnist world-view, Islam was not a source of law, but rather a source of inspiration, a personal matter to be left to each individual's conscience. This proposal, though, ran into the stubborn opposition of Islam's representatives who, from the outset, refused to abandon the possibility of a special position for Islam in the new state. In response to the significant and persistent disagreements between nationalists and Islam's representatives, all the members of the Committee for Preparatory Work for Indonesian Independence (Badan Penjelidik Usaha-Usaha Kemerdekaan Indonesia, BPUKI) who were still present in Jakarta met again to nominate a special committee of nine members who were given the task of drawing up a compromise solution to this thorny problem. It came up this on 22 June in a document which Yamin subsequently called "the Jakarta Charter" (*Piagram Jakarta*). The charter was supposed to be the preamble to the future Constitution of an "Indonesian state which is a republic resting upon the people's sovereignty and founded on the belief in God, *with the obligation for adherents of the Islamic faith to abide by Islamic laws*, in accordance with the principle of righteous and just humanity, the unity of Indonesia, and a democracy led by wise guidance through consultations, ensuring social justice for the whole Indonesian people."[8]

In the absence of any specific detail on the nature of the duty owed by Muslims—it was unclear if the duty was a legal one or simple a moral one—and given the vagueness surrounding the notion of Islamic laws, the practical implications of these "seven words"[9] for the country's new institutions were entirely dependent on its interpretation and concrete application by those in power.

But in august 1945, with the imminent arrival of Allied troops, it was obvious that Dutch soldiers would soon return to the country with the intention of restoring the Netherlands' colonial authority there. On 17 August 1945, Soekarno and Mohammad Hatta declared independence; on the same day, the latter, at the request of Admiral Mayeda, received a visit from a Japanese naval officer who

---

**8** The complete text of the charter can be found in B.J. Boland, *The Struggle of Islam in Modern Indonesia, op. cit.*, p. 243.

**9** In Indonesian, "*dengan kewadjiban menjalankan sjari'at Islam bagi pemeluk-pemeluknja*" ("*with the obligation for adherents of the Islamic faith to abide by Islamic laws*").

alerted him to the violent opposition of the Christian community on the edges of the archipelago to the "seven words" of the Jakarta Charter (Anshary 1983). This threat of secession was raised by Soekarno and Hatta during their meeting with the representatives of Islam in the Constituent Assembly in the early hours of the morning of the 18th. It was, therefore, to ensure national unity that Muslim leaders agreed to sacrifice the demands of their political group. Indonesia was to be founded on a belief in God, but the "seven words" which defined an obligation specific to Muslims were replaced in the preamble and in article 29 by a much more neutral expression concerning the single nature of the divine being, *Ketuhanan yang Maha esa*.

Pancasila is thus an extremely clever blend of Javanese, Muslim, Western, and Oriental influences. This can also be seen in the manner in which Pancasila's first principle was enunciated. To use Sanskrit (*maha esa*) to express a strong tribute to the Muslim *tauwid* is for me the symbol of Indonesian ingenuity, an ingenuity that acknowledges a diversity of influences and refuses to occult any part of the country's history, and by so doing wishes to formulate a common basis for all spiritualities. The *Ketuhanan yang maha esa* principle reflected a deep-rooted religious reality, mainly elaborated in Java and later disseminated to the entire country. The spiritual vision, which "inspired" Soekarno on the day he delivered his famous speech of June 1945, was the product of a complex religious legacy which he elaborated on some years later. He explained that his grandfather had been initiated into Javanese mysticism, his father into Islam and theosophy, while his mother had been brought up surrounded by Buddhism and Hinduism. In addition, during his exile in 1934 on the Catholic majority island of Flores, he regularly visited the missionaries there who allowed him access to their library.

Apart from Soekarno's own personal history, the roots for his vision also came from a "religious imaginary" forged in Java during the first decades of the twentieth century. An imaginary which can be linked to Charles Taylor's "social imaginaries" (2004) which, according to the Canadian philosopher, embodied the theory of multiple modernities developed by Shmuel Eisenstadt (2002). Its formulation found its roots in what has been masterfully described by the historian Merle Ricklefs as a 'mystic synthesis' elaborated from the sixteenth century onward between a Hindu-animist substratum and Islam (Ricklefs 2006). This mystic synthesis was based on the increasing affirmation of Islamic identity in Java as well as on a growth in the observance of Islamic rites. It also included, however, the recognition of older local spiritual forces which were invoked both amongst the nobility and the peasant classes. An example of this synthesis can be found in the mystic experience of union with the divine which characterizes pre-Islamic monism and which was revived through Sufism. This inclusive Javanese spirituality had been threatened by the spread of Muslim reformism from the 1880s onwards but responded both by becoming more radical and also by reaching out to other sources of inspiration. From the beginning of the twentieth century, for example, it was enriched with Christian religious elements, which were gradually adopted from the European circles to which they had been confined until then (Ricklefs 2007).

It was the two principalities (*vorstenlanden*) of Sukarta and Yogyakarta, vestiges of the Javanese kingdom of Mataram, that saw the most accomplished form of that remarkable consensus which would give birth to the *Ketuhanan yang maha esa* principle. At the dawn of the twentieth century, the two principalities' capitals were the scene of a remarkable hive of intellectual and spiritual creativity. This vibrancy turned them into unlikely laboratories for an alternative form of modern spirituality which strived to keep the demands made on it by Muslim and Western values at arm's length.

The repercussions in Java of the arrival of what one could call, for want of a better word, European modernity (the rapid rise of colonial influence, the development of its administration, the spread of literacy, and a more complex division of labour), had a particular effect in the Javanese principalities. Unlike the case of other South-East Asian colonized territories, the colonial government allowed the former Mataram territories to be the scene of a unique form of religious emulation. Such a development would have been difficult in Malaysia, where the British gave a protected status to Islam, or in the Philippines where the Spanish and the Americans both fostered Christianity, or even in other parts of the Dutch East Indies where the colonial government was wary about the fierce competition that could arise between religions.

Numerous religious communities (Muslims, Hindus, Buddhists, Christians, Theosophists and mystics) lived side by and thus helped foster the idea that being modern meant being inspired by religious pluralism. The overlapping of religious identities—one could be Muslim and a theosophist, or Christian and an adept of Javanese mysticism—foreshadowed the approach of the future Indonesian state. This could also be seen in the complete rejection of religious exclusivism, which had been established under the authority both of the colonial government and the four ruling families who had been allowed to keep possession of the Mataram kingdom's royal burial place.

There was also an eminently political aspect to the religious consensus established by virtue of the role played by many of the religious organisations in the emergence of the nationalist movement which would eventually spread from Java to the rest of the archipelago. It was this consensus that Soekarno encapsulated ingeniously in his famous speech given on 1 June 1945: Islam constituted an overwhelming majority in the country and should have a special status, but not to the exclusion of other religions. The Muslim religion was recognised as a part of a spiritual legacy which included other beliefs. The new Indonesian state's coat of arms reflected this delicate balance, in keeping with the principle of *Ketuhanan yang maha esa*. Pride of place was given to the star representing Islam in the centre of the shield, surrounded by four symbols, each representing one of Pancasila's principles. The eagle Garuda carrying the heraldry, however, was Vishnu's sacred mount, and it recalls, along with the nation's motto (*Bineka tungal Ika*) held in the eagle's claws and written in Sanskrit, both the long-standing and the important place of Hinduism in the country's heritage. Not only did Islam have to adapt itself in such a way as to make it compatible with local traditions and culture, it also, as Soekarno pointed out in his speech, had to ensure that it was consistent with the other principles of Pancasila, in particular that of "democracy by consensus":

> "If we are truly a Muslim people, let us do our best to ensure that the majority of the seats we are about to create will be filled by representatives of Islam. If the Indonesian population genuinely contains a majority of Muslims, and if Islam is to be a religion that is alive and well in our country, then we, its leaders, must capture the people's imagination so that it sends the greatest number of Muslim representatives possible to Parliament. Let us say that there are one hundred seats in Parliament, well then we must strive to ensure that sixty, seventy, eighty, ninety seats are occupied by Muslim figures. It will go without saying, then, that the laws voted by this assembly will be Muslim laws." (Bonneff et *al.*, 1980)

Muslims still had a duty, a compelling duty even, to assist in the triumph of their religion's values, but these values would be expressed in Parliament. Islamic values were not a given, they had to be fought for.

# 4 The Political Dimension of the State's Role in the Definition of Religion

This detachment from Islam, which was both in line with the syncretistic state of mind present in Java but also the result of a type of secularisation, went hand in hand with a very precise idea of how religion should be. The state's role in this definition reminds us of what Jean Baubérot (2014) defined as "laicity based on a state's sovereignty", (*laïcité régalienne*). Nonetheless, as the subtle negotiation exposed above showed, this secularisation also included a clear concession made in the direction of monotheistic religions, chief among which was Islam. Article 29 of the Constitution stipulated that "the state will guarantee the freedom of worship, each according to his or her own religion or belief". The freedom of conscience, then, was not provided for and atheism, in accordance with the first principle of Pancasila was, and remains, outlawed in Indonesia. What's more, by distinguishing between religion and belief, the Constitution opened the way for those two categories to be treated differently. The constitution preparation committee stipulated that religion (*agama*) must be understood as a monotheistic religion, while belief (*kepercayaan*) must be seen as based upon this religion (Yamin 1960, vol. III: 801–802).

With the creation of a Ministry of Religions in January 1946, *agama* gradually began to be defined in terms inspired by Islam that is to say monotheistic and possessing holy scripture, a prophet as well as a global character and recognition. Of the religions which went through the sometimes lengthy administrative procedures and political lobbying required to apply for official status, only the religions defined in such terms were allocated a division within the ministry, thus giving them access to the funds, which was the main motivation behind their application in the first place (Azra 1998). By the end of the 1940s, the Protestant and Catholic religions were granted divisions quite readily, though of course theirs was much smaller than that which had been allocated to Islam at the creation of the ministry. For the other major religions, however, divisions were obtained only after they had been forced to jump through an extraordinary number of theological hoops. In 1958, a special division for Hinduism was created and in 1965, President Soekarno issued a list of six recognized religions which included Buddhism and Confucianism, along with the four other religions already mentioned. It wasn't until 1980, however, that a Buddhist division was created, and the treatment received by Confucianism reveals the deeply political nature of the recognition procedure (Steenbrink 2015). The Confucians had gone to great lengths to conform to the requirements expected of them, resulting finally in their inclusion on the list issued in 1965, only to see Suharto remove them from it in 1978 in response to pressure arising from anti-Chinese sentiment In 2000, President Abdurrahman Wahid (Gus Dur) abrogated Suharto's 1967 Presidential Instruction, which banned open celebration of Chinese religion, belief and customary practices, and the Minister for Internal Affairs rescinded the 1978 Circular, which stated that only five religions were recognized. The rehabilitation of Confucianism was finally completed in 2006 when a division was created for it within the ministry, thus giving Indonesia's public policy on religions a greater semblance of coherence.

The state's approach to religion, then, was to a large extent dependant on political contingencies. The government always turned to Pancasila, in particular the *Ketuhanan yang Maha esa* principle, as a sort of civil religion, which would act as a sounding board allowing it to determine who was true to the nation and who, on the other hand, was merely posing as such. This aspect of Pancasila was highlighted during the two authoritarian regimes of independent Indonesia: Soekarno's Guided Democracy (1958–1965) and Suharto's New Order (1966–1998). During these two periods the defense of Pancasila was transformed into a constraining ideology subordinate to the government. In 1959, when disagreement between those who supported a broader role for Islam and the advocates of Pancasila led the constitutional assembly to an impasse, Soekarno decided to dissolve the assembly and to forcibly reintroduce the 1945 Constitution. The following year in 1960, invoking the necessity to defend Pancasila, he outlawed the major Muslim party, Masyumi.

Similarly, General Suharto's New Order imposed a strict interpretation of Pancasila, both to combat communism and to marginalize political Islam. Suharto also sacralised Pancasila, in order to justify his ruthless suppression of the communist movement, saying that "Pancasila has become a matter of life and death for our nation" (Ismail 1995: 143) and that "any group which would change Pancasila will meet with destruction" (Krissantono 1976: 25). The close symbolic association between the repression of the so-called coup d'état in 1965 and the defense of Pancasila, which could now be freed from its restrictive Soekarnoist interpretation, is reflected in the calendar of official celebrations in Indonesia. October the 1$^{st}$ became the Sacred Day of Pancasila, celebrated every year at the "crocodile pit" (*lubang buaya*) into which the bodies of the assassinated generals were thrown. At the centre of the memorial a sacred Pancasila monument was erected, composed of a giant Garuda dominating the statues of the seven assassinated officers who lie on a five-sided pedestal inscribed with the principles of Indonesia's national ideology.

Under the National Committee for the Formulation of Pancasila, an official interpretation called the Guide for the Understanding and Practicing of Pancasila (Pedoman Penghayatan dan Pengamalan Pancasila—known as "P4") was widely circulated. Different interpretations were regarded as deviant and the P4 was taught from kindergarten and elementary school through university. All public servants were also required to pass a P4 training course. Finally, an 1985 law stipulated that Pancasila must be mentioned as the 'sole social principle' in the charter of all political, social and even religious organizations.

# 5 Towards Religious Community-based Laicity and *Agamaization*

The state's strict oversight of Pancasila's regulation contributed to a less expansive expression of spirituality and corralled Indonesians increasingly towards the main religions. The first reason was the fight against communism after the dreadful events of 1965, when a wave of repression cracked down on anyone who seemed in any way linked to Marxism, which for the state was synonymous with atheism.[10] In order to escape from this, most Indonesians "sought refuge" amongst the main religions which had been recognized by the state. It became obligatory to include on your identity card which of those religions you belonged to, making it difficult for the still numerous smaller religious communities in the country to survive. In the 1970s, these *aliran kepercayaan* strived to be recognised officially by the state so as to be granted the associated legal protections and in 1978, they succeeded in being included in the National Policy Guidelines (*Garis Besar Hukum Negara, GBHN*). However, faced with protests by Muslim organisations, the Minister for Religions transferred responsibility for the *aliran kepercayaan* to the Ministry of Education and Culture to assuage Muslim groups' fears that those communities would be treated as religions.

By thus, confirming the existence of a hierarchy between religions and spiritual movements, the state fostered a process which Sven Cederroth (1996) has called "agamization". The idea gradually took root that the adherents of indigenous religions were not yet sufficiently religious to be "agamized". This change was reinforced by the marriage law of 1974 which stipulated that all unions had to be celebrated according to the rules of each couple's religion. This new legislation sounded the death knell for civil marriage ceremonies and it also effectively led to a ban on inter-religious marriages.

This shift in attitudes affected the fluidness which had long characterized the field of religion, and in particular inter-religious relations. Each religious community soon perfectly understood the role of arbitrator played by the state and accordingly they set about prioritizing their own relations with it to the detriment of their relations with other faiths. This deterioration in relations was particularly noticeable between Muslims and Christians whose representatives, following independence, had joined forces in a relentless struggle against communism and had often found a common platform in order to influence public opinion. After 1965, relations between the two communities soured. Muslim

---

[10] On the evening of 30 September 1965, six generals and a lieutenant were captured and executed by a group of "progressive" officers. On the morning of 1 October, their leaders spoke on behalf of the "30$^{th}$ of September Movement," stating that they had acted to thwart the plans of a "council of generals" who were preparing, with the help of the CIA, a coup d'état to overthrow President Soekarno. In a few short days, the putsch was quashed by general Suharto and the failed putsch provided a golden opportunity for those who had striven for years against the growth of the Communist party and the increasing influence it held over Soekarno. With nearly 500,000 dead, the anti-communist repression was one of the most atrocious massacres of the twentieth century (Cribb 1990).

organisations who had found themselves marginalized politically, notably the reformists, now criticized the Christian community for taking advantage unfairly of their close ideological proximity to the regime and for using their financial strength to encourage people to convert.

In order to stop this dispute from becoming acrimonious, the state decided that it had to take charge of interdenominational relations and created an interreligious board in 1967. In 1969, a further measure was taken when a joint decree was issued by the Ministry of Religion and the Interior Ministry, regulating the establishment of new places of worship so as to prevent any potential conflict. This dialogue between the authorities and the country's different religions led each denomination to organise itself in such a manner as to speak with one voice in order to better defend their interests in their negotiations with the government. While Protestants and Catholics had already established unifying structures with the creation of the Council of Churches and the Episcopal Conference during the 1950s, the Muslim community still remained divided. It was composed of two groups: Nahdlatul Ulama represented traditionalist Islam and Muhammadiyah comprised reformists. Since independence, these two major associations had been jockeying for position to curry favour with the government and they regularly came to loggerheads over who should be appointed minister of religions. In 1975, the government encouraged the formation of an Indonesian Ulema Council (*Majelis Ulama Indonesia—MUI*) which would include all of Indonesia's Muslim organisations. It served as an influential representative for Suharto's New Order regime within the Muslim community, providing enlightenment but also serving as an informal intermediary for the New Order's religious policy and reconciling the sometimes-contradictory positions of the big organisations, especially on the issue of the start of the Ramadan. Funded by the state but independent of the Ministry of Religions, MUI received in the mid-1980s a way to greatly supplement its income through the attribution of the halal.

The period which covers the first twenty years of the New Order (1966–1985) had in the past been characterised as "secularism with limited religionization" (Ichwan 2011). But it is possible to find, during that period, elements of the "community based laicity" (*laïcité communautaire*) described by Jean Baubérot (2014). The imposition of Pancasila as the basis for the organisation of religions seemed to mark the apogee of the state's role as arbitrator between the different religious communities. However, it was this very imposition which, paradoxically, signalled the decline of "secularisation" for reasons particular to the regime itself.

## 6 Towards an Identity-Based Laicity through a Political Orchestration of Islamic Values

Faced with a dwindling power base, Suharto decided it was time to turn again to religion. From the mid-1980s, his rapprochement with the Muslim organizations in order to overcome the growing criticism of his regime within the army prevented the new devout middle classes and the proletariat from joining forces. With the establishment of the All-Indonesia Association of Muslim Intellectuals (Ikatan Cendekiawan Muslim se-Indonesia – ICMI) founded in 1990 and chaired by his Minister of Technology, B.J. Habibie, Suharto acquired, at little cost, a new religious endorsement in exchange for a few stipends and a symbolic recognition of the modernizing role of Islam (Hefner 1993). This clever manipulation allowed him to redirect popular Islamic discontent towards targets that were non-strategic for him, namely the Christian and the Sino-Indonesian minorities. He then supported various kinds of Islamization policies: in 1989 a law on (Muslim) religious courts was accepted, followed in 1991 by a presidential decree that a Compilation of Islamic Law in Indonesia, formulated by experts of the Ministry of Religion should be used in all these courts. The same year the first Islamic bank, Bank Muamalat Indonesia was created (Hefner 2000).

In 1998, the fall of the Suharto regime allowed the return of democracy and the beginning of a period, called *Reformasi*, which permitted new debates around Pancasila. In April 1999, the Government announced that Pancasila indoctrination (P4) courses were to be discontinued and the BP-7 (the agency responsible for administering the Pancasila courses) was to be abolished. The People's Consultative Council (Majelis Permusyawaratan Rakyat — MPR) repealed the previous MPR Decree on Pancasila as the sole basis of mass organizations, but did not eliminate the Law on Mass Organizations on which the obligation was based. Most Islamic organizations and parties adopted Islam as their ideological principle, but did not reject Pancasila, at least not explicitly, as the foundation of the state. In 2000 and 2002, despite strong pressure from a few Islamic parties demanding the "seven words" of the Jakarta Charter be inserted into the preamble and Article 29 of the Constitution, the MPR—backed by the two biggest Muslim organizations, Nahdlatul Ulama and Muhammadiyah—kept the "*Ketuhanan yang Maha Esa*" unchanged.

This steadfast loyalty to the Pancasila doctrine did not, however, stop the holier-than-thou approach to many policy areas concerning Islam which had also marked the final ten years of Suharto's reign. It is true that the state continued to proclaim its attachment to a form of secularism which would treat all religions equally, but at the same time the democratization and decentralization allowed by the *Reformasi* permitted the proponents of an inegalitarian secularism, (i.e. one favouring Islam), to attempt to impose their views in many areas by claiming that they were the spokespeople of a silent Muslim majority. The state was powerless to arrest this new development which was in large part due to the political harnessing of an underlying social and religious transformation that had been at work for several decades. In this respect, it was merely the logical continuation of the New Order's decision, in its final years, to sacrifice Pancasila's egalitarian secularism in favour of the demands of a section of the Muslim community. Far from becoming a more secular society, Indonesia underwent a significant religious revival marked by an increase in the visible signs of people's faith.

Since the end of the 1960s, and even more so since the 1990s, the country has experienced a significant process of Islamization, which has been widely noted by observers of Indonesian society (Liddle 1996; Van Bruinessen 2013; Ota et al. 2010). Places of worship with their easily recognizable oriental-style chrome-plated onion domes have sprung up across the country and there has been such a marked increase in calls to prayer and improvised sermons broadcast by the crackling loudspeakers perched on *mushollas* that they have now become an accepted part of the soundscape of urban Indonesia. Indonesia's Muslim identity is also visible outside the observance of the pillars of Islam. The headscarf, which was worn relatively rarely until the 1970s, apart from its traditional regional manifestations (the *kerudung* in Java, for example, which used to cover the hair only partially), is now much more common among younger generations and has become standardized (*djilbab*). At a broader level, a consumer market has emerged geared specifically towards Muslims, notably in the food sector, where stocking *halal* products has become a necessity, and in the clothing sector, which has seen a sharp rise in the sale of Arabic-style clothes, sold mainly by the "Islamic corners" which have sprung up in the country's shopping malls (Rudnyckyj 2009; Fealy § White 2008).

Strangely, this apparent desecularisation of society has had no direct effect politically as the parties claiming to be Islamic have, by and large, been in decline since 1999. The hardline groups who wish to call into question the spirit of Pancasila, notably through the reintroduction of the Jakarta Charter, have been particularly affected. However, there have been a number of significant knock-on effects caused by this social change. Although there has been important progress in the democratization of the country over the past twenty years, a political class formed under the new Order, or at least inspired by its corrupting and nepotistic practices, has been able to stay in power. This has made it easier for to capitalise politically on the afore-mentioned Islamic revival. The increase in displays of religious devotion by public representatives, which were motivated by a complex mixture of conviction, opportunism, and pusillanimity, led to an Islamization of public norms that was muddled and often nefarious. The ambient mediocrity brought about by widespread administrative misrule, betrayal of principles, and corruption scandals has contributed to a shameless race to occupy, for political purposes, the religious high ground. The politicians who have tried to usurp Muslim values for their own ends are the very ones who fear moral and religious condemnation of their behavior.

This evolution could be observed on several levels. Nationally, it was marked by a certain number of debates, including on the law imposing the implementation of Sharia in Aceh in 1999 (a local requirement rather than a national initiative) on the law against pornography between 2005 and 2008, and on the possible abrogation of blasphemy as an offense between 2010 and 2011. During these debates the whole political class, apart from the PDIP, aligned its position with that of the Islamist organizations. Locally, this orchestration of Islamic values has been much more disorderly and far less democratic. Although the 1999 decentralization laws gave local authorities no mandate in religious matters, several provincial, regency, and municipal authorities have passed decrees imposing respect for the obligations of Islamic law. Studies carried out on this phenomenon of *perda sharia* (from local regulations, peraturan daerah, or 'perda', that are said to be influenced by sharia, such as requiring women to wear a jilbab, or obliging local civil servants to observe Muslim prayers, for example) have shed light on the Islamization process of Indonesian law and more broadly on certain aspects of the country's religious revival. Firstly, the increased enthusiasm for Islam in Indonesia has manifested itself mainly through a desire to moralize society, thus echoing the "moral panic" movement characteristic of this revival. These "anti-vice regulations" were aimed mainly at prostitution, gambling, and the consumption of alcohol; they sometimes, though not always, corresponded to the dictates of Islam, and they did not always make reference to religious norms. Secondly, these Sharia-inspired regulations have contributed significantly to the blurring of boundaries between Muslim parties and secular parties. Locally, most of the *perda sharia* were instigated by secular parties—Golkar in particular which was the governmental party under the New Order,—or by moderate Muslim parties such as the PKB or the PAN rather than by Islamist parties such as the PKS, the PBB, or the PPP (Bush 2008). These regulations are in reality rarely implemented and what's more they are unconstitutional in the eyes of Indonesian law as religious questions do not come within the competence of local authorities. However, they clearly reveal the growing place of Islam in public debate and undermine the first principle of Pancasila upon which Indonesian-style secularism is founded. Most of the regulations are based upon the Jakarta Charter which set out an obligation for Muslims to respect the principles of Sharia law but which, as we have already seen, never received any official recognition.

This evolution of Indonesian society has been enthusiastically encouraged by the Indonesian Ulema Council. The Council receives state subsidies and as such its semi-official role gives particular weight to its twin demands of an Islamisation of society and an increased orthodoxy within Islam itself. It was not the only institution to participate in the transformation we are describing however. The justice system has shown on several occasions that it is not immune from the pressure imposed on it to confer a more Islamic hue to the religious status quo. A clear indication of this has been the broader implementation of the blasphemy law which was adopted in 1969. The law was issued in the form of a presidential decree issued by Soekarno in 1965 but had almost never been applied until 2004. In 2010, in response to the increasing rise in the number of convictions for "insulting Islam", several human rights defence groups who had criticised this broader application of the law and its criminalisation of religious differences filed an application before the constitutional court. The court's hearing took place amid impassioned public debate as well as demonstrations in front of the court building by Islamist militia groups. In an unprecedented ruling, the court suggested that the Indonesian Constitution struck a compromise status for the country between a secular state and an Islamic one and that the limitations of freedom of religion were thus based on firm legal grounds. In May 2017, the conviction of Jakarta's first non-Muslim and ethnic Chinese governor, Basuki Tjahaja Purnama, known as "Ahok', was very much in line with this new broader definition of blasphemy. It reveals the influence of this new Islamic purism on the judiciary and was a shock for Indonesians attached to the religious status quo. For his supporters, Ahok symbolized the political renewal necessary for the continuation of the *Reformasi*. Elected vice-governor alongside Joko Widodo, (commonly known as Jokowi) in 2012, he succeeded the latter when he was elected to the presidency of the Republic in 2014, and was candidate for a second term as governor when he was arrested. In September 2016, Ahok had denounced instructions being circulated in mosques to prohibit Muslims (83% of the voters in the capital) to vote for him on the basis of Verse 51 of the Al-Maidah Surah (the table spread with food), a declaration which led to his conviction for blasphemy.

In response to this manipulation of religious tensions, supporters of a less identity-based and more liberal vision of Pancasila have on several occasions over the past ten years sought to renew the religious pact adopted at independence. On 1 June 2006, a demonstration celebrating the anniversary of Soekarno's foundational speech was attended by the then president Susilo Bambang Yudhoyono and included a wide spectrum of participants ranging from liberals and representatives of NGOs to religious minorities and proponents of Javanism (Raillon 2011). They were gathered to reaffirm the cultural roots of Indonesia's pluralism in response to the exclusive approach to religion of a growing number of the Muslim community. Since then, successive governments have regularly taken initiatives to remind the public of the state's attachment to the compromise struck in 1945. In 2017, after Ahok conviction, President Jokowi had little choice but to resort to the sort of measures which had not been seen since Suharto's fall. He launched, for example, an important organization to promote Pancasila with the support of the army staff who were worried about past tensions resurfacing that could affect the armed forces. Later that year, for the first time since 1998, an Islamist movement the Hizbut Tahrir Indonesia (HTI) which had been deeply involved in the demonstrations against Ahok was dissolved. This organization had been one of the most actively involved in the struggle against secularization which its president Muhammad Ismail Yusanto called "the mother of all destruction". This dismantling of the HTI was effectuated via a legally binding presidential decree concerning the dissolution of "anti-Pancasila" organisations which had been adopted one week previously rather than by using the much longer legislative procedure normally required. The decree was accompanied by precise instructions sent to university presidents aimed at eradicating the HTI's influence on their campuses. At the beginning of 2018, supporters of a liberal interpretation of Pancasila also won a major victory. A governmental decree and then the Supreme Court allowed Indonesian citizens to have their "traditional beliefs" (*aliran kepercayaan*) mentioned on their identity cards in place of one of the six recognized religions. In the future, they may even be able to not mention any religion, breaking with an obligation in force since 1966. These prospects are of great concern to the militant networks of conservative Islam because, beyond the imaginary danger of resurgent Communism, they could allow Indonesians to escape the growing pressures of orthopraxy within the Muslim community.

# 7 Conclusion

Pancasila constitutes an original solution for the political treatment of religious affairs, whether at a global level or at the level of the Asian continent. By gathering the main religions present within its borders under the premise of the "belief in a unique God" enshrined in its institutions, Indonesia refused to renounce either the primordial role played by the nation-state or the "sacred canopy" (Berger 1967) under whose shade the people found solace. The malleability of this principle with its many possible interpretations opens a space for exchange which corresponds perfectly to Paul Ricoeur's notion of a space for "reasonable disagreement", which he adapted from John Rawls and used to characterise French laicity (Ricœur 1995: 195). In Indonesia, as in most Muslim countries, a powerful religious revival movement has been calling into question a certain secularisation of society which they consider to be part of the colonial legacy. Though this revival has not managed to undermine the religious status quo adopted in Indonesia at independence, it has affected its application. At the same time, however, the advocates of a more liberal interpretation of Pancasila are well able to mobilise both arguments and people in defence of what they consider to be the core of the nation's identity. The study of the Indonesian case thus gives us a good illustration of what André Laliberté (in this volume) writes about the concept of multiple modernities. Laliberté's sees this concept as "an important corrective to the idea of a hegemonic and unchallenged Western modernity asserting its supremacy over non-Western civilizations that stood by passively". In light of this, the strength and originality of the Indonesian model is to have been able to draw from various sources of legitimacy. By not confining itself to the clash between Islamic references and Western secularism, Indonesia has reached an original compromise in which the invention of a religious modernity draw on the plurality of the past.

# References

Anshary, H. Endang Saifuddin. 1983. *Piagam Jakarta 22 juni 1945 dan sejarah konsensus nasional antara nasionalis islami dan nasionalis "sekular" tentang dasar negara republik indonesia, 1945–1959*. Bandung: Pustaka.
Aritonang, Jan Sihar. 2004. *Sejarah Perjumpaan Kristen dan Islam di Indonesia*. Jakarta: BPK Gunung Mulia.
Assyaukanie, Luthfi. 2009. *Islam and the Secular State in Indonesia*. Singapore: Institute of Southeast Asian Studies.
Azra, Azyumardi. 1998. "H. M. Rasjidi, BA: Pembentukan Kementerian Agama dalam Revolusi". In Azyumardi Azra and Saiful Umam, eds., *Menteri-menteri Agama RI: Biografi Sosial-Politik*, p. 6. Jakarta: INIS, PPIM, Badan Litbang Agama Departemen Agama RI.
Baubérot, Jean. 2014. "Laïcité(s), sécularisation(s), Quelques hypothèses". Colloque du GSRL, Paris, 26–27 juin.
Berger, Peter L. *1967. The Sacred Canopy: Elements of a Sociological Theory of Religion*. Garden City/New York: Doubleday and Company, Inc.
Boland, B. J. 1982. *The Struggle of Islam in Modern Indonesia*. The Hague: Nijhoff.
Bonneff Marcel et al. 1980. *Pantjasila, trente années de débats politiques en Indonésie*. Paris: Édition de la Maison des sciences de l'homme.
Bush, Robin. 2008. "Regional Sharia Regulations in Indonesia: Anomaly or Symptom?". In Greg Fealy and Sally White, eds., *Expressing Islam: Religious Life and Politics in Indonesia*, pp. 1–15. Singapour: ISEAS.

Cederroth, Sven. 1996., "From ancestor worship to monotheism: politics of religion in Lombok". *Temenos*, 32: 7–36.

Cribb, Robert, ed. 1990. *The Indonesian Killings of 1965–1966*. Clayton, VIC: Monash University.

Darmaputera, Eka. 1988. *Pancasila and the Search for Identity and Modernity in Indonesian Society: A Cultural and Ethical Analysis*. Leiden: Brill.

Dijk, C. van. 1981. *Rebellion under the Banner of Islam: The Darul Islam in Indonesia*. The Hague: Martinus Nijhoff.

Fealy, Greg and Sally White, eds. 2008. *Expressing Islam: Religious Life and Politics in Indonesia*. Singapore: ISEAS.

Feillard, Andrée and Rémy Madinier. 2011. *The End of Innocence? Indonesian Islam and the Temptation of Radicalism*. Singapore: NUS Press, Honolulu: University of Hawaii Press.

Hefner, Robert W. 2000. *Civil Islam: Muslims and Democratization in Indonesia*. Princeton, NJ: Princeton University Press.

Ichwan, Moch Nur. 2011. "Secularism, Islam and Pancasila: Political Debates on the Basis of the State in Indonesia". *Bulletin of the Nanzan Center for Asia-Pacific Studies*, 6: 1–43.

Ismail, Faisal. 1995. *Islam, Politics and Ideology in Indonesia: A Study of the Process of Muslim Acceptance of the Pancasila*. Ph.D Thesis: McGill University.

Kafrawi, R. Mohammad. 1956a. "Indonesia's Religions". *Atlantic*, 197 (June): 165.

Kafrawi, R. Mohammad. 1956b. *Islamic Education in Indonesia*. Jakarta: Ministry of Religious Affairs.

Krissantono, ed. 1976. *Pandangan Presiden Soeharto tentang Pancasila*. Jakarta: CSIS.

Liddle, R.William. 1996. "The Islamic Turn in Indonesia". *The Journal of Asian Studies*, 55 no. 3: 613–634.

Noer, Deliar. 1973. *The Modernist Muslim Movement in Indonesia 1900–1942*. Oxford: Oxford University Press.

Ota Atsushi, Okamoto Masaaki and Ahmad Sueady, eds. 2010. *Islam in Contention: Rethinking Islam and State in Indonesia*. Jakarta: Wahid Institute, CSEAS and CAPAS.

Raillon, François. 2011. "The return of Pancasila: secular vs. Islamic norms, another look at the struggle for state dominance in Indonesia". In Michel Picard and Rémy Madinier, eds., *The Politics of Agama in Java and Bali*, pp. 92–113. London/New York: Routledge.

Ricklefs, Merle C. 2006. *Mystic Synthesis in Java. A History of Islamization from the Fourtheenth to the early Nineteenth Centuries*. East Bridge: Norwalk.

Ricklefs, Merle C. 2007. *Polarising Javanese Society. Islamic and other visions (c. 1830–1930)*. Leiden: KITLV Press.

Ricœur, Paul. 1995. *La Critique et la Conviction*. Paris: Éd. Calmann-Levy.

Ridwan, Nur Khalik. 2018. *Negara Bukan-Bukan – Prisma Pemikiran Gus Dur Tentang Negara Pancasila*. Jakarta: Ircisod-Diva Press.

Rudnyckyj, Daromir. 2010. *Spiritual economies: Islam, globalization and the afterlife of development*. Ithaca/New York: Cornell University Press.

Rudnyckyj, Daromir. 2009. "Market Islam in Indonesia". *Journal of the Royal Anthropological Institute* no. 15: 183–201.

Sidjabat, W.B. 1965. *Religious Tolerance and the Christian Faith. A Study of the Concept of Divine Omnipotence in the Indonesian Constitution in the Light of Islam and Christianity*. Jakarta: BPK.

Steenbrink, Karel. 2015. "Pancasila as an Ambiguous Instrument for Interreligious Harmony and Development in Indonesia, 1945–2015". *Bulletin of the Nanzan Centre for Asia-Pacific Studies* no. 10: 15–36.

Van Bruinessen, Martin, ed. 2013. *Contemporary Developments in Indonesian Islam: Explaining the Conservative Turn.* Singapore: ISEAS.

Yamin, Muhammad. 1959–1960. *Naskah Persiapan Undang-Undang Dasar 1945*, 3 vol., Jakarta: Jajasan Prapanca.

Yayasan Proklamasi. 1978. *The Guide of the Living and the Practice of Pantja Sila and GBHN, the Broad Outlines of the State Policy.* Jakarta: Centre for Strategic and International Studies.

Michel Picard
# Religion, Secularization, and Counter-Secularization in Bali

**Abstract:** Once they had become Indonesian citizens, in 1950, the Balinese people were informed that they "did not yet have a religion". This implied that they were expected to convert to either Islam or Christianity, the only "religions" (*agama*) then recognized by the Ministry of Religion. Consequently, if the Balinese did not want to become the target of Muslim or Christian proselytizing, they had to make their own religion eligible for the status of *agama*. As it happened, Balinese social and intellectual elites had started to assess the foundations of their religious identity in the 1920s, when they were confronted with Orientalists, colonial administrators, Muslim schoolteachers and Christian missionaries. Until then, they had no notion of a system of beliefs and practices that could be separated from other aspects of their life that could be labelled "religion". This chapter investigates, first, how the word *agama* took on the meaning of "religion" in Bali, and second, how the Balinese came to assert that their religion was "Hinduism" (*agama Hindu*). It contends that the appropriation of the category *agama* implied for the Balinese an unprecedented distinction between the religious and the secular, amounting to a process of secularization. And it concludes by identifying an opposing process of counter-secularization, aiming at closing the gap between the religious and the secular that had been opened by the obligation imposed upon the Balinese people to have a proper *agama*.

## 1 Introduction

Once their island had become part of the Republic of Indonesia, in 1950, the Balinese people were informed that they "did not yet have a religion" (*belum beragama*). They were therefore expected to convert to either Islam or Christianity, the only religions (*agama*) then recognized by the Ministry of Religion (Kementerian Agama Republik Indonesia).[1] Indeed, in accordance with what Jean Baubérot characterizes as "regalian laicity," the Indonesian state imposes on society

---

[1] See Rémy Madinier's chapter in this volume.

**Michel Picard** (Centre Asie du Sud-Est)

https://doi.org/10.1515/9783110733068-006

its definition of what religion is, with the result that *agama* refers to a much more restricted semantic field than does the common understanding of the word religion. Thus, in order for a religion to be formally acknowledged as a legitimate *agama* by the Ministry of Religion, it has to conform to an Islamic understanding of what defines a proper religion—that is, divine revelation recorded by a prophet in a holy book, a codified system of law for the faithful, congregational worship not confined to one ethnic group, and a belief in the one almighty God. Consequently, if the Balinese did not want to become the target of Muslim or Christian proselytizing, their only recourse was to rationalize their religion and redefine it in monotheistic terms, in order to make it eligible for the status of *agama*.

The Balinese elites had not waited for the Ministry's rebuff to reflect on their religion. They had started to assess the foundations of their religious identity back in the 1920s, when they were confronted with Orientalists, colonial administrators, Muslim schoolteachers, and Christian missionaries. Since that time, they had faced protracted difficulties agreeing on what the "Balinese religion" is about, as they had no previous notion of a system of beliefs and practices that could be demarcated from other aspects of their life and labeled "religion," and to which one could "convert" (Picard 2017). For the Balinese, the appropriation of the category "religion" implied an unprecedented distinction between the religious and the non-religious, between that which belongs to "religion" and that which pertains to the "secular."

Rather than being objectively found, such a religious-secular divide had to be produced discursively. Hence, the matter at hand is to elucidate who determines what counts as religious, what counts as secular, and what is dismissed as superstition, and to establish what is acknowledged as a legitimate exercise of religion and what is not. In that respect, one could refer to the requirements of the Ministry of Religion as "religion-making from above" whereas the Balinese construction of their religion could be qualified as "religion-making from below" (Mandair & Dressler 2011: 21–22). In other words, what constitutes "religion" and what constitutes the "secular" is socially contested in Indonesia, as these categories are subject to power struggles, rhetorically deployed for various purposes by competing sets of actors with particular ends in mind, within specific sociopolitical contexts.

It must be stressed at the outset that there was no native terminology to translate these categories into Balinese. While Balinese opinion leaders took up the Sanskrit loanword *agama* to construe their "religion," they did not resort to a vernacular term that could be glossed as "secular."² Yet, although the Balinese never created a terminology to deal with the secular field proper, a twofold process of secularization and counter-secularization can nonetheless be identified in contemporary Bali.³

## 2 *Agama:* From *Dharma* to "Religion"

*Agama* has not always meant "religion" in Indonesia. In Sanskrit, the word *āgama* signifies "that which has come down to the present" and refers to "anything handed down as fixed by tradition," according to Indologist Jan Gonda in his study of *Sanskrit in Indonesia* (Gonda 1973: 499–500). As such, *āgama* is one of the sources of knowledge—the *pramāṇa*—which vary according to the different "points of view" (*darśana*) that comprise Hindu philosophy. *Āgama-pramāṇa* refers to authoritative scripture as a means of valid cognition and is usually considered equivalent to *śabda-pramāṇa* (revealed knowledge). Additionally, *āgama* is the name of a genre of non-Vedic scriptures that specific Hindu orders regard as revelation, and which became prominent during the early medieval period. This genre includes the Shaiva *āgama*, the Vaishnava *samhitā*, and the Shakta *tantra* centered on the cult of the Goddess. More specifically, the term *āgama* applies in particular to the canonical texts of the Śaiva-Siddhānta order.⁴

Surprisingly few Indonesianists appear to have wondered how such a Sanskrit loanword, laden with Indic references, could have come to designate an Islamic conception of what "religion" is about. Granted, one encounters a few references to the importance of the Shaiva *āgama* in Java and Bali (Hooykaas 1966: 156; Brunner 1967: 416; Staal 1995: 45; Becker 2004: 16). Yet this leaves many questions unanswered, since in Śaiva-Siddhānta *āgama* does not signify reli-

---

**2** The notions of secular, secularity, secularization and secularism were appropriated into Indonesian in the 1980s by means of English, as *sekuler*, *sekularitas*, *sekularisasi*, and *sekularisme* respectively. But these terms are not commonly used in Bali.
**3** Besides, it should be pointed out that rather than conceiving an explicit polarity between the sacred and the profane, the Balinese differentiate two complementary fields of experience—the manifest world (*sakala*, "what lies within the bounds of human sensorial perception") and the unmanifest world (*niskala*, "that which lies beyond the realm of the senses") (Rubinstein 2000: 49).
**4** Śaiva-Siddhānta, "the final truth of Shiva," is the most important of all the Shaiva schools, predominantly in Tamil Nadu. The primary sources of Śaiva-Siddhānta are the *Śaivāgama*, a body of Sanskrit texts that are treated as authoritative because they claim to have been revealed by Shiva to his *śakti* Parvati. On Śaiva-Siddhānta and the *Śaivāgama*, see Davis (1991).

gion, a notion that was unknown to the Indian world before the nineteenth century.

Although it is difficult to establish exactly when the word *agama* came to mean religion in Indonesia, we know that in Javanese and Balinese literary traditions the generic title *Agama* was "used to refer to a range of texts dealing with moral, religious and legal sanctions and practices" (Creese 2009a: 242, n. 2; see also, Lévi 1933; Sarkar 1934; and Hoadley & Hooker 1981 and 1986). These texts were mainly drawn from the Sanskrit *Mānava Dharmaśāstra*—the "Laws of Manu"—the most prominent of the treatises on *dharma*, in which legal and religious features are not distinguished (Rocher 2003; Holdrege 2004). According to epigraphic and textual evidence, from as early as the twelfth century, law codes in use in the Indic courts of Java and Bali were thus modeled on Hindu legal thought, thoroughly adapted and contextualized to suit indigenous needs.

The basic premise of Hindu law is the concept of *dharma*, which may be defined as that which upholds the socio-cosmic order. In the *dharmaśāstra*, the word *dharma* refers particularly to the *varnāśramadharma*, the duties incumbent on Hindus according to their social class (*varna*) and their stage of life (*āśrama*). *Dharma* is thus an exclusive and personal norm, both considerably broader and much more specific in scope than the category "religion." However, when Christian missionaries in India translated the Bible into Sanskrit in the early nineteenth century, they chose the term *dharma* as a gloss for the term religion and began to proclaim Christianity as the "true *dharma*" (*satyādharma*) (Halbfass 1988: 340). Faced with this Christian challenge to their *dharma*, which the missionaries expounded as a false religion, Hindus themselves started using the word *dharma* in the sense of religion, with the result that the Hindu *dharma* became one religion among others, to be compared and opposed to the Christian *dharma* or the Muslim *dharma*.

Now, if *agama* is equated with *dharma* in Javanese and Balinese legal texts from the twelfth century onward, we know moreover that in Malay chronicles dating back to the fourteenth century the term *agama* is systematically associated with Islam and used in a sense equivalent to that of *dīn*. Therefore, one has to conclude that for centuries the word *agama* had two distinct denotations in the Indonesian Archipelago, that of *dharma* as well as that of *dīn*, according to the context and language in which it occurred. By appropriating the word *agama*, Indonesian Muslims endowed it with new meaning, namely, the exclusive worship of the one and only God, and the requirement to convert to a foreign doctrine whose teachings are contained in a holy book propounded by an inspired prophet. As a result, a sharp distinction was drawn between "heathens" and "true believers." Later on, through its adoption by Christian missionaries, *agama* became associated with an ideal of social progress, while "pagan" beliefs were scorned as antiquated superstitions and viewed as a cause for shame.

As *agama* came to mean "religion"—in a process similar to that which occurred with the category *dharma* in India—the term was not only dissociated from "law" but also from "tradition," which was one of its original senses in Sanskrit. In Indonesia, this notion is rendered by the Arabic loanword *adat*, commonly translated as "custom." But this translation does not do justice to the importance of *adat* in traditional Indonesian societies, where it refers at once to the cosmic order and to social life abiding by this order. The traditionally comprehensive scope of *adat* was fragmented through a series of reductions. First by Islamic proselytizers—Christian missionaries later followed suit—who strove to curtail the religious import of *adat* by confining its significance to the habits and customs of a people (*adat kebiasaan*). By thus qualifying as *adat* those customs that do not have an explicit religious legitimation, they could be neutralized; no longer considered as a challenge to *agama*, they were reduced to superstitions and old-fashioned ways. In particular, the word *adat* entered the language of Islamized populations to refer to indigenous "customary law" as opposed to Islamic "religious law" (*hukum*). Subsequently, Dutch jurists codified the indigenous customary laws (*adatrecht*, translated as *hukum adat* in Malay) of the various peoples on whom they had imposed their colonial empire (Van Vollenhoven 1928; Korn 1932). By thus attributing to each ethnic group its own *adatrecht*, the Dutch colonial policy widened the divide between "tradition" and "religion."

Such a dissociation between *adat* and *agama* entailed certain consequences that are worth considering. Whereas in *adat*, practices are followed inasmuch as they have been handed down from generation to generation, in *agama* they are held to be motivated on the basis of prior belief. And while different *agama* make exclusive claims about being the true revelation, attributing the predicates "true" and "false" to *adat* would be a category mistake. Moreover, *adat* as a fixed set of practices inherited from one's ancestors is tied to a particular ethnic group which it differentiates from others, contrary to *agama*, which explicitly aims to transcend ethnic and national boundaries. Last but not least, the detachment of a transcendent divine from the immanent concrete of ancestor worship amounts to a process of secularization.

This is, in short, how *agama*, *hukum*, and *adat* have come to mutually define each other in Indonesia, the boundaries of each category being continually redefined through the process of their interaction (see Van der Veer in this volume). Whereas in the past, the semantic field of the word *agama* encompassed that which Indonesians characterize respectively as *hukum* and *adat*, today "religion" is dissociated from both "law" and "tradition," particularly in Islamized and Christianized societies. The emergence of the category *agama* in the sense of religion thus amounts to its differentiation from the categories *hukum* and *adat*, that are then construed as pertaining to the secular. As such, instead of assuming the autonomy of these concepts, it is only by addressing their interrelationships that their respective semantic fields can be appropriately circumscribed and analyzed.

However, in contrast to Islamized or Christianized areas of Indonesia, in Bali the word *agama* has retained its original polysemy. This is attested by Balinese-Indonesian dictionaries, which translate *agama* as (1) *agama* (religion), (2) *hukum* (law), and (3) *adat* (tradition).[5] The question, then, is to investigate how the Balinese came to differentiate these semantic fields and, specifically, to determine how they appropriated the conceptual dichotomy between the religious and the secular.

## 3 The Emergence of Secularity in Bali

If we understand "secularity" in the sense of "explicit forms of distinction between religious and non-religious spheres and practices in society" (Burchardt & Wohlrab-Sahr 2013: 606), its emergence in Balinese society is clearly an outcome of the colonial encounter.

Bali was one of the last regions of the Indonesian Archipelago to be subjugated by the Dutch; while Dutch forces first attempted to conquer the island in 1846, they did not obtain full control until 1908. The colonial takeover put an end to the Balinese kingship, whose power was manifested through rituals that comprised closely interwoven political, social, and religious features. The villages (*desa*) were linked to the ruling houses (*puri*) by means of complex and competing networks of personal relationships between lords and followers. Considering these bewildering local variations an impediment to the requirements of rational administration, Dutch colonial officials imposed a uniform administrative structure throughout Balinese society. The Village Act of 1906 established a new type of village, the "administrative village" (*gouvernementsdesa*, later renamed *desa dinas*, from the Dutch word *dienst*, referring to the obligations and services to be rendered for the colonial government), typically consisting of several "customary villages" (*adatdesa*, which became known as *desa adat* and more recently as *desa pakraman*) grouped together under a new name (Schulte Nordholt 1991: 11–16; Hauser-Schäublin 2011: 196). By instigating

---

[5] On the other hand, the Balinese religious scholar Sri Reshi Anandakusuma translates *agama* as *dharma* in his Indonesian-Balinese dictionary (Anandakusuma 1986: 234).

a dichotomy between customary matters, which they left to the Balinese, and administrative authority, which they appropriated, the Dutch thought they could rule Bali while leaving its traditional order untouched. But in doing so, they initiated an unprecedented distinction between religious tradition and secular power.

Despite the Dutch attempt to insulate Balinese society from disturbing outside influences, Bali actually underwent rapid and profound changes as a result of the colonial confrontation. In particular, the demands of an effective administration were instrumental in the emergence of a Balinese intelligentsia, since the colonial state needed educated natives to mediate between the local population and their European masters. These Dutch-educated Balinese strove to make sense of the situation brought about by the opening up of their world to what they viewed as the advent of "modern times" (*zaman modern*).

In the 1920s, the first generation of Balinese educated in colonial schools founded formal organizations and started publishing periodicals, a complete novelty in Bali. These publications were written in Malay, the lingua franca of trade and Islam in the Archipelago, which the Dutch adopted as the language of education and administration, and would soon become the channel of Indonesian nationalism. The use of Malay, rather than Balinese, to address Balinese topics intended for a Balinese readership, indicates that the intelligentsia were conscious of being an integral part of a larger entity, as a result of the incorporation of their island into the colonial state. Thus, the same process that prompted the Balinese to question their identity dispossessed them of their own words, by inducing them to think about themselves in a language that was not their own, but that used by both their fellow countrymen and their colonial masters. Such a linguistic substitution marked a reflexive distancing from the Balinese socio-cosmic order, which was decontextualized, relativized, and homogenized in the process.

In these publications, the Balinese defined themselves as a Hindu minority threatened by the proselytizing of Islam and Christianity, as well as a particular ethnic group characterized by their own customs. More precisely, they construed their identity—which they called their "Balineseness" (*Kebalian*)—as being based on *agama* and on *adat*. The very fact that Balinese resorted to these terms to define their identity is a testament to the conceptual shift occurring on the island after its takeover by a foreign power.

The word *adat* was introduced to Bali by the Dutch. In due course, it replaced a diverse terminology for locally variable customs, which had "a field of meanings covering ritual obligation, social institution, legal regulation, and ancestral evocation" (Warren 1993: 4). These customs governed the relationships between social groups and sanctioned the sense of communal solidarities in the villages. The appropriation of the term *adat* by the Balinese entailed a twofold consequence. First, it created a new conceptual category, that of "tradition," which initially was not contrasted with "religion" but with "administration," or that which came under the authority of the colonial state. Second, the incorporation of a miscellaneous assortment of local customs into this generic term altered their meaning for the Balinese. What had until then been an interplay of significant and deliberately fostered differences between villages was becoming the locus of Balinese ethnic identity, in the sense of a customary body of inherited institutions and values which governed the lives of the Balinese people.

As such, "tradition" was not clearly distinguished from "religion." Indeed, *adat* pertains to the religious world view of the Balinese, in the sense that it refers both to an immutable cosmic order and to the social order instituted accordingly by their ancestors, at once describing the ideal order and prescribing the behavior required to achieve it. Unlike the world religions that have a core of abstract basic tenets meaningful to people of diverse cultural backgrounds, Balinese ritual life is highly localized, connecting specific groups of people to one another, to their ancestors, and to their territory. It consists in a series of transactions with entities from the invisible (*niskala*) world, in which human beings give offerings and worship in order to ensure the renewal of life and the regeneration of nature. Participation in these rituals is a customary obligation for the Balinese, which sanctions membership in a village community, a kinship group, and a temple congregation. Accordingly, the Balinese are far more concerned with appropriate behavior (orthopraxy) than with the right beliefs (orthodoxy). What's important for them is not theology but efficacy. Such evidence led Indologist Frits Staal to conclude that, "Balinese ritual is a classic case of ritual without religion" (Staal 1995: 31).

Admittedly, we don't know when the Balinese started using the word *agama* in the sense of "religion"—nor when they actually chose to label their own *agama* as *Hindu*. But we do know that long before the Balinese began defining themselves as Hindus, Orientalists had already "Hinduized" them, at a time when they had yet to learn the word "Hindu" (Guermonprez 2001: 272). As it happened, before Dutch colonial administrators began to engage with Balinese society, Orientalists had viewed it as a "living museum" of Indo-Javanese civilization, the one and only surviving heir to the Hindu heritage swept away from Java by the coming of Islam. In their view, Hinduism had been brought to Bali in the fourteenth century by Javanese conquerors from the kingdom of Majapahit, who had also imposed the division of society into four "castes," in accordance with the Indic model of the *varna*. When Majapahit fell to Islam at the turn of the sixteenth century, the Javanese nobility who refused to embrace the new faith were said to have found refuge at the courts of their coreligionists on Bali, where they nurtured the Indo-Javanese civilization as a precious heirloom.

Thus, in the report of his brief visit to Bali in 1814, the British Orientalist John Crawfurd had taken for granted that the Balinese were Hindus and, moreover, he used the word *agama* in the sense of religion (Crawfurd 1820: 129; see further, Raffles 1817; Van Hoëvell 1848; Friederich 1849–50). Yet this begs the question whether the word *agama* already meant religion for the Balinese in the nineteenth century, as this would have required them to have been secularized, so as to be able to discriminate between the respective senses of *agama* as "religion," "law," and "tradition." I think this is unlikely, as *agama* still retained the meaning of *dharma* in Bali during the Dutch colonial period.

Hence, the *Agama* texts continued to be used for the administration of justice in the Balinese courts of law, which were presided over by a council of *brahmana* priests (*pedanda*) called *kerta*. When the Dutch established their authority on the northern part of the island in 1882, they took over the Balinese legal system and adapted it to their colonial needs by setting up courts of law which they renamed Raad Kerta (Korn 1932: 42; Creese 2009b: 525). Then, once they had imposed their rule over the entire island in 1908, Dutch colonial officials had the main *Agama* law codes edited and translated, first into Balinese (1909) and later into Malay (1918), as they deemed that the priests sitting at the courts of law were unable to adequately understand the archaic language of these texts. By thus homogenizing and fixing the *Agama* codes in printed editions, the very essence of Balinese judicial practice, based on exegetical textual traditions open to flexible interpretation, was fatally undermined (Creese 2009b: 545).

Further evidence that *agama* still had the common denotation of *dharma* in Bali during the colonial period is provided by the Kirtya Liefrinck-Van der Tuuk, the library that the Dutch administration set up in 1928 to preserve traditional manuscripts. In the library catalogue, established by Balinese scholars, the entry *agama* refers not to "religion" but to law codes related to the Indian *dharmaśāstra*. There is no entry corresponding to the category "religion"—neither is there one for *adat* or for *hukum* (Kadjeng 1929). However, in *Bhāwanāgara*, the journal published by the Kirtya from 1931 to 1935, we find both the legal and the religious meanings of the term *agama*. The religious meaning is glossed in Balinese as *Kasewasogatan*, from *Sewa*, Siwa's worshippers, and *Sogata*, Buddha's devotees, in reference to the two categories of *brahmana* priests in Bali, the *pedanda Siwa* and the *pedanda Buda*.

On the other hand, it is no coincidence that it was precisely when the Balinese were assessing their identity—in Malay this time—that they started to use the word *agama* in the sense of "religion." Indeed, they were seeking to promote their own religion on a par with Islam and Christianity, in an attempt to resist Muslim and Christian proselytism. For the Balinese, Islam and Christianity were seen not only as a threat, but also as a model of what a true religion should be. Faced with Muslim schoolteachers and Christian missionaries, they were under pressure to formulate exactly what their religion was about. In that respect, Christianity appears to have been more determinant than Islam in prompting the Balinese to construe their own religion, as unlike Muslims, who had long been integrated within the indigenous socio-cosmic order (Couteau 1999), the presence of newly converted Christian families in their villages brought about a dichotomy between the ritual and social spheres, by making it necessary to distinguish between domains of interaction in which "religion" was relevant and others where it was not (Ottino 2000).

The point is, *agama* could not become a boundary marker for the Balinese people until they began to view Islam and Christianity as a threat (Vickers 1987; Hauser-Schäublin 2004). In this regard, we should pay attention to the controversy that divided the Balinese intelligentsia over the proper name for their religion, as it reveals serious contention over the main points in debate, that is, how *agama* is related to *adat* on the one hand and, on the other, how Balinese religion is connected to Indian Hinduism.

## 4 In Search of a Name for the Balinese Religion

The name to be given to the "Balinese religion" proved to be a highly controversial issue. It triggered a protracted conflict between the Balinese who intended to retain their local traditions and those who strove to reform them in accordance with what they assumed Hinduism—as a "world religion" (Masuzawa 2005)—was about. This conflict set the rising elite of educated commoners (*jaba*) against the conservative nobility (*triwangsa*)[6]—with the periodicals *Surya Kanta* (1925–1927) and *Bali Adnjana* (1924–1930) as their respective mouthpieces—in their attempts to hold sway over the religious life of the Balinese people.

While commoners and nobility shared a common reference to *agama* and *adat* as the foundations of Balinese identity, their opinions diverged concerning the respective domains of these two categories. While the *triwangsa* were de-

---

[6] The Balinese nobility is composed of the *triwangsa* (the "three peoples": *brahmana*, *satria*, *wesia*), as opposed to the *jaba* (the "outsiders," that is, those who are outside the sphere of the courts), who make up the bulk of the population. According to their myth of origin, the *triwangsa* claim to be the descendants of the Javanese conquerors from the kingdom of Majapahit who subjugated the island of Bali in the fourteenth century.

termined to reinforce both tradition and religion, the *jaba* wanted to reform *agama* while ridding *adat* of all the customs they deemed obsolete. For the *triwangsa*, Balinese religion was based on the customary social order, within which *agama* was inseparable from *adat*. Whereas for the *jaba*, religion could and should be dissociated from a traditional order seen not only as unfair but also as a hindrance to progress. Yet they proved unable to differentiate between that which belongs to *agama* and that which pertains to *adat*.

In 1925, a dispute erupted between commoners and the nobility over the name of the Balinese religion. As mentioned above, the Balinese formerly had no generic name to designate what would later become their "religion." Once they adopted the word *agama* for this purpose, they referred to their religion simply as *agama Bali*. Afterward, the Balinese started using a variety of names for their religion, such as *Tirtha, Siwa, Buda, Siwa-Buda, Kasewasogatan, Trimurti, Hindu Bali, Bali Hindu*, and *Hindu*.[7]

The *triwangsa* proposed to call their religion *agama Hindu Bali*, stressing the fact that the Balinese people had appropriated and reinterpreted *agama Hindu* to such an extent that it had become indigenous to their island. In this way, they were clearly trying to preserve the established socio-religious order of yore, by endorsing the religion that the Balinese actually practiced. Whereas in defending the name *agama Bali Hindu*, the *jaba* claimed that the Balinese were truly Hindus, even if their religious practices were corrupted by superstition (*takhyul*) owing to their ignorance of the true nature of their religion. Consequently, in order to become the true Hindus they were supposed to be, the Balinese should discard all indigenous accretions that contaminated their religious practices. Hence, the *triwangsa* accused the *jaba* of attempting to promote a form of Hinduism similar to that found in India. This, they claimed, amounted to inventing a new religion, which was alien to the Balinese because their religion originated not in India but in Majapahit. It was therefore the duty of the Balinese to remain faithful to the religion their ancestors had brought to Bali at the peril of their lives, when they were fleeing the propagation of Islam in Java after the fall of Majapahit.

---

**7** *Agama Tirtha* refers to the holy water required for most religious rites. *Agama Siwa* and *agama Buda*, like *Kasewasogatan*, pertain to the two categories of *brahmana* priests—the *pedanda Siwa* and the *pedanda Buda*—while *agama Siwa-Buda* points more specifically to the Tantric fusion of Shaivism and Buddhism that originated in East Java in the thirteenth century. The name *agama Trimurti* designates the Hindu triad Brahma, Wisnu and Iswara. Finally, we find *agama Hindu Bali*, *agama Bali Hindu*, and *agama Hindu*. In that respect, we should bear in mind that it is only through the work of Dutch Orientalists that educated Balinese elites became acquainted with the word "Hindu" in the twentieth century.

While in the 1920s the context of religious debates had remained essentially Balinese, during the 1930s it became increasingly Indonesian. The questions regarding the Balinese religion re-emerged more pressingly than ever in a new periodical, *Djatajoe* (1936–1941), the organ of the organization Bali Darma Laksana. By then the Balinese were clearly on the defensive, as the controversy was no longer due solely to disagreement among themselves, but to the fact that they were at a loss as to how to reply to accusations of paganism by Indonesian Muslims and Christian missionaries (Kraemer 1933), not to mention some Dutch administrators (Korn 1932: 62). This was particularly the case of young Balinese studying outside Bali, who felt embarrassed whenever they were asked about their religion, with some going so far as to convert to Islam or Christianity for fear of being branded as "idolatrous" or "animists" by their schoolmates. In the eyes of religious reformers, the problem was that most Balinese did not know their religion. The reformers therefore urged their coreligionists to investigate the meaning of their religion so as to be able to refute the charges that foreigners held against it.

Thus, when the leaders of Bali Darma Laksana held their first congress in 1937, they commissioned a committee of *pedanda* and literati to compile a "Holy Book" (*Kitab Suci*), which would represent for the Balinese what the Koran is to the Muslims. They felt that once the Balinese knew what their religion was actually about, they would be in a better position to defend it against accusations of heathenism by Muslims and Christians alike, and would thus be less tempted to embrace another faith. Unfortunately, three years later, the readers of *Djatajoe* were informed that the attempt to compose a Holy Book had failed. The reason given was that in Bali, *agama* could not be divorced from *adat*, and *adat* differed from one village to the next; hence the members of the committee could not agree on a religious canon that would be valid for the whole island. The religion of the Balinese was not (yet) a religion of the Book (Picard 2004).

## 5 From *Agama Hindu Bali* to *Agama Hindu*

Although the first generation of Balinese intellectuals fell short of an agreement on how *agama Bali* was related to *adat* on the one hand, and to *agama Hindu* on the other, their debates had nonetheless prepared the Balinese people to face the pressures imposed upon their religious identity once their island had become part of the Republic of Indonesia. What happened during the colonial period was not simply that the former unity of *agama* and *adat* had started to disintegrate due to the colonial confrontation, since these categories were alien and had to be appropriated by the Balinese for their own purpose. It was not even that the Balinese had taken refuge in their religion, after having been threatened by Muslim and Christian proselytism. Rather, it was the conjunction of two distinct processes of differentiation which resulted in the formation of the categories of *agama* and *adat*—on the one hand, the Dutch-enforced separation between religious tradition and secular administration, and on the other, the growing urge to dissociate religion from tradition on the part of educated, reform-minded Balinese.

This conceptual separation of *agama* and *adat* had actually started when Balinese reformers were attempting to find a name for their religion, thereby initiating an objectification of religion as a separate field of beliefs and practices. Yet while the Dutch had de-politicized *adat* by dissociating political power from customary authority, religion was still merged with tradition in the colonial period. Once the Balinese had become Indonesian citizens, they would be compelled to distinguish explicitly between "religion" and "tradition." In order for their rituals to attain the status of *agama*, they had to be detached from what was considered as belonging to the domain of *adat*. Such a replacement of disparate local rituals by a de-territorialized universal religion amounted to a process of "secularization," in the sense of a functional differentiation of the institutional spheres of the "religious" and the "secular." Specifically, this process constituted a twofold invention: in the first place, that of a "Balinese religion" (*agama Bali*) proper, and second, that of the Balinese religion as "Hinduism" (*agama Hindu*).

The first question to be settled was for the Balinese leaders to agree on the name of their religion. After lengthy debates, they resolved in 1952 to call it *agama Hindu Bali*[8]—the name championed by the *triwangsa* in the 1920s. It appears that the name *agama Hindu Bali* became customary only after Balinese had started to convert to Islam or Christianity, in order to differentiate *Hindu Bali* from *Islam Bali* or *Kristen Bali*.

However, even if the Balinese had finally reached an agreement among themselves, they still had to convince the Ministry of Religion of the legitimacy of the

---

[8] By the same token, they adopted the name Sang Hyang Widi to designate the one and only God of the Balinese religion. This term had long been known among the literati and was popularized in the 1920s by the religious reform movement as an equivalent to the Malay word *Tuhan*, meaning "Lord." According to Jan Gonda, "in modern Bali *Vidhi* (*Viddhi*)—the Indian designation of 'rule, destiny' which is also applied to some individual gods—denotes that principle which, representing the unity of the universe, is beyond all plurality and acts as the guardian of the cosmic and moral order" (Gonda 1975: 23). The polysemy of the name meant it could comply with the conception of a personal God characteristic of the religions of the Book, as well as with the notion of *dharma*, which implies the prevalence of the Cosmic Law over the gods and of the gods over humans.

*agama Hindu Bali*. Consequently, over the following years, they kept pressing the Ministry to recognize their religion. While some religious leaders were looking for the seeds of regeneration in their own indigenous traditions, young Balinese who were studying in India urged their coreligionists to return to the fold of Hinduism, which they presented as the source of their rituals. Stressing the theological import and the ethical implications of religion, they attempted to restrain the Balinese ritualistic leanings, while construing their Hindu heritage in accordance with Islam and Christianity.

In 1958, after years of lobbying, a *Hindu Bali* section was finally established within the Ministry of Religion, a few weeks after Bali had become a full-fledged province of the Republic of Indonesia (Picard 2011a). The next step was to decide who should be in charge of the *agama Hindu Bali* now that the Republican government had replaced the former kings who had previously been the patrons of the religious ceremonies on the island. For that purpose, a council was set up in 1959 to coordinate the religious activities of the Hindu Balinese—the Parisada Dharma Hindu Bali (PDHB, Hindu Bali Dharma Council) (Bakker 1993: 225–291; see also, Ramstedt 2004).[9]

With the backing and subsidies of the provincial government, the Parisada undertook to translate Indian sacred scriptures, compile a theological canon (*Panca Çraddha*) (Punyatmadja 1970), publish a Hindu catechism (*Upadeśa*) (Mantra 1967), devise a Hindu prayer (*Tri Sandya*) as an equivalent of daily Islamic prayers (Lanus 2014), standardize rituals, formalize the priesthood, and provide religious instruction to the population. This endeavor amounted to a "scripturalization" of Balinese religion, a shift in focus from ritual to text. Unlike the kings and the priests, who merely interceded on behalf of their subjects and clients, the Parisada was now instructing the Balinese on what to believe and how to practice their religion.

Such a Hinduization of indigenous ritual practices rested on a democratization of religious knowledge that constituted a drastic break with traditional ideas of forbidden knowledge (*aja wera*),[10] as the Balinese had to understand their re-

---

[9] Note that instead of the word *agama*, rejected on account of its Islamic connotation, the Indian-educated Balinese responsible for naming the council retained the word *dharma* to convey the normative idea of "religion."

[10] Traditionally in Bali, knowledge was perceived as dangerous, inasmuch as it dealt with the mysterious powers (*sakti*) of the world beyond the senses (*niskala*). Hence, manuscripts pertaining to religious matters were shrouded in secrecy and protected by prohibitions (*aja wera*, literally "do not divulge"). Access to them was restricted to those persons who had been duly purified and had acquired the appropriate skills to study them, thereby becoming immune to *niskala* forces.

ligion if they wanted to defend it from the questioning of followers of other religions. Thus, for the first time, Balinese other than priests and literati were enjoined to find in their religion a logically coherent set of moral values and theological principles. Furthermore, the newly instituted monotheism implied that, instead of transactions with multiple entities from the *niskala* world, Balinese Hindus were expected to establish a personal relationship of faith and devotion with their one and exclusive God—Sang Hyang Widi. This in turn entailed a twofold differentiation, between "gods" and "ancestors" and between the "divine" and the "demonic." While formerly there were no clear lines of demarcation between ancestors and gods, but rather hierarchical ideas of more or less purified ancestors who eventually became united with divinities, now there had to be an absolute dichotomy between human ancestors and a transcendent God. Besides, whereas *niskala* entities were inherently ambivalent, potentially malevolent as well as benevolent, Sang Hyang Widi had become an entirely positive figure.

In the 1960s, the growing presence of Balinese communities outside their own island enabled the Parisada to extend its influence across the Archipelago. Cut off from their temple networks and their deified ancestors, these Balinese migrants needed a delocalized and scriptural religion that they could carry with them. In these circumstances, the Parisada leaders who had studied in India advocated giving up the exclusive ethnic flavor of the label *Hindu Bali* in favor of the more inclusive *Hindu Dharma*, as a means to strengthen the position of their religion vis-à-vis Islam and Christianity. As a result, at its first congress in 1964, the Parisada Dharma Hindu Bali changed its name to Parisada Hindu Dharma (PHD, Hindu Dharma Council), forsaking any reference to its Balinese origins. And the following year, when President Sukarno specified the religions that would qualify for official recognition, it was *agama Hindu* and not *agama Hindu Bali* that was retained.[11]

Thus it was through their struggle to obtain recognition for their religion that the Balinese came to define their ethnic identity in terms of *agama Hindu*. But it is precisely from the moment they began to identify themselves most explicitly as a Hindu island in a sea of Islam that one can date the premises of the disjunction between the Balinese religious and ethnic identities. This is because their identification of ethnicity and religion would soon be foiled by a twofold process of Indonesianization-cum-Indianization: on the one hand, the affiliation of other

---

**11** *Penetapan Presiden n° 1/1965 tentang Pencegahan Penyalahgunaan dan/atau Penodaan Agama* (literally, "On the Prevention of the Misuse and/or the Besmirching of Religion"). This decree made it illegal to slander, interpret falsely or promote teachings that depart from the core teachings of any of the state-sanctioned religions.

Indonesian ethnic groups with *agama Hindu* dissociated it from the Balinese, while on the other hand, the growing influence of Indian neo-Hinduism on *agama Hindu* rendered the link between religion and ethnicity ever more problematic for the Balinese.

Indeed, once expressly detached from any ethnic reference, *agama Hindu* was no longer the sole property of the Balinese people, who had to open it up to other Indonesian ethnic groups. Its official recognition brought new recruits in the wake of the anti-communist massacres of 1965–66, which provoked the "conversion" to *agama Hindu* of Javanese nominal Muslims (*abangan*) for fear of being branded "atheists," an accusation synonymous with "communists" in Indonesia. In the following years, several ethnic minorities took refuge in the *Hindu* fold in the hope of being allowed to conserve their ancestral rites, *agama Hindu* being reputedly more accommodating in this respect than Islam or Christianity. To integrate the newcomers, the Parisada devised a rite of conversion to *agama Hindu* named *Śuddhi Wadāni* (Titib 1991), adapted from the rite of reconversion invented by the Ārya Samāj in the nineteenth century to bring back into the fold of Hinduism those Indians who had converted to Islam or Christianity (Jordens 1991).

The diffusion of *agama Hindu* outside Bali continued to such an extent that it seemed the Balinese might lose control of the religion they had themselves established.[12] But what some Balinese saw as the dispossession of their own religion, other Indonesian Hindus perceived as Balinese "colonization." Hence a tension, affecting the Balinese themselves, between the Balinization of the religious practices of various ethnic groups affiliated with *agama Hindu* and the Indonesianization of the Balinese religion aimed at detaching it from its ethnic origins.

It did not take long for this tension to concern the Parisada itself. After having established branches in every province of the country, at the time of its fifth congress in 1986, the Parisada Hindu Dharma became the Parisada Hindu Dharma Indonesia (PHDI, Hindu Dharma Council of Indonesia). As a consequence,

---

12 It is rather difficult to know with any precision the number of followers of *agama Hindu* in Indonesia, inasmuch as the religious composition of the population is a politically contentious matter. According to the 2010 census, there are around 4 million Hindus in Indonesia, a figure disputed by the Directorate of Hinduism at the Ministry of Religion, which puts the number at roughly 10 million, while the Parisada claims that there are 18 million. According to the census, Hindus composed 1.69 per cent of the Indonesian population and 83.5 per cent of the population of Bali. In the opinion of most Balinese religious leaders, the proportion of Hindus is deliberately underestimated at the national level, whereas it is overestimated for Bali so as to prevent the Balinese people from knowing the true weight of the Muslim population on their island.

a regional branch was opened in Bali. Eventually, in 1996, at the time of the seventh congress, the Parisada headquarters were relocated from Bali to Jakarta, leaving only the Balinese branch on the island.

During the 1990s, the Islamic resurgence in Indonesia aroused Balinese apprehension over their religious identity and triggered, in mimetic fashion, a "Hindu revival" (*Kebangkitan Hindu*) (Setia 1993). This revival resulted in the fragmentation of the Balinese religious identity. It appears that, from then on, neither the traditional religion, attached to the correct execution of rituals, nor its official version, concerned with ethics and theology, were able to satisfy a growing fraction of the Balinese middle class in search of religious devotion and personal conviction as well as universalism. At the same time, the Parisada was criticized for being more a pressure group of conservative members of the Balinese nobility than a genuine religious body, and for promoting a traditionalist conception of *agama Hindu* still very much affected by its original Balinese parochialism (Bagus 2004). Such criticism came from two socio-religious movements which pursued distinct aims but whose actors originated from the same milieux—the *warga* and the *sampradaya*.

The *warga* movement resumed the commoners' struggle against the privileges of the nobility initiated in the 1920s (Kerepun 2007). After Indonesia's independence, the main *jaba* title groups had set up formal organizations uniting all members of a kinship group who considered themselves the descendants of a common ancestor. Their aim was to have their rights acknowledged against the *triwangsa*'s privileges, and specifically to abrogate the *brahmana*'s monopoly on the initiated priesthood (Pitana 1999). Under the pressure of the *warga*, the Parisada decreed during its second congress in 1968 that all Hindus were entitled to undergo the ordination rite to the initiated priesthood and, furthermore, that all duly initiated priests had the same status and were thus equally qualified to officiate at all ceremonies. This decree did not settle the matter, however, as despite the Parisada's official position, some of its leaders continued to defend the exclusive privileges of the *pedanda*.

While supporting the *warga*'s demand that their priests be allowed to officiate on a par with the *pedanda*, Balinese reformers were no longer satisfied with a nationally recognized religion. Instead, they aspired to universalize their religious identity by fully embracing Hinduism as a world religion. They initiated a renewed turn towards India, marked by the promotion of Indian concepts and practices, such as vegetarianism or the performance of the revived Vedic ritual *Agnihotra*. Pilgrimages (*tirtha yatra*) were organized to the holy sites of India, where Indonesian Hindus were urged to seek their religious sources, in the manner of Muslims going on the *hajj* to Mecca. Most of all, this rapprochement with India in the 1990s was marked by the gradual establishment in Indonesia of neo-

Hindu devotional movements (*sampradaya*), such as Sai Baba and Hare Krishna, the most popular among them (Jendra 2007). The propagation of these movements in Indonesia met with some opposition from the Ministry of Religion as well as from the Parisada, who feared the rise of conflicts between rival sects that could undermine the Hindu community.

## 6 Back to *Agama Hindu Bali*

The spate of ethnic and religious identity politics and the radicalization of Islam unleashed by the fall of President Suharto in 1998 led to strife within the Parisada during its eighth national congress in September 2001. The Balinese branch of the Parisada objected to some of the decisions the congress adopted, namely the nomination of a layman to the Parisada's chairmanship, which had so far been monopolized by the *pedanda*, not to mention the massive presence in its management of *jaba* and non-Balinese, as well as prominent members of the *warga* and the *sampradaya*. In November of the same year, the Balinese Parisada convened its own congress at Campuan, near Ubud. This site was not chosen at random. It was there that the Campuan Charter had been signed forty years earlier, which stipulated that the Parisada would be presided by a *pedanda*. Accusing the national leadership of undermining Balinese identity by unduly Indianizing *agama Hindu*, the Campuan congress refused the admission of the *sampradaya* into the Parisada and demanded that a *pedanda* be nominated as chairman.

Soon afterward, the central Parisada disowned the Parisada Campuan and convened a competing regional congress in March 2002 at Besakih. Besakih is another site of highly symbolic value, as it is the main sanctuary on the island, representing the community of Indonesian Hindus in its entirety. After the Parisada Besakih had duly ratified the decisions of the eighth national congress, it was acknowledged as the official Balinese branch of the Parisada. In the years that followed, each of the two Balinese Parisada claimed to be the legitimate representative of the Balinese Hindu community. While the Parisada Besakih had the support of the middle-class urban intelligentsia and those Balinese living outside the island, the Parisada Campuan appeared to be more aligned with the village population.

In 2007, the Parisada Campuan convened its congress, which decided to return to the "true self" (*jati diri*) of the Balinese religion—that is, to *agama Hindu Bali*. At the same time, the congress resolved to revert to the name originally chosen by their founding fathers, Parisada Dharma Hindu Bali, thus reversing the globalization of the Balinese religion by re-localizing it. In that respect, the return to *agama Hindu Bali* reveals itself to be much more than a withdrawal into Balinese parochialism on the part of a group of die-hard reactionaries, as their opponents contended. The split in the Balinese Parisada illustrates a divide centered on two interrelated issues: the desire to preserve *brahmana*'s priestly authority, and the challenge to Balinese control over *agama Hindu* in Indonesia. Its promoters attempted to put an end to the dispossession of their religion by winning back management of the Parisada, which they had lost in the 1990s, as demonstrated by the displacement of the Parisada's center from Bali to Jakarta, the increasing ascendancy of non-Balinese and non-*brahmana* over its leadership, and its inclusion of the neo-Hindu devotional movements aimed at "purifying" traditional Balinese religious practices (Picard 2011b).

## 7 Concluding Remarks

In recent years, the conflict between the two Balinese factions appears to have faded somewhat, although the reasons for its initial outbreak have yet to be properly addressed. Be that as it may, the comeback of *agama Hindu Bali* might be regarded in retrospect as a return to a signification of *agama* untainted by its Islamic and Christian interpretations, when *agama* had not yet been separated from *adat*. One could say that the Parisada Dharma Hindu Bali reappropriated the power to identify as *agama* that which pertained to *adat* for the Parisada Hindu Dharma Indonesia, just as the latter had claimed the power to designate as *agama* that which the Ministry of Religion had classified as *adat*. One could further say that this determination to reappropriate the Balinese religion amounts to a process of counter-secularization, aimed at closing the gap between the "religious" and the "secular" that had been opened by the obligation imposed upon the Balinese people to have a proper *agama*.

## References

Anandakusuma, Sri Reshi. 1986. *Kamus Bahasa Bali [Dictionary of the Balinese Language]*. Denpasar: C.V. Kayumas.

Bagus, I Gusti Ngurah. 2004. "The Parisada Hindu Dharma Indonesia in a society in transformation". In M. Ramstedt, ed., *Hinduism in Modern Indonesia. A minority religion between local, national, and global interests*, pp. 84–92. London and New York: RoutledgeCurzon.

Bakker, Frederik Lambertus. 1993. *The Struggle of the Hindu Balinese Intellectuals. Developments in Modern Hindu Thinking in Independent Indonesia*. Amsterdam: VU University Press.

Becker, Judith. 2004. *Gamelan Stories. Tantrism, Islam, and Aesthetics in Central Java*. Tempe: Arizona State University (1st edition, 1993).

Brunner, Hélène. 1967. "À propos d'un rituel balinais". *Journal Asiatique* 255 no. 3–4: 409–422.

Burchardt, Marian and Monika Wohlrab-Sahr. 2013. "'Multiple Secularities: Religion and Modernity in the Global Age' – Introduction". *International Sociology* 28 no. 6: 605–611.

Couteau, Jean. 1999. "Bali et l'islam: 1. Rencontre historique". *Archipel* 58: 159–188.

Crawfurd, John. 1820. "On the existence of the Hindu religion in the island of Bali". *Asiatick Researches* 13: 128–170.

Creese, Helen. 2009a. "Old Javanese legal traditions in pre-colonial Bali". *Bijdragen tot de Taal-, Land- en Volkenkunde* 165 no. 2–3: 241–290.

Creese, Helen. 2009b. "Judicial processes and legal authority in pre-colonial Bali". *Bijdragen tot de Taal-, Land- en Volkenkunde* 165 no. 4: 515–550.

Davis, Richard H. 1991. *Ritual in an Oscillating Universe: Worshipping Śiva in Medieval India*. Princeton: Princeton University Press.

Friederich, Rudolf H.Th. 1849–50. "Voorlopig verslag van het eiland Bali" [Provisional report on the Island of Bali]. *Verhandelingen van het Bataviaasch Genootschap voor Kunsten en Wetenschappen* 22: 1–63, 23: 1–57.

Gonda, Jan. 1973. *Sanskrit in Indonesia*. New Delhi: International Academy of Indian Culture (1st edition, 1952).

Gonda, Jan. 1975. "The Indian Religions in Pre-Islamic Indonesia and their Survival in Bali". In *Hanbuch der Orientalistik, Part 3: Indonesien, Malaysia und die Philippinen*, pp. 1–54. Leiden and Köln: E.J. Brill.

Guermonprez, Jean-François. 2001. "La religion balinaise dans le miroir de l'hindouisme". *Bulletin de l'École française d'Extrême-Orient* 88: 271–293.

Halbfass, Wilhelm. 1988. *India and Europe: An Essay in Understanding*. Albany: State University of New York Press (1st edition, 1981).

Hauser-Schäublin, Brigitta. 2004. "'Bali Aga' and Islam: Ethnicity, ritual practice, and 'Old-Balinese' as an anthropological construct". *Indonesia* 77: 1–28.

Hauser-Schäublin, Brigitta. 2011. "Spiritualized politics and the trademark of culture: political actors and their use of *adat* and *agama* in post-Suharto Bali". In Michel Picard and Rémy Madinier, eds., *The Politics of Religion in Indonesia. Syncretism, orthodoxy, and religious contention in Java and Bali*, pp. 192–213. London and New York: Routledge.

Hoadley, Mason C. and M.B. Hooker. 1981. *An Introduction to Javanese Law. A Translation of and Commentary on the Agama*. Tucson: The University of Arizona Press.

Hoadley, Mason C. and M.B. Hooker. 1986. "The law texts of Java and Bali". In M.B. Hooker, ed., *The Laws of South-East Asia. Volume 1: The pre-modern texts*, pp. 241–346. Singapore: Butterworths.

Holdrege, Barbara A. 2004. "Dharma". In S. Mittal and G. Thursby, eds., *The Hindu World*, pp. 213–248. New York and London: Routledge.

Hooykaas, Christiaan. 1966. *Sūrya-Sevana: The Way to God of a Balinese Śiva Priest*. Amsterdam: N.V. Noord-Hollandsche Uitgevers Maatschappij.

Jendra, Wayan. 2007. *Sampradaya. Kelompok Belajar Weda, Aliran dalam Agama Hindu dan Budaya Bali [Sampradaya. Veda Study Groups, A Current in Hindu Religion and Balinese Culture]*. Denpasar: Panakom.

Jordens, J.F.T. 1991. "Reconversion to Hinduism: The Shuddhi of the Arya Samaj". In G.A. Oddie, ed., *Religion in South Asia. Religious Conversion and Revival Movements in South Asia in Medieval and Modern Times*, pp. 215–230. New Delhi: Manohar.

Kadjeng, Njoman. 1929. "Voorloopig overzicht der op Bali aanwezige literatuurschat" [Provisional overview of existing literary collections on Bali]. *Mededeelingen van de Kirtya Liefrinck – van der Tuuk*, 1: 19–40.

Kerepun, Made Kembar. 2007. *Mengurai Benang Kusut Kasta. Membedah Kiat Pengajegan Kasta di Bali [Disentangling the Mix-up of Castes. Dissecting the Defense of Castes in Bali]*. Denpasar: Panakom.

Korn, Victor Emanuel. 1932. *Het Adatrecht van Bali [The Customary Law of Bali]*. 's-Gravenhage: Naeff (1st edition, 1924).

Kraemer, Hendrik. 1933. *De strijd over Bali en de Zending. Een studie en een appel [The Controversy About Bali and the Missions. A study and an appeal]*. Amsterdam: H.J. Paris.

Lanus, Sugi. 2014. "*Puja Tri Sandhyā:* Indian Mantras Recomposed and Standardised in Bali". *The Journal of Hindu Studies* 7 no: 2: 243–272.

Lévi, Sylvain. 1933. *Sanskrit Texts from Bali*. Baroda: Oriental Institute.

Mandair, Arvind-Pal S. and Markus Dressler. 2011. "Introduction: Modernity, Religion-Making, and the Postsecular". In M. Dressler and A.-P. S. Mandair, eds., *Secularism and Religion-Making*, pp. 3–36. Oxford and New York: Oxford University Press.

Mantra, Ida Bagus et al. 1967. *Upadeśa Tentang Adjaran-Adjaran Agama Hindu [Instructions Regarding the Teachings of the Hindu Religion]*. Denpasar: Parisada Hindu Dharma.

Masuzawa, Tomoko. 2005. *The Invention of World Religions. Or How European Universalism Was Preserved in the Language of Pluralism*. Chicago: The University of Chicago Press.

Ottino, Arlette. 2000. "Conflict avoidance and cohabitation of different religious groups in Bali". In H. Warsilah and R. Koestoer, eds., *International Symposium on Management of Social Transformation in Indonesian Society: In Search of Models for Conflict Prevention*, pp. 69–84. Jakarta: MOST-UNESCO and PMB-LIPI.

Picard, Michel. 2004. "What's in a name? *Agama Hindu Bali* in the making". In M. Ramstedt, ed., *Hinduism in Modern Indonesia. A minority religion between local, national, and global interests*, pp. 56–75. London and New York: RoutledgeCurzon.

Picard, Michel. 2011a. "Balinese Religion in Search of Recognition: From *agama Hindu Bali* to *agama Hindu* (1945–1965)". *Bijdragen tot de Taal-, Land- en Volkenkunde* 167 no. 4: 482–510.

Picard, Michel. 2011b. "From *agama Hindu Bali* to *agama Hindu* and back. Toward a relocalization of the Balinese religion?". In Michel Picard and Rémy Madinier, eds., *The Politics of Religion in Indonesia. Syncretism, Orthodoxy, and Religious Contention in Java and Bali*, pp. 117–141. London and New York: Routledge.

Picard, Michel. 2017. *Kebalian. La construction dialogique de l'identité balinaise*. Paris: Cahiers d'Archipel.

Pitana, I Gde. 1999. "Status Struggles and the Priesthood in Contemporary Bali". In R. Rubinstein and L.H. Connor. *Staying Local in the Global Village. Bali in the Twentieth Century*, pp. 181–201. Honolulu: University of Hawai'i Press.

Punyatmadja, Ida Bagus Oka. 1970. *Panca Çraddha [The Five Articles of Faith]*. Denpasar: Parisada Hindu Dharma Pusat.

Raffles, Thomas Stamford. 1817. *The History of Java*. London: Black, Parbury and Allen.

Ramstedt, Martin. 2004. "Introduction: Negociating identities – Indonesian 'Hindus' between local, national, and global interests". In M. Ramstedt, ed., *Hinduism in Modern Indonesia. A minority religion between local, national, and global interests*, pp. 1–34. London and New York: RoutledgeCurzon.

Rocher, Ludo. 2003. "The Dharmaśāstras". In G. Flood, ed., *The Blackwell Companion to Hinduism*, pp. 102–115. Oxford: Blackwell Publishing.

Rubinstein, Raechelle. 2000. *Beyond the Realm of the Senses. The Balinese Ritual of Kekawin Composition*. Leiden: KITLV Press.

Sarkar, Himansu Bhusan. 1934. *Indian Influences on the Literature of Java and Bali*. Calcutta: Greater India Society.

Schulte Nordholt, Henk. 1991. *State, Village, and Ritual in Bali*. Amsterdam: VU University Press.

Setia, Putu. 1993. *Kebangkitan Hindu Menyongsong Abad ke-21 [The Hindu Revival Faces the 21st Century]*. Jakarta: Pustaka Manikgeni.

Staal, Frits. 1995. *Mantras between Fire and Water. Reflections on a Balinese Rite*. Amsterdam: Koninklijke Nederlandse Akademie van Wetenshappen.

Titib, Made. 1991. *Pedoman Upacara Śuddhi Wadāni [Guide to the ceremony Śuddhi Wadāni]*. Denpasar: Upada Sastra.

Van Hoëvell, Wolter Robert Baron. 1848. "Recent Scientific Researches on the Islands of Bali and Lombok". *The Journal of the Indian Archipelago and Eastern Asia* 2: 151–159.

Van Vollenhoven, Cornelis. 1928. *De Ontdekking van het Adatrecht [The Discovery of Customary Law]*. Leiden: E.J. Brill.

Vickers, Adrian. 1987. "Hinduism and Islam in Indonesia: Bali and the Pasisir World". *Indonesia* 44: 31–58.

Warren, Carol. 1993. Adat *and* Dinas. *Balinese Communities in the Indonesian State*. Kuala Lumpur: Oxford University Press.

Pascal Bourdeaux
# States, Religions and Modernities for one Nation: Historicizing a Converging Secularization in Twentieth Century Vietnam

**Abstract:** On January 1, 2018, Vietnam's first Law on Belief and Religions came into effect. Before this law was drafted, a former Ordinance (2004) and decrees defined religious policy and practices with the same aims: first, strengthening national unification and, second, international integration. This process started in 1986 with the proclamation of the Đổi mới policy, in other words, the acceptance of a socialist-oriented market economy. Five years later, religious policy was updated to regulate a so-called religious revival, or desecularization as theorized by some sociologists. From this period, state secularism came under pressure from churches and, even more so, from diffuse spiritual dynamics expressed within the society. To present the religious situation of Vietnam on the eve of this new era, I propose to historicize the concept and process of secularization in Vietnam by expanding the time-frame and considering overlapping political spaces (multiple states and regions in one nation). I then form the hypothesis that present-day Vietnam is characterized by an ongoing converging secularization which has to deal simultaneously with different models of religious pluralism, modernity and secularity. This confirms the genealogy of secularization in its dual legacy, as a political project and as a sociological process.

## 1 Introduction

When considered through the lens of religious life and history, Vietnam appears ambivalent. On one hand, the country shows intense and pluralistic practices, Buddhist traditions, peculiar religious innovations, and a strong Christian community. But on the other hand, spiritual pragmatism, the lack of institutionalized religious organizations and the recurring debate on the real nature of the premodern—and modern—states (divine Confucianist monarchy and imperial cult as state religion, Buddhism as official or predominant religion) have always raised questions about the real effects of moral precepts on politics and the interiority

---

**Pascal Bourdeaux** (EPHE-GSRL-PSL)

https://doi.org/10.1515/9783110733068-007

of convictions or faith on social habits. These issues are central to current debates over whether the genealogy of the secular state corresponds to a continuous and linear history or to a more fragmented one. Did this secular state appear due to modernity (supposedly Western colonial modernity) or did it draw its authority and legitimacy in immanent local traditions? Did Vietnamese society ever live outside the bounds of religious temporality and theological conceptions? As a consequence, did a premodern secularity exist? Or is secularization consubstantial to a kind of post-colonial, liberal and/or socialist modernity?

From an external point of view, Vietnam is also ambivalent if we compare the strength of revivalism and nativist religious movements with international bodies' recommendations and criticism concerning Vietnamese government regulations believed to infringe on religious freedom. International criticism peaked in 2005–2006, when the USCRIF[1] put the country on its list of *Countries with Particular Concerns* while Vietnam was negotiating its integration into the WTO. This decade saw intense reflection on how to adapt the Vietnamese religious system of registered organizations and turn the Ordinance of 2004 into the first real Law on Beliefs and Religions. After many years of preparation and a very short and controlled public debate, the National Assembly passed the law, which officially came into effect on January 1, 2018. The rule of law is therefore confirmed but many questions are yet to be answered: will this law stabilize good state-church relations? Will it facilitate or limit internal religious autonomy and the registration of new religions and denominations? Beyond its political functionality, will the law result in better recognition of the social and cultural claims of contemporary Vietnam's different religions? What of the historical and cultural legacies of ethnic and ethnoreligious communities? These questions require us to look at the multiple aspects of the secular, as a political project (secularism), as a sociological and legal process (secularization), and as a concept (theory of secularization).

These aspects interact in Vietnam as elsewhere, but the gap between their temporalities appears to be fairly specific. One general aim of this chapter is to discuss the interval between the political project and the deeper transformation of religious life. To do so, I take into consideration the main research stemming from Talal Asad's anthropology of the secular by "suggest[ing] that this secularism is best explored through its rifts, aporias, problems and tensions" (Bubandt & Van Beek 2012: 3). I also want to situate the analysis of the current situation in a larger historical background and consider the history of secularity in Vietnam by defining the main milestones.

---

[1] United States Commission on International Religious Freedom (https://www.uscirf.gov).

I do this in order to recall, first, the conflict-ridden past and the many attempts to lay the groundwork for a new socialist state and society, and second —a more fundamental aim but also a more complex one—for the reunification of a temporarily fragmented nation.

Secularization is about state-building and religious policy. These aspects have been studied fairly extensively and with more objectivity than before, especially if we consider attempts to disconnect secularization and democracy or to focus more broadly on its relations with other political regimes. Vietnam entered a new era with the proclamation of the *đổi mới* policy (or "Renovation policy") in 1986. The imposition of a socialist-oriented market economy had consequences for the state management of religious life but also for research. *Đổi mới* only indirectly affected the spiritual domain—more precisely the status of religions in Vietnamese society and the nature of their relationship to a socialist state that had always recognized the freedom to believe or not believe. Some changes were already discernible from the first socioeconomic transformations, with the opening up of the country, the mobility of overseas Vietnamese and, finally, a global context in which the planned secularization of modern democratic societies and the willed secularism of former socialist countries (including the People's Republic of China) were called into question by a so-called religious revival.

In 1990, Resolution 24 of the Vietnamese Communist Party overturned the prevailing paradigm in the fields of religious policy, spiritual life, and scientific knowledge. In acknowledging that, "for a part of the population, religion is a moral necessity that has existed for a long time, that will continue to exist for a long time, and that follows the same path as the nation and socialism," this resolution began to withdraw from state atheism and recognize the historical nature, social utility, and vital diversity of religions. New debates erupted over the definition of "religions" and "beliefs" and how these could loyally fit with the imperatives of Vietnamese national politics. Since then, the legal framework (Ordinance of 2004, Law on Beliefs and Religions of 2016) has sought to clarify the policy of official recognition of religious organizations and the conditions for practicing religion with respect to fundamental liberties. These new conditions have enabled an increase in academic research through a new classification of religious phenomena (institutionalized religions, indigenous religions, new religious movements, popular forms of worship, and so forth) reinforced by a multidisciplinary approach.

Simultaneously, a new international academic interest in Vietnamese religious matters has emerged. In order to jettison strictly Western conceptions of the "religious question," an epistemological renewal has taken place over the last few decades. In the case of Vietnam, scholarship needed to be liberated from three constraints: colonial domination, wartime politicization of religious forces, and the bureaucratization of religious organizations since the establishment of the Socialist Republic of Vietnam. Theoretical and institutional frameworks for research on religious studies have been redefined, and international cooperation has increased. The field of religious studies nonetheless remains subject to numerous ideological constraints, whether that pressure emanates from the state, from religious communities, or from international organizations within civil society. But the vitality of religious life in Vietnam is undeniable.

As a result, religion is no longer a marginal topic focused solely on relations with the state. Religion is once again considered as a social phenomenon, as shown by the historiographical evolution of the field and all the debates around secularization (*thế tục hóa*) and desecularization (*giải thế tục hóa*). This vernacularization in local discourse is a second aspect of recent research. As Nils Bubandt and Martijn Van Beek rightly explain, "the relationship between vernacular forms of secularism and world religion is full of tension, often because there are both competing versions of secularism and multiple religious positions vying for the same political space" (2012: 10). Retracing the genealogy of archaic vocabulary, the reuse of terms, and the standardization of neologisms at different times and under different regimes can help to understand those traditional vocabularies and neologisms. As Reinhart Koselleck explains, combining historical semantic and social history sheds light on broader intellectual, social and institutional dynamics at a given time (2016: 127–148).

Another concept that must be brought into play here is the nation. I entirely agree with Peter Van der Veer and Harmut Lehmann when they write, "The location of religion in the modern world should, in our view, be addressed in relation to the historical emergence of the modern idea of the nation and its spread over the world" (1999: 4). Once the idea of the nation is understood as an ongoing process (*nation building*) and as a resource of sacrality (legitimacy and sovereignty), we then need to specify how it appeared in the case of Vietnam, how it was challenged by various ideologies during the twentieth century, whether Vietnamese nationalism is intrinsically secular, or if (and how) religious beliefs also supported anticolonial, modernist and patriotic movements.

As a third contribution, this essay tries to define the chronological framework of this history of secularity. Defining a panoramic view of twentieth-century Vietnam is the first step in moving beyond a classic historical approach to secularism and methodological nationalism in order to rethink the nation and secularization in the light of different trends of thought and political experimentation.[2] It is of

---

2 "One problem that plagues many of these analyses is that they operate with the teleological

course necessary to study the dynamics of secularization/desecularization in the *đổi mới* era, especially by questioning the religious transformations and compromises from the former perspective of atheist secularism.³ The *đổi mới* is clearly an historical event that determines the current religious situation. But we need to go back to colonial times and alternative postcolonial experiences to show the secularization process in its full complexity.

Indeed, I maintain that secularization in Vietnam is not a linear process, which was once driven by ideological conflicts and is now driven by their attenuation. Although we can't deny the high level of bureaucratization and some antireligious trends during modern times, I propose to call this long-term process a gradual converging secularization, in which the Vietnamese state has tried to adapt and integrate other conceptions of what religion is (and, consequently, what secularism is) in reshaping its own policy. Nation-building experienced multiple modernities over the last century. And different states—successive states or rival states—were confronted with different ethno-religious substrates and religious pluralisms, especially when the country was politically and geographically divided. This situation reinforced a certain asymmetry in terms of religious policy, religious revivalism and diversification, collective consciousness and national awareness. After a contextualized authoritarian unification of the nation in the 1980s, the redefinition of a secular model on the eve of the twenty-first century does not only express a detachment from or a decline of historical materialism; it also means a more pragmatic and open approach to religious diversity and religious conceptions of the world in a stronger, unified postwar nation. Converging thus means that even as the state continues to promote its religious policy and make it acceptable to civil society, it also tries to take a more neutral outlook on alternative religious practices and religious policies that were implemented before reunification. Finally, converging means that the secular state is also trying to unify the nation through recognition of religious identities; in other words, by achieving parity between a secular culture (*văn hóa thế tục*) and a coexisting religious culture. This situation necessarily creates some discontents. But in Vietnam, secularization seems to be understood in a more neutral sense.

---

and ahistorical language of modernization theory and therefore have difficulty dealing with the cross national variability and historical contingency of most secularization processes," (Gorski and Altinordu 2008 : 59).

3 See Ngo & Quijada 2015. The introduction of this book on ("Atheist Secularism and its discontents") reminds with acuity the dialectics between religion and communist project and the necessity to write a "new history of secularism" (5).

## 2 Genealogy of a Concept: Secularization/*thế tục hóa* and the Background of a Lexical Field

Let's look briefly at the old words and characters used to shape the modern terms of secularization, *thế tục hóa*, or *tính thế tục* for secular:

*Thế* (世) in its usual sense means life, in the world, generation
*Tục* (俗) in its usual sense means habits, custom, common
*Hóa* (化) means evolution, changes
*Tính* (性) means quality, disposition

As a disyllabic word, *thế tục* means what is mundane, profane, secular, worldly. It seems that this expression has increasingly evolved from denoting customs and habits to the definition of the secular world. It has also become the most common, although other words express this same idea, such as:

*Trần* (塵) in its usual sense means dust, dirty. Combined with *thế*, *trần thế* means the human world (the world of dust and rains) as opposed to the divine world.

*Phàm* (凡) means rude, mortal and is opposed to *tiên* (immortal). Combined with *trần*, *phàm trần* (or *cõi phàm*) means the mortal world as opposed to the immortal world.

*Gian* (間) means area. Combined with *thế*, *thế gian* is another way to name the world, and *thế giới* the universe.

One would have to conduct a systematic study of collections of texts and books to delimit the lexical field of secularity, but a quick overview can offer some initial impressions. In the imperial annals, *Khâm Định Việt sử thông giám cương mục* and *Đại Nam Thực lục*,[4] the term *thế tục* only appears five times to express the proper "customs" toward the monarchy. The study of two mid-nineteenth century texts by a Confucian poet confirms this usage: in his famous *Lục Vân Tiên*, Nguyễn Đình Chiểu speaks about the human condition (*sự thế*; *thế sự*) made up of ontological sufferings and the will to fulfill oneself according to humanistic values.[5] In his lesser-known *Dương Từ Hà Mậu* (an original disputation between a Buddhist and a Christian), he uses the term *thế tục* three

---

**4** For an introduction to the religious policy at the ancient and premodern times, see Nguyễn Thế Anh 1997 ; Nguyễn Ngọc Quỳnh 2012.
**5** Verse 1004: *Gẫm trong sự thế, thêm âu cho đời!*
[The more I have meditating on the human condition the more it saddened my existence]
　　Verse 1102 : *Gẫm trong thế sự, lắc đầu, thở than*
　　[Meditating on the human condition, he shakes his head and sighs]

times to mean the world and the human status of *Dương Từ* before he became a monk and lived in an isolated pagoda.[6]

As for "religion," no equivalent word was known in Vietnamese until modern times. More than the word, it was the concept of "religion" that the Christian missionaries introduced to Vietnam in the eighteenth century. First translated into Japanese (*shūkyō*), then Chinese (*zonggiao*), it engendered the Vietnamese word *tông giáo*, which finally became *tôn giáo*. It was not until the beginning of the twentieth century that it spread through the different levels of society and was juxtaposed to the more local and popular expression *thờ cúng*.[7] The appearance and imposition of religion as a concept needs more historical investigation, but two general remarks can be made: the monarchy and the Confucianists formerly used other terms to denote rituals, religious practices and teachings. Examples include the paradises (*cõi Phật* or *cực lạc*) or the legendary mountains of the immortals (*Tiên đảo Bồng Lai*) with respect to Buddhist or Daoist traditions. They also defined norms and values to preserve the good traditional customs (*đạo hằng*) as opposed to the evil cults (*đạo tà*); orthodox teachings (*chính giáo*) as opposed to heterodox ones (*dị giáo*); and social behavior to benefit the world (*nhập thế*) or leave it for a religious life (*xuất thế*). Generally speaking, a premodern idea of secularism can be perceived in the dualist conceptions of *tục* (profane) and *thiêng* (sacred), *thế* and *trời* (sky, divine) and, above all, *đạo* (path, then religion) and *đời* (the human life). This was the traditional way to distinguish our human world from other worlds, divided into different sacred spaces—skies, hells and heavens in which the human soul meet deities, superior entities or ancestors. Then this preexisting form of dualism started to be challenged by alternative Christian cosmology and soteriology. It was under the effect of colonial modernity and Westernization that the relations between this world and the other-worldly evolved. But while *tôn giáo* became widespread around one century ago, it was later still that *thế tục* became a conventional word to express that which is secular overall in contrast to the spiritual worlds,

---

**6** Verses 175/176: *Bao nhiêu thế tục gần xa, nhân tình ấm lạnh trải qua đã rồi*
  [All his good and bad human relations kept in this secular world are henceforth cut off]
Verse 353: *Bao nhiêu thế tục gác ngoài*
  [He abandoned all his common customs outside the place]
Verse 3416: *Thế tục lắm người con mắt thịt*
  [In this secular world, lots of people have crude eyes]

**7** According to Đặng Nghiêm Vạn, *thờ* (徐, written in chữ nôm) means showing respect towards high ranking officers or supernatural beings; *cúng* (供, written in classical chinese or chữ hán) is to make an offering. *Thờ cúng* is thus the oldest vernacular expression to refer to various kinds of religious activities (2007 : 691–742).

and sometimes in opposition to religious attitudes and beliefs. And it is only during the colonial decades that different forms of secularity started to be explained and defined.

Looking at dictionaries is also an enlightening way to detail the genealogy of the word secular and the synonymy between Western languages (Latin, Portuguese, Spanish, French, English) and Vietnamese (Sino-Vietnamese then Romanized Vietnamese or *quốc ngữ*). Initiated by Western missionaries during the seventeenth century (1651) with the active support of their Vietnamese interlocutors, the publication of dictionaries improved in the nineteenth century and really took off in the twentieth century.[8] From the first dictionaries, we can sketch an initial comparative overview of the main words relative to the secular field (see appendix 1). The vocabulary was stable until the 1930s but seems to have evolved as a consequence of colonial transformations (scientific progress, religious modernity, printing press, Western education, etc.) as well as with the improvement of lexicological knowledge (see, in particular, the precisions of Cordier, Hue and Gouin).

# 3 Towards a Reappropriation of a Modern Concept

## 3.1 The Colonial Turn and the "Question Laïque"

The making of French Indochina, especially after the establishment and stabilization of the Third Republic, is a period in which the Vietnamization of the concept of "religion" sparked new debates on local and world religions, state-church relations, the religious rejection of modernity or, on the contrary, interest for new science and technology to accelerate a positivist modernity. To sum up, a lot of research has been done on religion under colonial rule (in order to legitimate the conquest by defending missionary action or the development, on the contrary, of a secular and anticlerical "*mission civilisatrice*"), religious comparatism, cultural transfers, and religion and the colonial regime before and after the proclamation of the 1905 Law on the Separation of Church and State.

---

[8] The most convincing introduction to the history of Vietnamese dictionaries was written by Pierre Pencolé (1957). His study needs to be continued and updated.

As in France, colonial society was divided over religious or republican values.[9] Discussions emerged about whether the 1905 Law should be exported to the colonies or not (Delisle 2009, Keith 2005, Lange 2005). In the end it would not be implemented, but debates arose and developed over the legal status of religious organizations, the status of missions, the management of places of worship, land and property, social activities, and the categorization and institutionalization of religious practices.

Following the trauma of the First World War, the 1920s and 1930s were certainly the most transformative period for the religious field. Following the evolution of the education system, from traditional to Western pedagogy and modern teaching programs, and from local colonial schools to the overseas experiences of new generations before and during the interwar period (France, Japan, and later the Soviet Union), the Vietnamese elite seized upon the "religious question" from different perspectives. Among this elite were classical Confucian literati, bourgeois influenced by anticlerical positions, progressives who wanted to reform local traditions, and patriots increasingly attracted to different forms of political radicalism—socialism in particular (Trinh Van Thao 1990, Marr 1971 and 1981, Hue Tam Hô Tai 1996, Buchenau 2015). The common people were less concerned by these intellectual debates. They generally maintained their village customs (*phong tục*) and traditional beliefs (*tín ngưỡng dân gian, lễ hội truyền thống*) without making a strict separation between the sacred and profane aspects of their social life. To summarize the situation, I propose to define four main trends: a Confucian neo-traditionalism which tried to promote a new secular morality; a revival of popular religiosities, expanded through the appearance of new religious movements;[10] the reconfiguration of the Christian faith due to the indigenization of the clergy and the rivalry with Protestantism; and a deep modernist movement which tried to unify a national Buddhism.

The religious question in colonial Vietnam is quite well documented and useful for broadening our understanding from a strict political history to a more peculiar conceptual history of secularism. As we know, the French Revolution and the French model of *laïcité* interested not only the Vietnamese revolu-

---

**9** "En effet, qu'est-ce donc que la mission émancipatrice dont se réclama la République pour coloniser les peuples, sinon la laïcisation d'un projet missionnaire ?" (Chanet & Pelletier 2005 : 9).
**10** Let's note here that the renewal of Buddhism, the birth of Caodaism and the settlement of the first protestant denominations aroused the interest of progressive Republicans in order to defend the liberty of conscience and to promote religious pluralism (see, for example, the archives of the Ligue des droits de l'Homme, Bibliothèque La Contemporaine, Université de Paris-Nanterre).

tionaries but the majority of modern intellectuals, who would also play a part in the independence movement and the building of a postcolonial state. How the Vietnamese elite went about reappropriating *laïcité* still requires more study. Instead of focusing only on anticlericalism and Christian deconfessionalization, such an approach would opt for a wider account of religious diversity (institutionalization of Buddhism, emergence of new religious movements) to analyze the roots of the modern secular process using empirical evidence as well as theory.

The dictionaries (appendix 2) show that the notion of secularity was still vague during the first half of the twentieth century. For instance, according to Ravier and Dronet (1903), the adjective *laïque*/lay indicates that which is "without sacred function" and *séculier*/secular that which "belongs to the human world at large." In the 1930s, the eminent scholar Đào Duy Anh[11] endeavored to specify his translations of the concepts of secularization and *laïcité*.

**Table 1:** Đào Duy Anh, *Dictionnaire français-annamite*, Huế, 1936

| | |
|---|---|
| Laïc/laïque | Tục thế tục |
| (habit laïc, enseignement laïque) | |
| Les ecclésiastiques et les laïcs | Tăng và tục |
| La Laïque ou l'école laïque | Thế tục học hiệu |
| Laïcal | Thuộc về thê tục |
| Laïcat | Thân phận, người tục |
| Laïcisation/Laïciser | Hóa ra tục, tục hóa/ Dứt quan hệ với giáo hội |
| Laïciser une école | Tục hóa một trường học |
| Laïcisme | Tục tính; tục hóa chủ nghĩa |
| Laïcité | Tục tính |
| Sécularisation/séculariser | Hoàn tục, tục hóa, hóa thành thê tục |
| Séculariser les moines/l'enseignement | Hoàn tục cho tu sĩ/giáo dục |
| Sécularisme | Duy tục chủ nghĩa; Hiện thế chủ nghĩa |
| Sécularité | Tục gian thánh chức; Thực sự tài phán quyền |
| Séculier | Thuộc về thế tục, về tục gian (1): thế gian, xã giao (2) |
| Clergé séculier | Tục gian tăng lữ |
| Juridiction séculière; bras séculier | Phổ thông (thế tục) tài phán quyền |
| Vie séculière et nullement chrétienne | người tục |

---

[11] On Đào Duy Anh's contribution to the emergence of religious studies in Vietnam, see Đỗ Quang Hưng 2009.

His examples and clarifications attempt to show how the meaning of the secular had shifted from defining the relationship between religions and society to the relationship between religions and the state, which implies the possibilities of irreligion and separation. But historical events from the late 1930s onwards impeded the stable institutionalization and legal redefinition of the religious field in the colonial context.

## 3.2 The Postcolonial Crossroads: Reshaping Secularism in Different Ways

In Vietnam, as in other Asian or African countries, the issue of secularism arose concomitantly with the question of post-colonial nationhood, as Partha Chatterjee has mentioned in his research.[12] In spite of the August Revolution of 1945 and the proclamation of the Democratic Republic of Vietnam (DRV) on September 2, French aspirations to take the country back provoked a violent colonial war, which turned into a cold war involving foreign countries from the end of 1949 (Soviet Union, Popular Republic of China, USA). While the various Vietnamese political and religious "forces" unanimously agreed to fight against colonialism and reunify the nation,[13] they were divided over the way to attain independence and proclaim the legitimacy of the new state, and over the choice of political regime. International tensions and the wave of claims for national independence reinforced the fault line between a strict secularist revolution based on atheism and other revolutionary movements more respectful of or allied to religious traditions.

The independence movement that lasted from 1945 to 1975 had to deal with many politico-religious conflicts, which also created religious and geographical fault lines in the Vietnamese nation. From an ideological perspective, socialist and liberal theories defined the nature of secularism and the teleology of secu-

---

**12** Quoted in Bubandt and Van Beek (13). I agree with these authors that, "Nation-states grapple with similar challenges and come to very different 'solutions' that can be understood by careful analysis not only of the global genealogy of secularism, but also, crucially, of the affordances and constraints of specific local, non-state imaginaries of the spiritual and of secularism"(15).

**13** Remember that Vietnam in its broadest geographic sense, as we know it today, was reunified in the late eighteenth century by the Tây Sơn dynasty but effectively only in 1802 with the rise of the Nguyễn Dynasty. Before this, the country was divided into two principalities. Under colonial rule, it was divided into three *kỳ* or regions with different status (colony, protectorate and municipalities). This situation explains the different ways in which religious life and religious conflicts evolved locally (prohibition of missionary activities in Protectorates for instance).

larization differently. Although churches and other religious organizations tried to remain neutral vis-à-vis political movements, they were obliged either to obtain a legal personality (liberal state) or accept their subordination to patriotic organizations and mass movements (socialist state). It is therefore crucial to consider the perceptions and effectiveness of the secularization process in the light of divergent local contexts and political experiences. Two main characteristics should be underscored: first, the overlapping of multiple modernities and states that lead to a more balanced periodization of post-colonial Vietnam; second, increasing asymmetry between North and South Vietnam in terms of theoretical approach, regional regulation of religious diversity (functionalization of limited religious organizations in the North versus regulation of a modern religious pluralization in the South) and, eventually, regulation of cultural life and religious consciousness.

**Table 2:** Genealogy of polical regimes since 1802

| | | |
|---|---|---|
| **Imperial Vietnam under the Nguyễn dynasty (1802–1945)** | | |
| **Colonial Vietnam (1862–1945) [From Cochinchina to Indochine française]**<br>– Régime des Amiraux (1862–1879) [military authority]<br>– Third Republic (1879–1940) [civil government]<br>– Decoux Administration following the Vichy Regime (1940–1945) | | |
| **Democratic Republic of Vietnam** (2/9/1945)<br>Central Government (Hanoi) and local representatives, then local Administrative and Resistance Committees | French Military reconquest (1945) | |
| | Autonomous Republic of Cochinchina (1946–1947) | |
| | Provisional Central Government of Vietnam (1948) | |
| | État Associé de l'Union française (1948) [without Cochinchina] | |
| Geneva Agreements (1954) and temporary partition | | |
| **Democratic Republic of Vietnam**<br>North of the 17th parallel | **Republic of Vietnam** (1955–1975)<br>South of the 17th parallel<br>– First Republic (Ngô Đình Diệm and al.) (1955–1967)<br>– Second Republic (1967–1975) | **National Liberation Front** (1956–1976)<br>South of the 17th parallel<br>– Maquis then liberated zones |
| | | **Provisional Revolutionary government of the Republic of South Vietnam** (1969–1976) |
| **Socialist Republic of Vietnam** (since 1976) | | |

With regard to the first characteristic, the table shows that the constitutional history of Vietnam is more complex than the official historiography suggests. Alternative forms of nation building appeared alongside the DRV over its 30-year existence. Each regime or political project, however short-lived, had to express a doctrine defining state-church relations. The Socialist Republic of Vietnam (SRV) claims to be a natural descendent of the Democratic Republic of Vietnam. All current developments should therefore be looked at on a *continuum* that begins with the proclamation of independence in September 1945. As such, the DRV becomes the main point of reference that serves to justify the transition of the socialist state, particularly when it comes to explaining changes in the SRV's religious policy. But if we are to gain a more comprehensive understanding of the history of secularism in Vietnam, it is also necessary to study all the past "southern" experiments. This will clarify the current trend, which I call a "converging secularization." A recent book clearly backs up this opinion:

> We [Vietnamese] haven't studied the position of the French and American colonialists on this topic [State-Church relations] enough [.../...] The Saigon regime promulgated several decrees recognizing religious organizations that we would do well to reevaluate [my translation] (Nguyễn Hồng Dương 2014: 219–221).[14]

Behind the official phraseology ("colonialists"; "Saigon regime" rather than the Republic of Vietnam, considered illegitimate and non-existent), this quotation shows a pragmatic evolution in the way of understanding religious regulation and plurality. Indeed, it implicitly proposes taking a closer interest in the Republic of Vietnam's two constitutions, that of 1956 and of 1967.

To clarify the second characteristic, let us provide a brief overview of state-church relations between 1945 and 1975 in the Democratic Republic of Vietnam, the State of Vietnam, and then the Republic of Vietnam (Bourdeaux 2015).

From 1945, the *Việt Minh* Revolution aimed to unify the nation by funding the DRV. The government tried to reassure religious groups in order to strengthen national solidarity under a single anti-colonialist engagement; but the Cold War provoked many disasters and psychological warfare ended up reinforcing ideological conflicts. The central government imposed representative institutions and mass organizations on the whole society. Religious organizations were asked to

---

[14] As Mark Sidel has explained few years before, "The role of constitutions and constitutionalism in the former Republic of Vietnam [...] have a distinct role in Vietnamese constitutional development that is now being explored by constitutional drafters and scholars throughout Vietnam. Two constitutions were drafted in South Vietnam in the 1950s and 1960s and an energetic constitutional dialogue went on during part of that era" (2009 : 7–8).

join the *Liên Việt* and some religious leaders were asked to enter the political apparatus. After 1954, religious organizations in North Vietnam were obliged to join the Patriotic Front. Until 1977, the decree signed by President Hồ Chí Minh in 1955 (14/6) confirmed the liberty to believe or not believe and the secular nature of the state. While the state fought feudal customs and superstitions over these three decades, it also insisted on the moral and social dimension of religious activities to prove their compatibility with socialist ideals.[15] Secularism above all meant the emancipation of individual and social conscience strengthened by materialism. On this point, the model was similar to the Chinese one prior to the Cultural Revolution.

Meanwhile the State of Vietnam tried to control religious groups and prevent any dissidence by organizing *de facto* religious plurality, especially in the southern provinces. It also spread propaganda to ward off the danger of the atheist project that the DRV was supposedly trying to promote. Under the Republic of Vietnam, the situation changed with the rise of religious conflicts (exodus of Catholics from North to South—*cuộc di cư 54*—, "war against the sects", Buddhist crisis -*biến cố Phật giáo*-[16]). The presages of an interfaith dialogue emerged, especially after the creation of a committee of religions in 1964, which included all the main religions (Catholics, Baha'i, Hòa Hảo Buddhists, Cao Đài, Confucians, Buddhists) except, at that time, for Protestants and Muslims. With the proclamation of the second Republic (Nguyễn Văn Thiệu), religious organizations (or religious denominations under the new American influence) established official relations with the secular state, which guaranteed religious pluralism and tried to promote the emergence of a public sphere. But taking advantage of the lack of popular support for what communist propaganda termed a "puppet regime," the DRV and the National Liberation Front (NLF) combined their efforts to overthrow the regime. In addition to the DRV's diplomatic and military activities, the NLF enlarged some liberated zones, integrated religious communities into the national salvation organizations, and proclaimed its loyalty to the DRV.[17]

Comparing these two political systems highlights their different conceptions of secularism, which nonetheless interacted with each other. Atheism in North

---

15 "The focus here should not be on the extent to which atheistic ideas conquered the hearts and minds of individuals but rather on the way it affected people's understanding of the role of religion in society." (Thibault 2015 : 18).

16 The conflict broke out when the government forbade the use of the Buddhist flag in public spaces.

17 This policy was called *tôn giáo vận* and the organizations were dubbed *cứu quốc* (for example *Hội phật giáo cứu quốc*, Buddhist association for national salvation).

Vietnam fundamentally questioned the role of religion in Vietnamese society at large; and religious diversity in South Vietnam necessitated a clear position on pluralism. A more discerning semantical analysis based on theoretical texts and dictionaries would enrich this debate. But research on this period is still too limited from this point of view. Looking at Bauberot's typology, we can nonetheless propose some considerations: from the birth of independent Vietnam, the aim was to establish a secular state and control religious organizations. The war obliged the DRV to concentrate on other vital objectives, so it would be apt to speak of "regalian laicity,"[18] with maybe a short "anti-religious" episode at the very end of 1950, after the *nhân văn giai phẩm* Affair (similar to the Chinese *Hundred Flowers Campaign*) and the misdeeds of the agrarian reform. At the same time, the Associated State of Vietnam tried to adopt a "collaboration laicity." The elite were indeed French educated and their patriotism was partially influenced by *"valeurs laïques."* But this form of *laïcité* was also adopted owing to the weakness of the state. Then the Republic of Vietnam under the presidency of Ngô Đình Diệm adopted an "identitarian laicity" strongly influenced by the Catholic factor. Finally, religious policy under the Thiệu regime can be considered a "liberal laicity."

# 4 National Reunification and Secularization since 1976

For three decades, each regime framed the issue of secularization as a demand for "liberation," understood in different ways: freeing society from religious domination, freeing the nation from colonial or imperial domination with the support of religious forces, and freeing religious life and belief from political oppression. With the end of the war in 1975 and the proclamation of the Socialist Republic of Vietnam in 1976, the secularization question was subsumed under the new requirement for state centralization and national reunification. The government, the Communist Party and the Popular Army sought to ensure the stability and durability of the new regime and regional security before resolving internal conflicts. The regime also had to balance the myriad regional asymmetries to build a united socialist society. This meant imposing the same standard of living, widespread collectivization of the economy, political re-education, the privatization of religious life on the one hand and the functionalization of religious organizations on the other.

---

**18** For a definition of this term, see Bauberot's article and typology.

## 4.1 Đổi Mới of Religious Policy in Three Thresholds

What position did the southern religious organizations take in the reunification process? How did they merge into new national institutions or churches (Buddhists, Catholics, Protestants, Muslims) and new regional religious expressions (Cao Đài, Hòa Hảo Buddhists, Baha'i, local Buddhist organizations, evangelical churches) without risking being provincialized? All these questions were crucial at the end of the war but, at the time, efforts were concentrated on the internal pacification of society and purging the administration. Above all, the government still had to fight against antagonistic forces and anti-revolutionary enemies around and within the country. As a consequence, security issues and the call for the greatest possible national unity and solidarity (*Đại đoàn kết*)[19] were of course prioritized. Decree 297 signed by Prime Minister Phạm Văn Đồng in November 1977 outlined the new policy in very general terms and confirmed the liberty of conscience—which the new Constitution of 1980 upheld—but in accordance with the principles of socialism and under the guidance of the Communist Party. In reality, what ensued was a strict privatization of belief, the replacement of public religious celebrations (considered to have a negative influence on the masses) with compulsory patriotic celebrations, a rejection of superstitions, and a subordination of religious communities both to the state and to the religious institutions already affiliated to the state.[20]

After the first 15 years of strict reunification, a reform program was decided on as a consequence of economic collapse. A second threshold was crossed in 1991 when Decree 91 of March 21 broke with secularist views and the principle of the decline of religion. The Party-State defined its concordatory model and allowed for the trend toward a gradual reappearance of religious life in the public sphere and social activities. As Jane Werner rightly pointed out, "the Communist Party's accommodation of religion after 1986 is a return to previous policy rather a break with socialist ideals" (Ngo & Quijada: 22). During this period, debates about "Hồ Chí Minh thought" and national identity (*bản sắc dân tộc*) confirmed citizens' intangible loyalty towards the Nation State, while high-ranking officials

---

**19** A specific slogan was "đoàn kết tôn giáo, đoàn kết lương giáo," calling for religious solidarity (in the first half of the slogan), especially solidarity between Catholics and the other religions (in the second half).

**20** The Committee for Religious Affairs wrote in 1983: "Following the improvement accomplished by the religions in North Vietnam, those of the South progress day by day in the right direction …/… If the religious issue is still complex in our country, it is not because of the multiplicity of beliefs or the large number of followers; it is because historically, religions were manipulated by imperialists and reactionaries," (quoted in Maïs 1986: 9).

started to see the Party more as the embodiment of the Nation than the vanguard of the Revolution.

A third threshold was crossed with the Ordinance on Religions and Beliefs (November 15, 2004), which set out a new policy for the registration of religious organizations. Religious policy reform is still in progress but national priorities are increasingly linked to international interactions. Since the Ordinance, the national integration of religious beliefs and Vietnamese spiritualities has been concomitant with international integration. The new law passed in 2018 should pursue this evolution.

Returning to Baubérot's typology, we can consider that during its first years of existence, the Socialist Republic of Vietnam sought authoritarian control of public religious life, especially in the southern part of the country where religious groups, more diverse than in the North and without any organic relation with the socialist state, were brought under the authority of the state apparatus (Patriotic Front, Religious Affairs Bureau). To call this secularist policy "anti-religious" would be excessive; it was above all assimilationist. The second period (1991–2006) seems to fit the criteria of "regalian laicity." Finally, since 2006, the registration policy has gone beyond a strict "regalian laicity" to move toward a more flexible "identitarian laicity." The way Vietnamese Buddhism has been promoted as a soft power in the last few years can be seen as a symbol of this phenomenon. On the other hand, patriotic forms of worship and nationalism maintain a prominent place but with an ambiguous aspect: while the historical, secular and national nature of celebrations are visible, they often hide popular spiritual traditions or new spiritual projects. Moreover, the socialist background can be leveraged in different ways. For instance, the socialist ideal can take popular religious forms, as in the north of Vietnam where socialist symbols or rhetoric have served to reactivate traditional millenarian beliefs. On the other hand, when the socialist ideal is rejected, it is the nation that is sacralized and spiritualized, with direct reference to Vietnamese soil and ancestors. Yet this nationalism is not really multiethnic; it is inherently based on "kinh" identity and, as such, state control of ethno-nationalist claims or transnational identities expressed at the local level explains the resurgence of authoritarian forms of secularism, but for more ethnic than religious purposes.

## 4.2 Đổi Mới of the Religious Field: Standardizing the Terminology of the "Secular"

Can we clearly distinguish between secularity and laicity in present-day Vietnam? The answer may still be unclear, but the question has been under debate for many years. Civil servants in charge of religious affairs, Party ideologists, semi-independent academics, religious leaders, Vietnamese diasporic intellectuals, foreign experts and observers have discussed independently, and sometimes together, the different theories of secularization and their implementation in the local context. While some parts of civil society have tried to join the debate, generally speaking the emerging public opinion doesn't make any social use of the issue, as can be the case in most democratic countries, particularly in Europe. A sociology of the actors and their social institutions is therefore crucial to understand this conceptualization process from the inside.[21] In addition, as Beckford has explained, certain actors have been key drivers of the secularization process in the Western world. This is clearly the case in Vietnam, where we now speak of "secularizing agents" (acteurs sécularisants, *những tác nhân thế tục hóa*), while other actors try to promote a kind of limited desecularization process. The secular question has expanded from its original focus on state-church relations to integrate different segments of civil society; and debates have increasingly moved from strict legal religious regulations to encompass ethical and cultural values. Baubérot described this phenomenon when writing about his third threshold of laïcization, as did Taylor, who analyses "Secularity III" as the new conditions of belief. In recent years, Jaffrelot proposed adding a new category called "Secularity IV" to explore the interactions between religions and national identities. This seems particularly appropriate in Vietnam where the state now clearly combines patriotic forms of worship—half-secular, half-sacred—to promote a unified national identity.

As mentioned above, the lexical field of secularization was still vague and limited largely to the academic world until the 1980s. Even if more investigation is needed to understand how politicians, intellectuals and religious leaders[22] spoke about secularization in South Vietnam before 1975, we can affirm that various state departments and agencies, including the Institute for Religious Studies founded in 1991, began working to define this lexical field during the late 1990s. The scientific vocabulary started to spread in the 2000s to analyze the general theory of secularization and its implementation in the case of Vietnam. Looking at a selection of recent books, academic reviews, and specialized dictionaries,[23] we can see new attempts to define words such as *secularization*, *sec-*

---

**21** According to Alfonso Perez-Agote, "Secularism is carried by social actors with specific interests" (2014: 887).
**22** Especially Catholics after Council Vatican II and part of the sangha linked with different forms of engaged Buddhism.
**23** In addition, I have analyzed two reviews in full: *Tạp chí nghiên cứu tôn giáo* (Religious Studies Review, a monthly publication of the Institute for Religious Studies launched in 1999 and

ularity, and *laicity*, facilitated by the improvement of social sciences in Vietnam. Reinterpreting old vocabulary, translating international concepts from different languages (French, Japanese, Chinese, and increasingly English) and standardizing these translations in Vietnamese is an ongoing process that has already produced fruitful analysis.

As a consequence of the establishment of the rule of law, the study of different models of secular states, and the translation and adaptation of the international legal and academic concepts, the vocabulary is more and more precise and the lexical field is expanding. Concerning the standardized vocabulary, I can mention a uniform translation of "secularization" as *thế tục hóa* or simply *tục hóa*. Starting with this word, I have listed other expressions from my readings that have appeared in recent years to distinguish the paradigm and the process:

> Theory of secularization (as defined by Berger): *học thuyết thế tục hóa* or *sự thế tục hóa*
> Secular principle: *nguyên lý / nguyên tắc thế tục*
> Secular trend: *xu hướng thế tục*
> Secularization process: *quá trình thế tục hóa*
> Desecularization: *giải thế tục hóa*
> Secularizing agents: *những tác nhân thế tục hóa*
> Secularization of Laicity (as defined by Willaime): *thế tục hóa nguyên tắc thế tục*
> Wordliness (as defined by Olivier Tschannen): *Tính trần tục*
> Mondanization: *trần thế hóa* as opposed to *thần thánh hóa* (divinization, canonization)
> Secular culture: *văn hóa thế tục*
> Secularity: *tính thế tục*

In recent years, the definition and translation of "laicity" has been the subject of intense debate and has generated several propositions that try to encompass the concepts of institution, secularity, and neutrality:

> *Tính thế tục trung lập thể chế* (translated by Nguyễn Kim Hiền)
> *Thế tục trung lập trung tính* (Nguyễn Hồng Dương, Nguyễn Quốc Tuấn)
> *Thể chế thế tục trung lập* or *Thể chế thế tục* (Đỗ Quang Hưng)

In line with this attempt to define the concept of "laicity," different expressions aim to specify its legal and sociological aspects in the current context of later modernity, for instance:

---

also published in an English version from 2007), *Tạp chí công tác tôn giáo* (Religious Affairs Review, publication of the Governmental Committee for Religious Affairs launched in 2005). Other theoretical reviews are worthy of interest, such as *Tạp chí cộng sản* (Review of Communism), *Tạp chí mặt trận* (Review of the Patriotic Front).

Modèle laïc (fr.): *mô hình thế tục trung lập trung tính* (Nguyễn Kim Hiền), *mô hình thể chế thế tục trung lập* (Đỗ Quang Hưng)
Secular control regime model (according to Cole Durham): *mô hình "nhà nước thế tục kiểm soát"*
Semi-laïcité (according to Baubérot, fr.): *mô hình nửa thế tục*
Conception laïque (fr.): *khái niệm lối đời*
Colonisation laïque (fr.): *thực dân theo lối đời*
Laïcisme agressif (fr.): *Chủ nghĩa thế tục cân thiệp*
Laïcité positive (fr.): *chủ nghĩa thế tục trung lập tích cực*

Alongside this translation process, some academics try to provide new definitions of premodern vocabulary through the lens of the secular issue, especially the terms "đời," and "đạo" and their combination to distinguish what is temporal (*đời*) or spiritual (*đạo*). The latter term can be understood as a generic and polysomic category for speaking about religion and spirituality (*sống đạo*) as implicitly and originally Daoist or as strictly Confucian (*đạo [nho] làm người*). Hồ Bá Thâm (2007) has tried to show how *đời* and *đạo* interact with each other, how together they constitute what is existential, how faiths and beliefs are composed of the coexistence of these two categories of reality. This is what some mottos clearly express, especially "lợi đạo ích đời" [Use Religion to benefit Life] and "sống tốt đời đẹp đạo" [Live in accordance with moral life and good religion]. While the theoretical research aims to create technical neologisms (experimental function) for use by researchers, others try to explain these concepts with simpler understandable expressions (pedagogical function). The paradox is that these explanations appear in a modern society where the distinctions between religions and spiritualities (as expressed by the locution "tôn giáo tín ngưỡng") are less and less visible.

# 5 Conclusion

Religious sciences emerged in Vietnam in the 1990s with the main objective of analyzing the nature and the expression of religious life in modern society so as to facilitate interactions between the state and church in the context of a reunited nation. What began with a functionalist approach and strictly applied research has expanded into a broader interest for religious phenomenon in terms of theoretical and multidisciplinary approaches. Political science, social science and the humanities offer different methods and points of view for defining the concept of religions and the demarcation of the religious sphere, and observing religious and spiritual modernities at large. If we look specifically at the field of history, religious history has increasingly sought to become independent from political history, more global or universal, moving beyond a strict national history. And beyond historical materialism, diverse conceptions of temporality and regimes of historicity serve to rethink religious phenomenon in space and time. The secular question has been a topical issue for at least two decades now, not only for academics but also for a large share of Vietnamese citizens, believers and non-believers alike. The visibility of religions in the public sphere is doubtless the expression of an emerging civil society. In the case of Vietnam, where religious historiography dominated in neither ancient nor modern times—unlike in Europe for instance—the current visibility of religious diversity doesn't really challenge the secular nature of the state. Rather it questions, on the one hand, the nature and meaning of these new religious dynamics and, on the other hand, the adaptability of the new rule of law and regulation of religious phenomena. We can observe an attempt to define, sociologically and legally, a regime of laicity appropriate to the current developments of the Vietnamese state and nation. Though this trend is still nascent, we also note an increased interest among Vietnamese academics in retaining experiences from the past and learning more about a premodern as well as a modern history of secularity. This is what I propose to call a converging secularization (*sécularisation de convergence*). It invites further study on the genealogy of states in the *longue durée* and on alternative postcolonial policies, which are not longer seen only as expressions of rivalry or failure but also as an instructive "field of experience." The sociology of laicity is crucial. But just as crucial is a history of laicity focused on semantics, collective representations, normative texts, and social practices.

Appendix 1 – Comparative study of classical vocabulary

| Dictionaries | Terms of reference | | | | | |
|---|---|---|---|---|---|---|
| | Đạo – (道) | Đời – (代) | Thế – (世) | Tục – (俗) | Thế tục (世俗) | Others |
| Alexandre de Rhodes (1651) | Ley, Lex | Seculo; Seculum seu huminis vita communis | Mundo; Mundus | Indecens; Inciuilis | – | |
| Pigneau de Behaine (1772) | Religio | Seculum; Vita; Mundus | Mundus; Seculum | Mos | Seculi mores | Trần tục, phàm tục: Mundus |
| Taberd (1838) Theurel (1877) | Religio; Regula | Saeculum; Vitae; Mundus | Mundus; Seculum; Auctoritas | Mos | Mores saeculi | |
| Legrand de la Liraÿe (1874) | Religion; Voie; Raison; Vertu; Règle | Siècle; Vie; Monde | Monde; Condition | Coutume | Usages du monde | |
| Paulus Cua (1895) | Lẽ phải; dạy việc thờ phượng [Règle; rendre un culte à] | Thân sống một người; thiên hạ; thế gian [homme vivant; gens du monde, monde] | Đời, cả và thiên hạ [Vie; Le monde dans son ensemble] | Thói quen [Habitudes] | Thói đời; tục đời [manières du monde] | |
| Génibrel (1898) | Religion; Raison; Règle; Condition | Siècle; Vie; Monde | Monde; Siècle; Génération | Coutumes | Les mœurs du siècle; Usages du monde | Trần tục: mondain Phàm tục: terrestre |
| Vallot (1904) | Voie; Doctrine; Règle; Religion | Siècle; Génération; Monde | Monde | Coutumes | | |

Appendix 1 – Comparative study of classical vocabulary *(Continued)*

| Dictionnaries | Terms of reference | | | | | |
|---|---|---|---|---|---|---|
| | Đạo – (道) | Đời – (代) | Thế – (世) | Tục – (俗) | Thế tục (世俗) | Others |
| **Cordier (1930)** | Religion; Raison; Règle; Condition | Siècle; Vie; Génération | Monde; Vie; Siècle | Habitudes; Mœurs; Coutumes | Monde terrestre; Les usages du monde | Trần tục: monde terrestre<br>Phàm tục: les mortels |
| **Hue (1937)** | Voie; Raison; Taoïsme; Religions | Vie; Monde; En langage religieux bouddhiste et chrétien le monde opposé à religion | Age; Siècle; Monde | Habitudes; Mœurs | Coutumes du monde | Hoàn tục: rentrer dans le monde; Phàm tục: monde profane opposé à religieux |
| **Gouin (1957)** | Chemin; Raison; Taoïsme; Religion en général | Vie; Génération; Existence; Monde; Monde opposé à religion | Âge; Siècle; Génération; Monde | Habitudes; Mœurs; Coutumes | Monde terrestre; Coutumes du monde | Đời tục: monde profane<br>Tục hóa: laïciser<br>Thế tục chủ nghĩa: sécularisme |
| **Hoàng Phê (1988)** | Đạo: [...]<br>Nguyên tắc mà người có bốn phận giữ gìn và thuận theo trong cuộc sống xã hội; Tổ chức tôn giáo | Đời: [...]<br>Xã hội loài người; Từ dụng trong công giáo đối lập với đạo để gọi chung những người không theo công giáo hoặc những việc ngoại đạo | | | Thế tục:<br>[...] Đời sống trần tục đối lập với đời sống tu hành | Phàm:<br>[...] Cõi đời trên mặt đất đối lập với cõi thần tiên |

Appendix 2 – Specifications of the lexical field

| Dictionnaries | Terms of reference | | |
|---|---|---|---|
| Ravier, H. Dronet, J.B. (1903) | Laïque:<br>Không có chức thánh, bổn đạo | | Séculier:<br>Thuộc về đời, thuộc về triều |
| Đào Duy Anh (1936) | Laïc/laïque:<br>Tục, Thế tục<br>Laïcité:<br>Tục tính | Laïciser, laïcisation:<br>Hoá ra tục, tục hóa, dứt quan hệ với giáo hội | Laïcisme:<br>Tục tính, tục hóa chủ nghĩa | Sécularisation, séculariser:<br>Hoàn tục, tục hóa, hóa thành thế tục | Sécularisme:<br>Duy tục chủ nghĩa<br>Sécularité:<br>Tục gian thành chức |
| Đào Đăng Vỹ (1963) | Laïc/laïque:<br>Thuộc về thế tục, ngoài tôn giáo, ngoại đạo<br>Laïcité:<br>Tính cách thế tục; ngoại đạo | | Laïciser: tục hóa<br>Laïcat: Hoàn cảnh ngoại đạo | Séculariser:<br>Tục hóa, hoàn tục | Sécularisme:<br>Chủ nghĩa thế tục<br>Sécularité:<br>Tính phàm tục |
| Đoàn Trung Còn (1963, buddhist) | Hoàn tục:<br>Những vị xuất gia trở lại thế tục | | Thế tục trí:<br>Đối với thánh trí là trí của bực tu hành, đắc đạo, cái trí không dùng vào việc lợi danh ở đời | | |
| Lê Văn Đức (1970) | Hoàn tục:<br>Trở lại đời, không tu hành nữa | Thế tục hóa (pháp):<br>Dựa theo phong tục mà đặt ra (những thủ tục pháp lý cho hợp với y thức dân chúng) | | Thế tục:<br>Thói quen của hầu hết thiên hạ | Thế tục trí [esprit laïc] |
| Viện ngôn ngữ học (1988) | Laïcité:<br>Tính không tôn giáo | Laïcisme:<br>Thuyết thế tục hóa | | Laïcisation/sécularisation:<br>Sự thế tục hóa | Séculariser:<br>Hoàn tục, thế tục hóa |
| Lê Khả Kế (1997) | Laïcité:<br>Tính không tôn giáo | Laïque:<br>Phi giáo hội, không tôn giáo, thế tục | | | |

Appendix 2 – Specifications of the lexical field (Continued)

| Dictionnaries | Terms of reference | | | | |
|---|---|---|---|---|---|
| Viện ngôn ngữ học (1997) | Laïc: Thế tục, không ở dòng tu Adj.: Thuộc đời sống dân sự | Laïcisation: sự thế tục hóa Laïciser: Thế tục hóa | Laïcisme: Thuyết thế tục hóa | Laïcité: Tính thế tục | Séculariser: Hoàn tục, thế tục hóa |
| Lê Khả Kế (1997) | Hoàn tục: Return to the secular life, give up the froke | | Thế tục: The way of the world; temporal | | Thế tục hóa: Secularize |
| Nguyễn Như Ý (1998) | Thế tục: Đời sống trần tục phân biệt với đời sống tu hành theo quan niệm tôn giáo, tránh xa thế tục [Secular life opposite to monastic life in a religious conception] | | | | |
| Trần Nghĩa Phương (2001) | Laïc: Thế tục, không theo đạo Laïcisation: Sự thế tục hóa | Laïcisme: Thuyết thế tục hóa, phong trào thế tục hóa | Religion séculière: Tôn giáo thế tục | Sécularisation: Sự tục hóa; hoàn tục Sécularisme: Thuyết duy thế tục; chủ nghĩa thế tục; phong trào thế tục hóa | |
| Minh Thông (2001, buddhist.) | Thế: loka (in the world) | | Thế tục: Samisa, Samvrti (Worldly) | Siêu thế: lokottara (supramundane) | |
| Học viện Đaminh (2014, christian) | Laïcism: Duy thế tục Laicization: Hồi tục | Secular: đời, trần thế, thế tục | Secularization: Tục hóa. Thoát ly khỏi sự kiểm soát của tôn giáo | Secularism: Quan điểm về thự tịa dưới khía cảnh thế tục, không đếm xỉa gì đến giá trị tôn giáo | |
| Ngô Minh, Nguyễn Thế Minh (2009, christian) | Laïc: Giáo dân, không tôn giáo | Laïciser/sécularisation: Thế tục hóa | | Laïcisme: Trào lưu/Thuyết tục hóa | Laïcité: Tính cái thế tục |

**List of dictionaries**

1. Rhodes de, A. (1651) — *Dictionarium Annamiticum et Latinum ope Sacrae Congregationis de Propaganda Fidei in lucem editor ab Alexandro de Rhodes e Societate Jesu, ejusdemque Sacrae Congregationis Missionario Apostolico*, Romae
2. Pigneau de Behaine, P. (1772) — *Vocabularium Anamitico-Latinum*, Pondichéry
3. Taberd, J.-L. (1838) — *Dictionarium latino-anamiticum*, Serampore
4. Theurel, J. (1877) — *Dictionarium anamitico-latinum, ex opere Taberd constans*, Ninh Phu
5. Legrand de la Liraÿe, T. (1874) — *Dictionnaire élémentaire annamite-français*, Saigon
6. Huỳnh Tịnh Paulus Cua (1895) — *Dictionnaire Annamite. Dai Nam Quôc âm Tu-vi*, Saigon, 2 vol.
7. Génibrel, J.F.M. (1898) — *Dictionnaire annamite-français comprenant 1°: tous les caractères de langue annamite vulgaire avec l'indication de leurs divers sens propres et figurés et justifiés par de nombreux exemples. 2°: les caractères chinois nécessaires à l'étude des Tu Tho,[= Quatre Livres classiques chinois]. 3°: la flore et la faune de l'Indochine*, Saigon
8. Ravier, H.; Dronet, J.B. (1903) — *Lexique Franco-Annamite*, Ke So
9. Vallot, G. (1904) — *Petit dictionnaire annamite-français composé sur le plan des dictionnaires de l'évêque d'Adran (éditions de Mgr Taberd et de Mgr Theurel) et à l'aide du dictionnaire franco-tonkinois*, Hanoi, 2e éd.
10. Cordier, G. (1930) — *Dictionnaire annamite-français à l'usage des élèves et des annamitisants*, Hanoi
11. Đào Duy Anh (1936) — *Dictionnaire français-annamite*, Huê
12. Hue, G. (1937) — *Dictionnaire annamite-chinois-français*, Hanoi
13. Gouin, E. (1957) — *Dictionnaire vietnamien chinois français*, Saigon
14. Đào Đăng Vỹ (1963) — *Việt Pháp Đại Từ điển*
15. Đoàn Trung Còn (1963) — *Phật học từ điển. Việt, Hán, Pháp, Phạn*
16. Lê Văn Đức (1970) — *Từ điển Việt Nam*, Nxb Từ điển Bách khoa
17. Viện Ngôn Ngữ Học (1988) — *Từ Điển Pháp-Việt*, Nxb Từ điển Bách khoa
18. Hoàng Phê (1988) — *Từ Điển Tiếng Việt*, Nxb Khoa Học Xã Hội
19. Lê Khả Kế (1997) — *Từ điển Pháp-Việt*, Nxb Khoa học Xã hội
20. Viện Ngôn Ngữ Học (1997) — *Từ Điển Pháp-Việt*, Nxb Từ điển Bách khoa
21. Lê Khả Kế, Phạm Duy Trọng (1997) — *Từ điển Việt Anh*, Nxb Thành phố Hồ Chí Minh
22. Nguyễn Như Ý (1998) — *Đại từ điển tiếng việt*, Nxb Văn hóa Thông tin
23. Trần Nghĩa Phương (2001) — *Thuật ngữ tôn giáo (anh, việt pháp)*, Nxb KHXH
24. Minh Thông (2001) — *Multilingual dictionary of Buddhism*

25  Ngô Minh, Nguyễn Thế  *Từ vựng triết thần căn bản (Pháp Việt – Anh Việt)*, Nxb Phương
    Minh (2009)          Đông
26  Học viện Đaminh (2014)  *Thuật Ngữ Thần Học Anh-Việt*, Nxb Tôn giáo

# References

Ban tư tưởng văn hóa trung ương. 2005. *Tài liệu bồi dưỡng chuyên đề vấn đề về tôn giáo và các công tác tôn giáo ở cơ sở* [Central committee for thought and culture, Explanatory documents on Religions and Religious Affairs at the basic level]. Hà Nội: Nxb CTGQ.

Bhargava, Rajeev. 2004. "India's Model: Faith, Secularism, and Democracy". *Open Democracy* (November 3). https://beta.opendemocracy.net/en/article_2204jsp/ (Accessed April 23, 2020).

Bourdeaux, Pascal. 2015. "Regards sur l'autonomisation religieuse dans le processus d'indépendance du Viêt Nam au milieu du vingtième siècle". *French Politics, Culture and Society* 33 no. 2 (Summer) : 11–32.

Bourdeaux, Pascal. 2010. "Réflexions sur l'institutionnalisation du bouddhisme Hòa Hảo. Remise en perspective historique de la reconnaissance de 1999". *Social Compass* 57 no. 3 (September) : 372–385.

Bubandt, Nils and Van Beek, Martijn (eds.). 2012. *Varieties of Secularism in Asia, Anthropological explorations of religion, politics and the spiritual.* London: Routledge.

Buchenau, Klaus. 2015. "Socialist Secularities: the diversity of a universalist Model". In M. Burchardt, M. Wohlrab-Sahr and M. Middell, eds., *Multiple Secularities Beyond the West: Religion and Modernity in the Global Age*, pp. 261–283. Berlin: De Gruyter.

Burchardt, Marian, Wohlrab-Sahr, Monika and Middell, Matthias, eds. 2015. *Multiple secularities beyond the West: Religion and Modernity in the Global Age.* Berlin: De Gruyter.

Chanet, Jean-François et Pelletier, Denis. 2005. "La laïcité à l'épreuve de la sécularisation 1905–2005". *Vingtième siècle* 87: 7–10.

Delisle, Philippe, ed. 2009. *L'anticléricalisme dans les colonies françaises sous la Troisième République.* Paris: les Indes savantes.

Đặng Nghiêm Vạn. 2007. "Réflexions sur quelques caractéristiques de la religion au Vietnam". In Đỗ Quang Hưng et Claude Langlois, ed., *Études de sciences religieuses en France et au Vietnam/Nghiên cứu tôn giáo Pháp và Việt Nam*, pp. 691–742. Hà Nội: Nxb KHXH.

Đặng Nghiêm Vạn. 2004. "Về chính sách tự do tôn giáo ở Việt Nam" [The Policy of Freedom of Religion in Vietnam]. In Viện khoa học xã hội Việt Nam, *Về tôn giáo và tôn giáo ở Việt Nam* [On Religions and Religions in Vietnam], pp. 292–312. Hà Nội: Nxb KHXH.

Đặng Nghiêm Vạn. 1998. *Những vấn đề lý luận và thực tiễn tôn giáo ở Việt Nam* [The religious question in Vietnam, theory and practice]. Hà Nội: Nxb KHXH.

Đỗ Quang Hưng et Langlois, Claude (éd.). 2007. *Études de sciences religieuses en France et au Vietnam/Nghiên cứu tôn giáo Pháp và Việt Nam.* Hà Nội: Nxb KHXH.

Đỗ Quang Hưng. 2014. *Chính sách tôn giáo và nhà nước pháp quyền* [Religious Policy and State of Rule.] Hà Nội: Nxb ĐHQGHN.

Đỗ Quang Hưng. 2009. "Nhận thức về tôn giáo nửa thế kỷ XX: trường hợp Đào Duy Anh" [Knowledge on Religion in the Mid-Twenty Century, the case of Đào Duy Anh.]. In Đỗ Quang Hưng, ed., *Nghiên cứu tôn giáo, nhân vật và sự kiện* [Religious Studies, Characters and Events], pp. 93–117. TpHCM: Nxb TpHCM.

Eisenstadt, Smuel. 2000. "Multiple Modernities". *Daedalus* 129 (Winter): 1–29.

Gheddo, Piero. 1970. *Catholiques et bouddhistes au Vietnam*. Paris: Altasia.

Gorski, Philip. 2000. "Historicizing the secularization debate: church, state and society in late medieval and early modern Europe, ca. 1300 to 1700". *American Sociological Review* 65: 138–167.

Gorski, Philip and Altinordu, Ates. 2008. "After Secularization?" *Annual Review of Sociology* 34: 55–85.

Haneda, Masashi (éd.). 2007. *Sécularisations et laïcités*. Tokyo: the University of Tokyo Center for Philosophy.

Hồ Bá Thâm. 2007. "Đạo và đời với truyền thống nhân văn Viet Nam" [*Đạo, Đời* and Traditional Humanism in Vietnam.]. *Tạp chí nghiên cứu tôn giáo* 10: 3–10.

Học viện Đaminh. 2014. *Thuật ngữ thần học anh-việt* [Theological terminology, English, Vietnamese.]. Hà Nội: Nxb Tôn giáo.

Hue Tam Hô Tai. 1996. *Radicalism and the Origins of the Vietnamese Revolution*. Harvard: Harvard University Press.

Jaffrelot, Christophe. 2018. "Secularity without Secularism in Pakistan: the Politics of Islam from Sir Syed to Zia". In M. Künkler, J. Madeley and S. Shankar, eds., *A Secular Age beyond the West, Religion, Law and the State in Asia, the Middle East and North Africa*, pp. 152–184. Cambridge: Cambridge University Press.

Keith, Charles. 2005. "Catholicisme, bouddhisme et lois laïques au Tonkin, 1899–1914". *Vingtième siècle* 87: 113–128.

King, Richard. 1999. *Orientalism and Religion, postcolonial Theory, India and the Mystic East*. London: Routledge.

Koselleck, Reinhart. 2016. *Le futur passé, contribution à la sémantique des temps historiques*. Paris: Ed. EHESS.

Krech, Volkhard and Steinicke, Marion, eds. 2011. *Dynamics in the history of religions between Asia and Europe, encounters, notions and comparative perspectives*. Leiden: Brill.

Lange, Claude. 2005. "La loi et ses conséquences en Indochine". In J.-P. Chantin et D. Moulinet, eds., *La Séparation de 1905. Les hommes et les lieux*, pp. 219–229. Paris: Éd. de l'Atelier.

Lange, Claude. 1976–1977. "L'église catholique au Vietnam (Sud) de la 'libération' à la 'réunification'". *Échanges France-Asie* 20 (septembre 1976), 24 (mars 1977) et 25 (avril 1977).

Langlois, Claude. 2007. "Concepts et vocabulaire du religieux". In Đỗ Qung Hưng et Claude Langlois (éd.), *Études de sciences religieuses en France et au Vietnam/Nghiên cưu tôn giáo Pháp và Việt Nam*, pp. 539–552. Hà Nội: Nxb KHXH.

Maïs, Jean. 1986. "1975–1985, dix ans de relations entre l'Église et l'État au Vietnam" *Échanges France-Asie* 5.

Marr, David. 1971. *Vietnamese Anticolonialism 1885–1925*. Berkeley: University of California Press.

Marr, David. 1981. *Vietnamese Tradition on Trial, 1920–1945*. Berkeley: University of California Press.

Morlat, Patrice, ed. 2003. *La question religieuse dans l'empire colonial français*. Paris: Les Indes savantes.

Ngo, T., Quijada, J., ed. 2015. *Atheist Secularism and its discontents. A comparative study of Religion and Communism in Eurasia*. Hampshire: Palgrave Macmillan.

Nguyễn Hồng Dương (chủ biên). 2014. *Tiếp tục đổi mới chính sách về tôn giáo ở Việt Nam hiện nay. Những vấn đề lý luận cơ bản* [Continuation of the Policy of Religious Reform in Vietnam, Theoretical Foundations.]. Hà Nội: Nxb Văn hóa Thông tin và Viện Văn Hóa.

Nguyễn Ngọc Quỳnh. 2012. *Chính sách tôn giáo thời Tự Đức (1848–1883)* [The religious policy under the reign of Tự Đức (1848–1883).]. Hà Nội: Nxb CTQG.

Nguyễn Quang Hưng. 2016. *Tôn giáo và Văn Hóa* [Religion and Culture.]. Hà nội: Nxb tri thức.

Nguyễn Thế Anh. 1997. "La conception de la monarchie divine dans le Viêt Nam traditionnel". *BEFEO* 84: 147–157.

Nguyễn Xuân Nghĩa. 2010. "Religion, État et Société: Trente cinq ans de sécularisme, sécularisation et désécularisation chez les catholiques de Hô Chi Minh-Ville (1975–2009)". Thèse de doctorat de l'Université de Toulouse.

Nguyễn Xuân Nghĩa. 2019. "Giải thế tục hóa: khái niệm và sự kiện (từ góc độ xã hội học)" [Desecularization, notions and events (from a sociological perspective).]. *Nghiên cứu tôn giáo* 181 no. 1: 3–31.

Pencolé, Pierre. 1957. "Dictionnaires vietnamiens". *Bulletin de la Société des Missions Etrangères de Paris* 99 and 100 (février, mars): 127–140 and 211–227.

Perez-Agote, Alfonso. 2014. "The notion of secularization: Drawing the boundaries of its contemporary scientific validity". *Current Sociology* 62 (October): 886–904.

Sidel, Mark. 2009. *The Constitution in Vietnam, a contextual analysis*. New York: Bloomsbury Publishing.

Taylor, Charles. 2011. *L'âge séculier*. Paris: Seuil.

Thibault, Hélène. 2015. "The Soviet Secularization Project in Central Asia: Accommodation and Institutional Legacies". *Eurostudia* 10 no. 1: 11–31.

Trần Văn Giàu. 1973. *Sự phát triển của tư tưởng Việt Nam thế kỷ 19 đến Cách mạng tháng Tám* [The Development of Thought in Vietnam from the Nineteenth Century until the August Revolution of 1945.] TpHCM, Nxb TpHCM.

Trinh Van Thao. 1990. *Vietnam, du confucianisme au communisme*. Paris: L'Harmattan.

van der Veer Peter and Lehmann Harmut, eds. 1999. *Nation and Religion. Perspectives on Europe and Asia*. Princeton: Princeton University Press.

Aminah Mohammad-Arif
# Indian Secularism: an Original Accommodation of Religious Plurality Endangered from Within?

**Abstract:** In this chapter, I will examine Indian secularism through the lens of the multiple layers of the "plural"—which may or may not intersect—starting with its raison d'être, i.e., religious plurality. As we shall see, the "plural" is also at play in the legal system, the sources mobilized by various actors, and the implementation and significance of secularism. These multidimensional and overlapping pluralities engender a system characterized by flexibility, which has perhaps ensured its survival but has also laid the foundations for its endangerment from within. In the process, I shall also refer to the interlinkage between secularism and secularization. I will first contextualize the emergence of secularism in contemporary India. Next, I will examine the prehistory of the term. Bearing in mind terminological issues, I will then address the specificities of secularism in India using two parameters, the (non)interference of the state, and citizenship. I will conclude with an attempt to decipher the "nature" or type of this secularism by drawing on some of the "global theories" with which the present volume is concerned.

## 1 Introduction

An attempt to address the fairly fuzzy notion of the "secular" in India across time and religions would be overly ambitious. Therefore, I will mostly focus here on Indian secularism, which deserves close attention given, on the one hand, that it has been established as a political doctrine and, on the other, that it is a very original understanding of the relation between state and religion compared to conceptions and practices elsewhere in the world.

What is the basis of this originality? What are its historical roots? How does Indian secularism differ from other attempts to regulate the relationship between the state and religions in a context of great religious plurality? Is it concerned by the criticisms of post-colonial writers who, following Talal Asad, consider that "secularism as a statist project aims to make religious difference inconsequential

---

**Aminah Mohammad-Arif** (CNRS-CEIAS)

https://doi.org/10.1515/9783110733068-008

to politics while at the same time embedding majoritarian religious norms in state institutions, laws, and practices?" (Mahmood 2016: 206)

Several researchers have of course already taken an interest in this question, one of the main authorities being Rajeev Bhargava (1998, 2012, 2013). His thorough analysis, which remains the most accomplished theorization of Indian secularism to date, includes the groundbreaking proposition that the specificity of Indian secularism rests on "principled distance", a notion to which we shall return. But does the explanation of the resilience of secularism through "principled distance" withstand the onslaught of Hindutva, the ideology of Hindu nationalists? Other authors have also contributed considerably to the reflection on secularism, notably through the question of its relevance and applicability in the Indian context (Nandy 1998).

Other authors have also contributed much to the reflection on Indian secularism. This is the case of Partha Chatterjee who analyzes very finely some of the "anomalies" (to quote him) in Indian secularism, such as the tension between the principle of freedom and the principle of equality. (1998: 358–366). He also pointed out that Hindutva did not have as its main objective the religionization of the state, and as such was not a threat to secularism: "The mature and most formidable statement of the new political conception of Hindutva is unlikely to pit itself at all against the idea of a secular state" (1998: 346). Twenty-five years later, now that Hindu nationalists have seized power with an absolute majority, how meaningful is this assessment?

While keeping these analyses in mind, I will try in this paper to give an account of the originality of Indian secularism, which is based on a genuine and inventive attempt to accommodate religious plurality, and then to highlight both its internal contradictions and the dangers that threaten it. To this effect, I will first contextualize the emergence of secularism in contemporary India. Next I will examine the prehistory of the term. Bearing in mind terminological issues, I will then address the specificities of secularism in India using two parameters, the (non)interference of the state and citizenship. I will conclude with an attempt to decipher the "nature" or type of this secularism by drawing on some of the "global theories" with which the present volume is concerned. In the process, I will discuss how Hindu nationalists in power undermine secularism without being unconstitutional.

## 2 Contextualizing Secularism in India

Secularism in India is rooted in a very singular context. First, India's religious diversity in terms of both beliefs and practices is unparalleled worldwide. It has a wide array of religious traditions (Hinduism, Buddhism, Sikhism, Jainism, "tribal" religions and so on), and the so-called Abrahamic religions (Islam and Christianity) came to Indian shores almost as soon as they were founded. Judaism and Zoroastrianism complete the picture, albeit in tiny numbers. All these religions have been comingling in the Indian landscape for centuries. Within religious groups, further plurality exists across castes, sects and ideologies. Second, the contemporary history of India was marked by a traumatic event (a "moral shock" to borrow James Jasper's phrase [1999]) that can be seen as a tragic culmination of the interlinkage between religion and politics, *i.e.*, India's partition and the creation of Pakistan. The two countries reacted to Partition in different ways. The founders of Pakistan had initially envisioned a secular state. Yet given the way religion was mobilized to lay claim to a new country, and the trauma and losses engendered by the division of India, it proved impossible to set religion aside when defining the identity of the newly founded nation-state. For India, the trauma had the opposite consequence: the founders of postcolonial India saw secularism as the sine qua non of the country's survival. Among the several reasons for this (including the personal belief of several leaders of the Congress Party that led India to independence, such as Jawaharlal Nehru (1889–1964) and Abul Kalam Azad (1888–1958)), demography was a core issue; whereas Pakistan could only claim 3 per cent of religious minorities, in India religious minorities represented almost 20 per cent of the total population, including the largest Muslim minority in the world.

After independence, the Indian state faced the challenge of managing religious plurality in a huge country already characterized by considerable regional diversity. The task was made all the more challenging by a particularly tense political context, which stretched on for decades after Partition. From the 1960s to the 1990s, riots frequently broke out between the two major religious groups, Hindus (80 per cent of the population) and Muslims (10 per cent at the time of independence in 1947, and 14 per cent today). Riots still occur today from time to time. This violence is so structural that a word has been coined for it: communalism. The term designates the propaganda or effective action of the members of one religious community against another for religious reasons. I will not go into this notion further, but it is worth mentioning here because the notion of "secularism" in India is so complex that it is frequently defined or understood as the antonym of "communalism."

Another major peculiarity of the Indian context is the salience of individual and collective religiosity and the significant role of religion (which is itself a late construct, especially as far as Hinduism is concerned) in defining social identity. In many situations, religious norms tend to be conflated with social norms. Indian society is therefore generally believed to be barely secularized, particularly in the restricted meaning of the decline of religion. Admittedly, secularization is a polysemic term that may include broader meanings, and refer to ideas of individualization, subjectivation, and rationalization of religious practice itself. In India, such ideas have their roots in the religious reform movements that emerged during the colonial period among both Hindus and Muslims, such as the Brahmo Samaj and the Aligarh movement. Both movements advocated conceptions of religion that would be more in tune with "modernity": they rejected caste observance and the mediation of traditional authorities; they sought the elimination of certain practices such as *sati*, and the relegation of religion to the private sphere. In postcolonial India, secularization is not so much a relegation of religion to the private sphere as an understanding of religion as a fluid and internally contested category, where, to quote Mohita Bhatia (2013: 106), "the boundaries between religion, culture, politics, caste and community are constantly drawn, challenged, redrawn or negotiated." The religious space can be simultaneously challenged and inhabited, and religious values can be appropriated as well as subverted (Bhatia 2013: 106). There are several examples of such processes, including religious practices (in Sufi shrines for instance) that cannot be apprehended through the strict categories of Hinduism or Islam. That said, the persistent salience of religion in Indians' daily lives, across religions, remains undeniable and has helped mold Indian secularism in singular ways.

# 3 A Prehistory of the Concept

As far as the interlinkage of politics and religion is concerned, another originality of the Indian experience lies in the fact that India has been ruled by people from very different religious backgrounds over the course of its history. Hindu dynasties first governed the country. Muslim rulers succeeded them in the thirteenth century and remained until the eighteenth century. A colonial power with a Christian background finally took over in the eighteenth century until independence in 1947 (although the British did not mobilize Christianity much as a religion during their rule, there was still a perception among the local population that the country was governed by a Christian power[1]). But interestingly, despite this religious diversity and although the connection between religion and politics has varied according to the rulers in place, similarities have been more salient than differences, and continuities more striking than breaks. The word

---

1 I thank Peter van der Veer for this pertinent remark.

"secularism" was a late invention, coined in 1851 by George Jacob Holyoake (in contrast with atheism; see Asad 2003: 23–24). It is useful to go further back in history, however, as some forms of secularity, defined in broad terms, had older roots in India. Besides, Indian secularism is different from the way the colonial power—i.e., Britain, with its formally established church—had conceptualized relations between state and religion on its own soil. In order to uncover the specificities of secularism in contemporary India, I will therefore briefly analyze the relation between religion and politics, and the place the state conferred to religion in the ancient and medieval periods. The study of political regimes before colonization thus shows that the state adopted a policy of accommodating religious plurality long before the modern period, irrespective of whether the ruler was Hindu or Muslim. Besides, whoever the ruler was, political unity was at no time built upon religious bases.

As far as Hindu rulers are concerned, we should first bear in mind that religious plurality is inherent to Hinduism, divided along the lines of caste, sect, and so on. So much so that the very notion of "Hinduism", as a religion, is a late construct, as mentioned above, dating back to the colonial period. Second, politics is theoretically subordinated to religion since, according to the caste system, the Brahmin (the equivalent of a priest in charge of religious functions) is situated at the top of the hierarchy while the Kshtriya (the caste of warriors the kings belong to) sits just below in second position. In order to claim legitimacy in ancient and medieval India, the king had to associate himself with Brahmins who enjoyed a superior ritual purity and embodied the ultimate values. In practice, however, the king could dispense with the Brahmins' tutelage for all matters that had no "obvious" religious connotation. The existence of autonomous social spheres suggested that the secular was, in a way, granted its own separate space. Moreover, Brahmins lived off the generosity of the king and hence were materially dependent on him. In order words, the relationship between kings and Brahmins was more one of interdependence than subordination: kings needed Brahmins for legitimacy while Brahmins needed the protection and the material support of the kings (Gaborieau 1999). Third, as Catherine Clémentin-Ojha points out, Hindu Law was characterized by multiple juridical sources: the Vedas coexisted with custom, which "was given priority in case of a conflict with written norms" (Clémentin-Ojha 2010: 327). The king was urged to respect the customs of his subjects (Lingat 1967: 272).

Muslim rulers established *sharia* in the regions they administered between the thirteenth and eighteenth centuries. However, although they needed the support of religious dignitaries to legitimize their governance, as Marc Gaborieau and others have pointed out, Islam occupied a fairly negligible space in the state apparatus, allowing Muslim rulers to adapt to the local context (Gaborieau

1994a & 1994b). Hindus were granted the status of *zimmi* (a protected minority under Muslim rule) although they were theoretically *kafir* (or "infidels" as per Islamic law) and not people of the Book (like Jews and Christians). This status gave them the right to retain their own legal system, and they benefitted from relative freedom of religion. Groups other than Muslims were associated with the state apparatus. The Muslim rulers' policy of accommodation explains in part why sultans and Mughal emperors were able to rule on a long-term basis over a population which, in its vast majority, professed other religions.

Accommodation did not only take the form of policies with pragmatic or strategic goals. It also translated into specific ways of thinking, through notions expressing religious universalism like the *sulh-i-kul*,[2] developed during the times of Mughal Emperor Akbar (1556 – 1605), or the *sarva dharma samabhava* promoted by Hindu philosophers such as Vivekananda (1863 – 1902) and later embraced by Gandhi (1869 – 1948).[3] As Sudipta Kaviraj points out, though, "this is a semantic of religious experimentation, not of secularity in the usually recognised sense of the word". [...] to have that disposition towards other religious paths required a deep but unusual interpretation of one's religious faith" (Kaviraj 2013: 94). Buddhism also has its promoters of the coexistence of religions. The prime example is Emperor Ashoka of the Maurya dynasty (third century BC), who worked for the glory of the religion he had embraced with all the zeal of a new convert, but who is nonetheless said to have promoted tolerance of other religions and mutual respect between them. Hence—though this may sound a little anachronistic—the way the ancient and medieval periods laid the foundations for accommodating religious plurality supports the idea that the basic notions of modern secularism in India were not purely exogenous but had some vernacular roots as well.

While the secular concept cannot be considered simply an imposition of the colonial power, the British nonetheless paved the way for secular with an "ism" in India; just as they had paved the way for the conceptualization of very diversified practices into a full-fledged religion, since then known, and claimed by the people concerned themselves, under the name of "Hinduism". A detour into legal questions will shed some light on the emergence of secularism in India and its singularity. When the British came to India in the eighteenth century and gradually took commercial and then political control of the country, they established a new legal system that included a hierarchy of courts in charge

---

[2] *Sulh-I kul* is a Sufi concept meaning "perfect reconciliation."
[3] *Sarva dharm samabhava* refers to the idea that all religious paths lead to the same destination.

of administering civil law and criminal law. Hindu and Muslim judges were increasingly replaced by British magistrates or by Indian judges trained in British law. Criminal law was also increasingly secularized while a large section of civil law was codified according to the British model. In family matters, however, the British opted for a policy similar to that of the Mughal emperors who ruled India from the sixteenth to the eighteenth century: religious communities could keep their own canonical laws for settling family disputes. Thus, as early as 1772, the British allowed each of the major religious groups to retain their own "personal law" for all matters related to marriage, divorce, inheritance, adoption, donations and *waqf* (charitable foundations). In other words, the law was gradually secularized, while religion was confined to family matters. Indian secularism finds its roots in this very process. So does the "contextuality" of secularism (to borrow the phrase of Rajeev Bhargava, 2013), to which we shall return later. For instance, during the eighteenth and nineteenth centuries, the British at times provided financial support to temples and mosques and banned Christian missionaries from proselytizing, while at other times strongly encouraged Christian proselytism.

Let us now turn to the development of secularism in postcolonial India, starting with terminological issues.

# 4 Secularism in Postcolonial India as per the Constitution and the Legal System

Secularism is of course an English word. What are the vernacular words in India? Are they simply translations of the English term or do they borrow from local notions? If there are only translations of the word, what do they convey of the vernacular understandings of the concept? Are they used in daily language?

The first and clear answer to these questions is that people in India (and Pakistan) mostly use English words to refer to "secular" and its derivatives, such as "secularism," including in official public documents and speeches. The vernacular translations of these words, often created with artificial neologisms, are hardly used; indeed, most people are unaware of their very existence and hence their meaning. This seems to vindicate Partha Chatterjee's claim that ""the continued use of the term 'secularism' is, it seems to me, an expression of the desire of the modernizing élite to see the 'original' meaning of the concept actualized in India" (Chatterjee 1998: 351).

These translations are nonetheless worthy of attention because they can convey very different meanings. In Hindi, the Indian national language, secularism is often translated as *dharma nirapekshta* (literally "indifferent to and independent from religion"), somehow implying the idea of a separation between the religious sphere and the political sphere. In Urdu, the Pakistani national language, secularism is translated as *ladiniyat* (literally "anti-religiousness," "non-religiousness") borrowed from Arabic. However, Arabic has other words to translate secularism, such as *almaniyya* and *laikiyya*, which do not necessarily confer the underlying meaning of an *opposition* to religion as *ladiniyat* does, but are instead related to ideas of the mundane and the profane (therefore implying the idea of different spheres rather than an opposition). Although other words exist in Urdu to translate "atheism" such as *la mazhab* or *munkar-e khuda*, the use of *ladiniyat* therefore suggests a conflation between secularism and atheism. The commentary on the notion of secularism in an online Urdu dictionary is fairly interesting:

> There are also several similar words to Secularism in our dictionary, which are Agnosticism, Apostasy, Atheism, Blasphemy, Defection, Disbelief, Dissent, Dissidence, Divergence, Error, Fallacy, Heterodoxy, Iconoclasm, Impiety, Infidelity, Misbelief, Nonconformity, Paganism, Revisionism, Schism, Sectarianism and Sin. Apart from similar words, there are always opposite words in dictionary too, the opposite words for Secularism are Agreement, Belief, Harmony and Orthodoxy.[4]

The underlying meaning of the word is symptomatic of the pressure of Islamists on the Pakistani state to give religion a central space. This is ironic considering that, as mentioned above, the founder of Pakistan, Muhammad Ali Jinnah (1876–1948), had originally envisioned a secular state: a country for Muslims rather than a Muslim country.

To get back to the development of secularism in India, the Constitution provides a starting point for assessing its significance. Although the epithet "secular" was introduced in the preamble of the Constitution as late as 1976 through the 42$^{nd}$ amendment, the basic principles of the Constitution lay the groundwork and hint at the singular meaning of secularism in the Indian context. Freedom of conscience, speech and religion have thus been inscribed in the Constitution since its inception in 1950, through a series of articles with converging effects. Article 15 prohibits any discrimination on the basis (among other things) of religion; article 16 applies the same rule to recruitment in the public sector and article 29 to entrance to a public school or a state-supported school. More specifically, article 25 states:

---

[4] https://www.urdupoint.com/dictionary/english-to-urdu/secularism-meaning-in-urdu/78790.html

(1) Subject to public order, morality and health and to the other provisions of this Part, all persons are equally entitled to freedom of conscience and the right freely to profess, practice and propagate religion.

There are also provisions for collective rights: the Indian State does not recognize any official religion, and considers each religion with an equal "benevolence." Articles 26 and 30 stipulate that:

26. Freedom to manage religious affairs Subject to public order, morality and health, every religious denomination or any section thereof shall have the right

(a) to establish and maintain institutions for religious and charitable purposes;

(b) to manage its own affairs in matters of religion;

(c) to own and acquire movable and immovable property; and

(d) to administer such property in accordance with law

30. Right of minorities to establish and administer educational institutions

(1) All minorities, whether based on religion or language, shall have the right to establish and administer educational institutions of their choice.

(2) The state shall not, in granting aid to educational institutions, discriminate against any educational institution on the ground that it is under the management of a minority, whether based on religion or language.

Although there is no uniform legislation regarding the practice of religion in the public sphere, Indian secularism thus stresses the importance of collective rights and the correlative respect of all religions in the public sphere. Far from separating state and religion, it grants official recognition to all beliefs. In accordance with its original purpose, Indian secularism thus represents a form of state acceptance of religious plurality: "unity in diversity" to quote Jawaharlal Nehru, one of its most iconic figures.

The legal system follows a dualistic logic inherited from the British, who themselves took inspiration from the Mughal rulers, and has its own provisions regarding religious rights. In independent India, religious groups have their own separate jurisdiction regarding family rights, succession rights and the rights of religious foundations. This means that the state applies a different legal system to the major religious groups. It does not try to eliminate any legal recognition of religious identities and accepts that religion may be freely exercised in civil society. In other domains (penal, administration and business), the state applies the same universal legal system to all its citizens.

# 5 Secularism in Practice

By "secularism in practice," I do not mean to oppose theory and practice but to examine some practices which are embedded within the Constitution, and, in doing so, to continue highlighting the specificities of Indian secularism. To do so, I will use two parameters: the (non)interference of the state, and citizenship.

## 5.1 The (non)Interference of the State

While the non-interference of the state does not lie at the core of Indian secularism, this principle is interesting to examine in more detail from a comparative perspective with other forms of secularism elsewhere in the world. As mentioned above, religious freedom is guaranteed by the Constitution provided that certain conditions— "public order, morality and health"—are respected. By mentioning these conditions, the Indian penal code has banned certain practices with a religious foundation, such as *sati* (the practice of widows immolating themselves on their husbands' pyre) and untouchability (as part of the caste system and its socio-religious basis). The banning of these two practices is a form of state intervention to prevent offenses against individuals. In a similar vein, another example of interference for the sake of social justice is the obligation to grant untouchables (or Dalits) access to the temples that had previously banned them in the name of ritual purity. Similarly, the state has reformed the Hindu personal law in areas related to women's rights, such as divorce (women can now legally ask for divorce) and inheritance (which was previously restricted to the men and boys of the family). Once again, social reform is the state's main argument to justify its action[5].

Besides the defense of public order, morality and health on the one hand, and social reforms on the other, a third constitutional principle enables the state to intervene in religious matters. It concerns the right of the state to regulate activities associated with religious practice (Clémentin-Ojha 2010: 348). Although the state avoids any interference in the organization of worship, it has a say in the administration of temples and can intervene in particular in cases of embezzlement or administrative malfunctioning. Some states, like Tamil Nadu,

---

[5] For more detailed examples of State intervention in religious matters in the name of social reform (like the Hindu reform bill), see Chatterjee 1998.

supersede religious authorities to manage Hindu temples directly, arguing that "managing temple funds and property are secular activities."[6]

Interestingly, as Marc Galanter rightfully points out (1997), the corpus used to justify such policies of social reform or of regulating religious activities may include both "secular" and religious sources: the Constitution and religious texts. The state, with the support of judges, may use these sources (either directly or through academic texts) to show for instance that a particular sect has a distorted interpretation of Hinduism.[7] The state thus endows judges with the authority to say what Hinduism is, and hence the judiciary is included among the bodies that regulate religion (Chatterjee 1998; Clémentin-Ojha 2010).

Education is a further example of the state's ambiguous relation to religion. The Indian educational system includes public schools, entirely private schools, and state-sponsored schools. Theoretically, reference to religion is prohibited in public schools. However, the visibility of religion on school premises calls this principle into question; for instance, religious symbols (through clothing or in other forms) are not banned in schools. The greatest ambiguity however lies in the place of religion in school programs. Religious education is prohibited in public schools but it is authorized in state-sponsored schools as long as it is optional. This implies that the state can sponsor religious education, albeit indirectly.

## 5.2 Citizenship

Let us now examine citizenship and its corollary, *i.e.* the prohibition of any discrimination. Article 15 of the Constitution protects citizens against any kind of discrimination based on religion, race, caste, or gender. It considers individuals as citizens and not as members of a particular religious group. In other articles, however, the Constitution derogates from this principle. First, the state has adopted a form of positive discrimination by introducing a system of reservation in the administration and in universities to improve the status of lower castes. Admittedly, in doing so, the state is seeking to eliminate structural inequalities, but this affirmative action is a de facto recognition of the caste system, and, in a way, of communitarianism, since it acknowledges caste-based identification. In theory, positive discrimination was meant to be implemented for a limited peri-

---

6 http://www.thehindu.com/opinion/op-ed/reforms-in-the-house-of-god/article5570711.ece?homepage=true
7 See for instance the Satsangi case. Cf. Clémentin-Ojha 2010.

od, but more than 70 years after independence, this system is still necessary to make up for the social gap between upper castes and lower castes, and has therefore been maintained.

Religious minorities, Muslims and Christians in particular, continue to have separate personal laws inherited from the colonial period. Like Hindus, Christians have seen their personal law partly reformed in recent times (2001), particularly regarding divorce.[8] Muslims, who form a much larger minority with a specific history—former rulers but now a largely stigmatized group—are more averse to such reforms. Since independence, their leadership, however heterogeneous it may be, has built up personal law into a major symbol of Muslims' religious identity. They perceive any attempt to reform this status as unacceptable state interference in their affairs and an infringement of their religious rights. The objective of the Constitution's promoters was the eventual adoption of a secular uniform civil code for all citizens beyond religious affiliation. Yet like positive discrimination, the personal status of religious groups is still in place, albeit for different reasons. Continued positive discrimination is motivated by a concern for social progress. Personal laws have been maintained with a view to protecting religious freedom and minority rights, but at the expense, in some cases, of social progress; the absence of reforms in the Muslim personal law has a bearing on women's rights for instance. While polygamy is prohibited for Hindus, it has been legal for Muslims for decades; and until December 2018 when a new law was passed by the Parliament (see below), women had very limited rights in terms of divorce while men, on the contrary, could easily repudiate their wife using triple *talaq* (or "instant divorce"). Interestingly, in Pakistan, the state reformed the Muslim personal law, similarly inherited from the colonial period, as early as the 1960s. These reforms guaranteed women the right to divorce and put an end to the practice of triple *talaq*.

In any case, the preservation of separate personal laws for each community is a transgression of the principle of non-discrimination by the state since the latter differentiates between Hindus, Muslims and Christians, thereby reifying religious categories and endorsing communitarianism. Indian secularism is thus characterized by tension between the defense of individual freedom and the recognition and protection of the particularities of religious communities. Symptomatic of this tension is the fact that groups with divergent interests may come together to support or oppose the abolition of personal laws and the establishment of a uniform civil code, albeit for different reasons and with different agendas. Some liberal and feminist groups support a uniform civil code in the name

---

[8] See Parashar 2008.

of certain principles underpinning secularism, such as the construction of a national identity beyond religion, caste and ethnicity, or women's rights. But so do Hindu nationalists, who may strategically put forward the argument of secularism but in fact wish to conflate a uniform civil code with a Hindu civil code. Other liberal, feminist and human rights groups oppose the uniform civil code precisely for this reason and argue that such a code would be imposed at the expense of minority rights (see Hasan 1994). This situation is worth recalling Partha Chatterjee's analysis articulating secularism and tolerance. Reflecting on the relationship of religious minorities to the State, he elaborated an understanding of the notion of "toleration", based on Foucault's concept of governmentality. "Toleration" is the acceptance that a group, going against governmentality, has the right to insist on its difference without giving a reason for it ("the right not to offer a reason to be different"). This proposal is not reducible to the acceptance of cultural relativism because there is in return the expectation of a democratization of the group from within (Chatterjee 1998: 370–379). It is an interesting proposal, but it assumes that religious minorities form fairly homogeneous groups within which democratic debates could be easily organized by a leadership whose authority is recognized. This is hardly the case among religious minorities in India.

# 6 Deciphering the "Nature" of Indian secularism

If we use the typology developed by Jean Baubérot, Indian secularism is situated at the crossroads of two forms of secularism. The first is liberal secularism (*laïcité libérale*[9]), because individuals' freedom of conscience is recognized and all citizens benefit from the same rights regardless of religion. Citizenship is thus defined in civic and universalist terms, and is not based on religious criteria. The second is communitarian secularism (*laïcité communautaire*), because for family law, succession and religious foundations, the legal system rests upon laws derived from the religious texts of the main groups. The system of positive discrimination also supports the idea that Indian secularism is in part a form of communitarian secularism. But with regard to Baubérot's typology, theoretically the state does not have privileged links with any one single religion.

A third concept developed by Rajeev Bhargava also has a definite heuristic value. Bhargava argues that Indian secularism is "a contextual secularism based

---

**9** Just as secularism is not easy to translate into French because it is not the exact equivalent of *laïcité*, *laïcité* is not easy to translate into English.

on the idea of a principled distance between the state and religious institutions and a shared search for a contextually grounded common ethic" (Berman, Bhargava, Laliberté 2013; see also Bhargava 1998). In other words, the state may intervene or not intervene in a given context depending on whether doing so would be compatible with the values of religious freedom and equality between citizens. Admittedly, this concept helps account for one of the most salient features of Indian secularism, i.e., its malleability and flexibility.

Yet what happens to the principled distance when the political context changes, and power lies in the hands of one group, like the Hindu nationalists who are now in power in India with an absolute majority? The religionization of the State may not be their main priority (Chatterjee 1998: 346–347). They may even refer to secularism (in its interpretation of separation between the State and religion and not in that of equidistance of the State with respect to all religions) for strategic reasons (as the example of triple *talaq* shows; see below). However, as is well known, they oppose many basic principles of secularism, in its meaning of equidistance with regard to all religions: Indian culture is defined as a manifestation of Hindu values, and the Indian nation as a Hindu nation. In this ethnic nationalism seeking its legitimacy in majoritarianism, not much space is given to religious minorities, particularly those whose religion came from outside India, such as Christians and Muslims. Since Narendra Modi came to power, the trampling of secular principles has reached unprecedented proportions. Overriding these principles is not new (the Congress Party has ignored them on occasion to win votes, particularly from minority groups) but never in the history of postcolonial India has it been done on such a scale, and accompanied by such tremendous violence. Let us look at a few examples. First, the proliferation and hardening of the beef ban; it may be of spiritual benefit for some groups but it represents a threat not only to the economic conditions of other groups (such as Muslim butchers and Dalit tanners) but to their very lives (as shown by the lynching of Dalits and Muslims accused of transporting beef).[10] A second example is the government's scrapping of the Hajj subsidy. This policy may be framed in the language of social justice and women's empowerment,[11] but since the state continues to pay out significant amounts for Hindu pilgrimages,[12] it represents a serious challenge to the idea of a "principled distance." A third example is the bill passed in December 2018 criminalizing triple *talaq* or instant divorce (the offending husband can

---

10 Muslims and Dalits were lynched in the wake of the beef ban.
11 The funds will instead be used to provide education for Muslim girls.
12 Details.

spend as long as three years in jail). Obviously, the Muslim practice of triple *talaq* is a severe violation of women's rights. However, unilateral divorce is a practice observed in other religious groups as well, including Hindus and Christians, but the offense in their case comes under civil law and not criminal law.[13]

Therefore, the question is whether this contextuality of secularism has paved the way to a form of "hijacking" of secularism by the state itself, allowing it to adopt policies that jeopardize the original aim of regulating religious plurality so as to avoid conflict between religious groups. The question is not so much whether Hindu nationalism as such challenges secularism or whether a political party can change the secular character of the Constitution "at its whims and fancies,"[14] but whether the flexibility of secularism is perhaps such that it allows the state itself to challenge the original spirit of secularism without being unconstitutional.

# 7 Conclusion

Despite its limitations, which include constant tension between universalism and communitarianism (particularly from a euro-centric perspective) and a recentness that still makes it a political experiment submitted to the "test of democracy" (Kaviraj 2013: 95–96), Indian secularism remains a fairly innovative crafting of the relationship between the state and religion. It responds to the numerous challenges of a religious plurality involving significant risks of conflict, combined with the urge to remedy social injustice that is partly embedded in religion itself.

Indian secularism is not much concerned with religiosity as such or with the relations between religion and (non)modernity. Compared to other forms of secularism, like *laïcité à la française* with its underlying assumption that religion (particularly in the public sphere) and modernity are practically incompatible, Indian secularism is neutral and indifferent ("non-judgmental") vis-à-vis religious conceptions and practices as long as they remain compatible with the state's definition of individual freedom and human rights. In other words, to borrow from Talal Asad, Indian secularism "does not have a narrative of progress from the religious to the secular" (Asad 2003: 1; see also Viswanathan 2008). Even though Niraja Gopal Jayal righly points out that the early debates were

---

[13] https://scroll.in/article/895448/civil-offence-for-hindus-crime-for-muslims-the-triple-talaq-ordinance-is-plainly-discriminatory
[14] https://scroll.in/article/862935/the-bjp-is-wrong-merely-removing-the-word-secular-from-the-constitution-wont-make-it-any-less-so

not exempt from the idea that there was a "natural citizen", mainly Hindu and male (Gopal Jayal 2013: 53), the way secularism is defined in the Constitution does not particularly imply that majoritarian religious norms are deep-rooted in the institutions and laws.

Relatively low levels of secularization in India also attest to the fact that secularism as a political doctrine is not "related to the secular as an ontology and an epistemology" (to quote Asad 2003: 21). Secularism in India is not a response to secularization as a sociological evolution, or, from an axiological perspective, as a desirable evolution. As Rajeev Bhargava points out, political secularism is not a precondition for "ethical secularism" (i.e., the belief that the fundamental bases of personal and collective conduct do not derive from the divine but from human sources; cf. Bhargava 2013). In fact, although secularism and secularization can converge and influence each other (through the elimination of some religious practices, for instance) Indian political secularism can even hinder the secularization of society inasmuch as it tends to reify religious categories, for instance by making Islam and Hinduism out as fixed and exclusive categories (Bhatia 2013:107), and by "flattening out heterogeneous religious histories" (Viswanathan 2008: 475).

Another of the originalities of Indian secularism lies in the different layers of the plural. In addition to the plurality of religion, there is plurality in the legal system (blending a British heritage and legal principles entrenched in older traditions), plurality in the sources mobilized by the state through the judiciary (combining "secular" and religious texts) and plurality born of the federal system implemented in India (the level of state intervention may differ from state to state). While these overlapping pluralities, embedded in a long history, are a way to respond to distinct (local) situations, they further amplify the flexibility of India's secularism. A flexibility, we shall hope, which will continue to provide the state with the tools to manage religious plurality and regulate conflict in the long run, despite the current onslaught of religious nationalism(s).

# References

Asad, Talal. 2003. *Formations of the Secular: Christianity, Islam, Modernity.* Stanford: Stanford University Press.
Berman, Bruce; Bhargava, Rajeev; Laliberté, André, eds. 2013. *Secular States and Religious Diversity.* Vancouver, BC:University of British Columbia Press.
Bhargava, Rajeev. 1998. *Secularism and its Critics.* Delhi: Oxford University Press.
Bhargava, Rajeev. 2012. "How has Secularism Fared in India?"In Christophe Jaffrelot & Aminah Mohammad-Arif, eds., *Politique et religions en Asie du Sud: le secularisme dans tous ses états?,*pp. 47–67. Paris: Editions de l'EHESS, collection Purushartha.

Bhargava, Rajeev. 2013. "Reimagining Secularism: Respect, Domination and Principled Distance". *Economic and Political Weekly* 48 no. 50: 79–92.

Bhatia, Mohita. 2013. "Secularism and Secularisation: A Bibliographical Essay". *Economic and Political Weekly* 48 no. 50: 103–111.

Chatterjee, Partha. 1998. "Secularism and Tolerance". In Rajeev Bhargava, ed., *Secularism and its Critics*, pp. 345–379. Delhi: Oxford University Press.

Clémentin-Ojha, Catherine. 2010. "L'insertion des convictions religieuses dans les droits positifs contemporains: le cas de l'Union indienne". *Convictions philosophiques et religieuses et droits positifs*, Textes présentés au colloque international de Moncton, 24–27 août 2008, pp. 324–366. Bruxelles: Bruylant.

Gaborieau, Marc. 1994a. "Akbar et la construction de l'Empire (1556–1605)". In Claude Markovits, ed., *Histoire de l'Inde moderne, 1480–1950*, pp. 97–114. Fayard: Paris.

Gaborieau, Marc. 1994b. "Les États indiens: les sultanats". In Claude Markovits, ed., *Histoire de l'Inde moderne, 1480–1950*, pp. 29–49. Fayard: Paris.

Gaborieau, Marc. 1999. "La tolérance des religions dominées dans l'Inde traditionnelle: ses prolongements modernes au Népal et au Pakistan". In G. Saupin, R. Fabre and M. Launay, eds., *La tolérance*, colloque international de Nantes (May 1998), quatrième centenaire de l'Edit de Nantes, pp. 451–461. Presses universitaires Rennes/Université de Nantes.

Galanter, Marc. 1997 [1989]. *Law and Society in Modern India*. New Delhi: Oxford University Press.

Gopal Jayal, Niraja. 2013. *Citizenship and its Discontents: an Indian History*. Cambridge: Harvard University Press.

Hasan, Zoya. ed. 1994. *Forging Identities: Gender, Communities and the State*. Delhi: Kali for Women.

Jaffrelot, Christophe, and Aminah Mohammad-Arif, eds. 2012. *Politique et religions en Asie du Sud: le sécularisme dans tous ses états?* Paris: Editions de l'EHESS, collection Purushartha, volume 30.

Jasper, James. 1999. *The Art of Moral Protest: Culture, Biography and Creativity in Social Movements*. Chicago: University of Chicago Press.

Kaviraj, Sudipta. 2013. "Languages of Secularity". *Economic and Political Weekly* 48 no. 50: 93–102.

Lingat, Robert. 1967. *Sources du droit dans le système traditionnel de l'Inde*. La Haye: Mouton and Co.

Mahmood, Saba. 2016. *Religious Difference in a Secular Age: A Minority Report*. Princeton, NJ: Princeton University Press.

Nandy, Ashish. 1998. "The Politics of Secularism and the Recovery of Religious Tolerance". In Rajeev Bhargava, ed.s, *Secularism and its Critics*, pp. 321–344.

Parashar, Archana. 2008. "Gender Inequality and Personal Religious Laws in India". *Brown Journal of World Affairs* 14 no. 2: (Spring-Summer): 103–112.

Taylor, Charles. 2007. *A Secular Age*, Harvard: Harvard University Press.

Viswanathan, Gauri. 2008. "Secularism in the Framework of Heterodoxy". *Modern Language Association*, 123 no. 2 (March): 466–476.

Eddy Dufourmont
# The Imperial "Civil Religion" and *seikyō bunri:* The Historical Process of Secularization in Modern Japan, from the Perspective of "Confucianism" (1868–1945)

**Abstract:** Since most of the studies of secularism in Japan have focused on the shintō and the so-called "State shintō" of modern imperial Japan (1868–1945), the article will contribute on the debate in two ways: first by discussing the historicity of the secularism in Japan from the point of view of Jean Baubérot's theory, second by discussing the role of Confucianism in the formation of imperial ideology. To achieve this goal, the article will focus on the formation of the word seikyō bunri (separation between State and religion) as translation word for secularism, and discuss this process of translation at crossroads between European philosophy and Chinese thought. With their Confucian background, their emphasis on Imperial restaurationism and their interest to French laïcité, Japanese Statemen imagined a State shintô as "civil religion", while some of their Democrat opponents, with the same background and same interest to French secularism, had a complete different political agenda and were even atheists. The result of this process of circulation of the word secularism and of this political struggle was the establishment of a State shintō, which pretended to definite Japanese State by a shintoist cult of the emperor while proclaiming freedom of belief. Thus, the imperial period can be characterized as what Baubérot calls "closed pluralism" in the process of secularization.

## 1 Introduction: Confucianism and Secularization as a Historical Process in Japan

The question of secularization in modern Japan have been addressed by a large number of studies, mainly focusing on the history of State shintō and comparison between the juridical system of Postwar Japan and United States or the links

---

**Eddy Dufourmont** (University Bordeaux Montaigne)

https://doi.org/10.1515/9783110733068-009

between politics and religions.[1] This developing research focus has heightened the need to analyze the Japanese case in a global context. One example of such an approach is the recent special issue of *Japan Review* edited by Aike Tors and Mark Teuween, which draws on the theoretical contributions of Talal Asad to probe the universality of the categories "religion" and "secular" by delving into their genealogy and history (Rots and Teuween 2017). Similarly, Mark Mullins has pointed out the importance of studying secularism as a "homegrown" process (Mullins 2012: 61–82). Before this shift in approach, the historiography of religion and secularism in modern Japan could be characterized by two features: first, a special interest in Shinto and the question of State Shinto (*kokka Shintō*), sometimes even limited to the Yasukuni controversy;[2] and second, more recently, a growing tendency to discuss the concept of "religion" itself as invention.[3]

Many efforts have been made to clarify the sociocultural process of secularization in Japan. In Japanese the term used for secularism as doctrine is *sezokushugi* 世俗主義 and *sezokuka* 世俗化 for secularization. The legal and political aspect of the separation of state and religion—that is, secularism, in Japanese *seikyō bunri* 政教分離, which means literary "separation between politics and religion" and is much more used than *sezokushugi*. The French word *laïcité*—has received less attention. Most discussion in historical perspective has focused on State Shinto. We would like to contribute to the discussion on two points: analyzing the process of *seikyō bunri* from the point of view of French theory of secularism and from the point of view of Confucianism, which have been both largely ignored.

Concerning the first point, Mark Teuween and the contributors to the recent issue of the *Japan Review* did well to draw on the work of Talal Asad. But although they start with Asad and follow more recent studies that no longer consider secularity and secularism as Eurocentric terms, they don't pay attention to the few efforts specialists have made to discuss the Japanese case from the

---

[1] In Japan see as for recent examples Ōie 1984; Abe 1989; Asoya 1990; Tamakake and Minamoto 1992; Hirano 1995; Sugihara 2001; Kirigaya and Fujita 2001; Wada 2014; Among the recent works in English see Fitzgerald 2003; Reader 2012: 7–36; Trent 2014; Thomas 2019; Ernils 2020.
[2] The most important contributions include Sakamoto 1994; Shimazono 2010; Isomae 2016. In English, Hardacre 1989. See also Okuyama 2011: 123–146.
[3] In Japanese, Isomae 2002 and 2016; Shimazono and Tsuruoka 2004; Hoshino 2012; in English, Isomae 2005: 235–248; Josephson 2012.

French theoretical point of view, particularly studies by Shimazono Susumu, Jean Baubérot, myself, and Date Kiyonobu (in chronological order).[4]

Of the four studies mentioned above, Jean Baubérot's is the most theoretical. The other three follow Baubérot's theory for approaching secularism as a historical process in Japan, but they have their weak points. Date is a specialist of French secularism and his study, based mainly on secondary sources, is limited to contemporary Japan. Shimazono and myself recognized the potential value of using Baubérot's theory in the case of Japan, but Shimazono's discussion was too short and lacked references, while I centered my discussion on the presence of Islam in Japan.

More studies are therefore needed to tie the Japanese case into a global theory of secularism. This contribution intends to address this need by focusing on the modern period (1868–1945) and on Confucianism. The first reason for this choice is the importance of the translation process during the Meiji era, when the word "religion" came to Japan and the nation-state was organized. Second, in the recent evolution of historiography as described above, whereas much research has been done on Shinto, Christianity and Buddhism, Confucianism is still the "poor relation," with very few studies focusing on it.

Warren Smith wrote a pioneering but isolated work on the history of Confucianism in modern Japan in 1959 (Smith 1959). It was not until 2002 that a group of scholars pointed out of the lack of studies on this topic (Elman, Duncan, Ooms 2002). Since then, Kiri Paramore, Takeshi Kojima, Ogyū Shigehiro and myself have made contributions,[5] with some attempts to clarify how Confucianism has been perceived as religion or as ethics/philosophy in Modern Japan. In fact, most of the research on religious history in this period neglects the role of Confucianism in the modern religious history of Japan.[6] Citing Jean-Jacques Rousseau, Robert Bellah was the first to use the concept of "civil religion" in relation to Japan (and in comparison with the US); later, Ian Reader and Okuyama Michiaki did so too.[7] While discussing the possibility of using the concept of "civil religion" from the perspective of sociology of religions, all of them focused mainly on Shinto and did not really give space to Confucianism or follow a historical approach. As Helen Hardacre stated, the early Meiji leaders were, because

---

[4] Shimazono 2009: 71–78; Baubérot and Milot 2011: 203; Dufourmont 2011: 161–181; Date 2015: 169–188.

[5] As for books, by chronological order, Kojima 2008; Dufourmont, 2010 and 2014; Paramore 2016a.

[6] Recently, Shimazono Susumu recognized Confucianism, "a spiritual culture", as part of State Shintō (Shimazono 2016: 31–46).

[7] Bellah and Hammond 1980; Reader 1994; Okuyama 2012.

of their Confucian background, "mostly atheist, this-worldly mindset" and were prepared to some extent to establish a secular State (Hardacre 2018: 90).

For a better understanding of the formation of secularism in modern and contemporary Japan, attention must be paid to three points: taking into account the French theories on secularism while discussing the Japanese case; rounding out previous research by focusing on Confucianism; and, at the same time, considering the words used in research, such as Confucianism, as invention, as a historical process. The goal of the present study is to provide a combined response to these three needs and thereby contribute to the understanding of secularism in Japan as a historical process.

## 2 The Historicity of Japanese Secularity: Reconsidering the Imperial Period (1868–1945)

### 2.1 Applying Jean Baubérot's Theory of Secularism: Pre-Modern and Modern Japan as a Period of "Limited Pluralism" (1600–1945)

Before even trying discuss the question of secularism in Japan through case studies in Japanese history, one basic question must be answered: is it actually possible to use the concept of secularism as a lens for looking into Japanese history?

Foreign researches also discussed the paradigm of secularization as a historical process.[8] These researchers have tried to discuss the paradigm of secularization from a global perspective, covering the entire history of Japan, but without a definition based on the theoretical literature. Among them, Jean Baubérot's work seems especially relevant since he recently conceived a theory of secularization as a historical process applicable to any country in the world (Baubérot and Milot 2011). Baubérot takes the word *laïcité* not as a phenomenon of secularization specific to France, but as a global phenomenon of separation of state and religions that is arrived at in different ways.[9] He also defines secularization as

---

**8** Rocher 2007: 183–202; Berthon 2010: 13–51; Paramore 2012: 19–30; Krämer, 2015; Paramore, 2016b: 129–143;. Rots and Teeuwen 2017.
**9** Baubérot and Milot define their concept of *laïcité* as the separation of state and religions, freedom of conscience and religion, equality between all citizens, believers or not, and neutrality of the state, which guarantees the fundamental liberties and freedom of conscience and religion.

a non-linear historical process in which a society starts from a stage where secularism does not exist, and finally reaches a stage where secularism is established. According to Baubérot, three thresholds mark the main steps in this process, starting with a situation of non-existent secularism (Baubérot and Milot 2011: 204–205):

1) The first threshold sees the appearance of a struggle for secularism. The movement contests the main religion's exclusive domination of society and the state. It gives a place to free-thinkers and religious minorities. Pluralism appears but in a form that Baubérot calls "closed pluralism," limited to certain religious groups which are recognized as legitimate to the exclusion of others. Religion continues to play a central part in socialization as the main source of public morals.

2) The second threshold sees the establishment of a form of secularism, either as separation of religions and state or as "civil faith" (or a mix of both). Religion is marginalized as an institution while areligious institutions (like school) become dominant. Pluralism opens up to all religious and areligious groups, and socialization through religion becomes optional.

3) The third threshold belongs to the late modernity of present times, in which secularism is called into question. The need for religion is recognized not as a social institution but as a cultural resource with which individuals can define their own identity.

So can this theory be applied to the case of Japan? In fact, since Baubérot approaches secularism as a global phenomenon, he tries to use research on every country. He included the Japanese case in his theory with reference to only a few studies. This is of course very few. Baubérot nonetheless proposed to set the start of the first threshold in 1889 (Imperial constitution) and the transition to the second threshold in 1945; he does not deal with the third (Baubérot and Milot 2011: 213, 225). While Baubérot is not entirely wrong, I disagree with him in seeing 1889 as the start of the first threshold.

In Japan, the religious landscape was dominated by Buddhism and the beliefs existing prior to its arrival during the sixth and seventh centuries, usually designated with the word *shintō*, did not really exist independently from Buddhism. Before 1868, it was common for monks to perform "Shinto" rituals and even to give "Confucian" lectures. Deities were shared between Shinto and Buddhism and the temples were mixed. Sanctuaries and temples were also secular powers with land, money and armies. What most people know as *Shinto* 神道

---

They distinguish six ideal-types of secularism in history: separatist laicity, authoritarian laicity, anticlerical laicity, laicity of civil belief, laicity of recognition, and laicity of collaboration.

is a creation of late medieval times, largely inspired by Buddhism, before its recreation in the modern period.[10] Taoism and Confucianism coming from China had a very limited impact on Japanese society before 1603 since they remained largely unknown outside the imperial court. In this context, secularism before Tokugawa regime did not exist at all, on public sphere, and religion and state were not separated[11].

Yet the establishment of the Tokugawa dynasty, which unified Japan, introduced changes that Baubérot did not see. First, the Tokugawa dynasty gained the monopoly on violence and created a central state to entirely dominate society. This change coincided with the arrival of Christianity in Japan, a religion made especially alien to the Japanese by its monotheism and intolerance of other beliefs. For this reason, and also for political aims, the Tokugawa forbade Christianity and destroyed it by force and repression, in a process very similar to the Spanish government's policy against Muslim *Moriscos*. Some Christians remained hidden until the end of the ban in 1873. It has been said that Confucianism, which gained a new and considerable role in Japanese society, had quasi-official status in Tokugawa ideology. This should be qualified, however, since it was only in 1780 that the Tokugawa State really adopted such an attitude, and even then, the institutionalization of Confucianism was limited (Kurozumi Makoto, "Tokugawa Confucianism and Its Meiji Japan Reconstruction", in Elman et *alii* 2001: 370–397; Paramore 2016 a: 66, 104–108). Thus, this period can be described as one of "limited plurality," including Confucianism and Christianity alongside the dominant pair of Buddhism-Shinto.

At the same time, the Edo period saw profound changes in the intellectual landscape, with what can be considered as the first manifestations of freethinking after 1700. Andō Shōeki (1703–1762), Tominaga Nakamoto (1715–1746), and Yamagata Bantō (1748–1821) are well known examples of intellectuals who proposed the first conceptions of the world completely free from religious references (and critical of religion). Ogyū Sorai drew on Confucian thought to develop his own political philosophy, which was the first to be based completely on human actions and not on the Heavenly order. Kaiho Seiryō is another example

---

**10** Kuroda Toshio was one the first to challenge the image of Shinto as an essence and the "national faith" of Japan. Following on from him, historians such as John Breen and Mark Teuween did further researches to clarify the historical process of Shinto's creation (Teuween, Breen 2000; Id 2010).

**11** This statement is not shared by all historians, in particular Christoph Kleine (Kleine 2019: 9–45) and also his earlier works. Kleine points out in Buddhist thinkers of Heian period discourses emphasizing the interdependence of ruler's law and Buddha's law, in which he sees a secularity *avant la lettre*.

of inventive freethinking in this period (Ansart 2014). Such freethinking constitutes another argument for considering the Edo period, at least after 1700, as having reached Baubérot's first threshold in which secularization appears.

If the secularist movement first appeared during the Edo period after 1700, how we should consider the period of Imperial Japan? With regard to the second threshold, that is, the establishment of secularism, 1945 is a key date since it was only with the 1947 Constitution that freedom of belief and separation of state and religion were really established. As Baubérot correctly noted, the institution of freedom of belief along with the establishment of State Shinto in the constitution of 1889 shows that Japan was in a situation of limited plurality, which is peculiar to Baubérot's first period. We can therefore consider that the modern period between 1868–1945 in fact represents a continuation of the Edo period. If we accept that secularization appeared in the first half of the seventeenth century, then the first period characterized by limited plurality and the birth of freethinking would be 1600–1945. Of course, this raises the question of the years 1868–1945, the period in which Japan modernized and entered into relations with the outside world, especially Europe. Yet did the changes that began in 1853 really mean an evolution for "closed pluralism"?

## 2.2 Translating "Secularism": The Invention of Religion in Modern Japan and the European-Inspired Secularist Movement.

The words secularization and secularism themselves have a history. Before trying to think about secularism as a phenomenon with regard to the entire Japanese past, we should therefore consider it as a word that entered Japan at a particular moment with a particular history. This approach follows the theory of "cultural transfer" developed by historian Michel Espagne. From this perspective, ideas are not essences that cross the borders between countries through a natural and self-evident process. The spread of ideas is itself a problem that needs to be analyzed, with a focus on languages as the medium in which the propagation takes place. Therefore, the people of the countries in which new ideas are disseminated are not passive; they do not simply receive the ideas. Rather they acquire them and play an active role in introducing the ideas into their countries (Espagne 2013: 1–21). So if we apply this theory to the Japanese case, we must ask how secularism entered Japan and why. What is the history of secularism as the product of cultural transfer?

Answering these questions entails a focus on the beginning of modern Japan, especially the Meiji era (1868–1912), because it was the crucial period for translation, mainly from European languages, and the creation of new words.

The word "religion" entered Japan in the context of the diplomatic treaties of the 1850s. Because no word existed in Japanese that corresponded to the Euro-American concept of religion, several words appeared: *shū* 宗, *kyō* 教, and *ha* 派. These could designate Christianity, a certain Buddhist school, differences between Confucianism and Daoism, or differences between schools of painting or mathematics. Later on, the words *shūmon* 宗門, *shūshi* 宗旨 and *shūhō* 宗法 appeared, but these still designated one specific group within what we would call a religion. The word *shūkyō* 宗教 itself, which finally became the equivalent of "religion," was first used as synonym for Christianity, and the central place of Christianity in the translation of religion has been underlined in previous research (Suzuki 1979: 13–17).

However, the use of *shūkyō* was not limited to Christianity; far from it. In fact, many discourses tried to rethink their own traditions as religion, *shūkyō*, or as a philosophy, which was also a new word (*tetsugaku* 哲学). In both cases, the crucial concern was Japan's access to civilization (*bunmei* 文明). Thus, the definition of a school of thought as religion or as philosophy became increasingly important for securing a future in modern society. The first intellectuals to translate and introduce philosophy and law were also the first to discuss religion and to mention freedom of conscience and freedom of belief. Fukuzawa Yukichi, the very first to publish a book on European and American societies, mentioned the freedom of belief in the United Kingdom and presented it as one of the six conditions for "civilized politics." (Fukuzawa [1866] 1958, vol.1: 290–291) The Christian Nakamura Masanao translated John Stuart Mill's *On Liberty* (*Jiyū no ri*, 1872), in which Mill advocated a minimal state and described freedom of conscience as a right of the individual. Freedom of belief was a freedom of personal faith (Mill 1927: 18–19, 24–30). Another intellectual, Katō Hiroyuki, proposed a different perspective with the translation of Johann Bluntschli's *Allgemeines Staatsrecht* (*Kokuhō hanron*, 1872–1876), in which Bluntschli recognized a personal right of belief but also a collective free choice of belief for groups. Because of this, the state also had a right to interfere in religious matters to protect public order (Bluntschli 1874, vol. 9: *jō*). Both Nakamura and Katō belonged to the Meirokusha (Meiji 6 Society), an intellectual society formed by proponents of modernization. Meirokusha's journal, *Meiroku Zasshi*, published several articles in 1874 concerning the relations between the state and religions in the context of the movement for Shinto as the only religion of Japan (see *infra*). Nishi Amane maintained that politics and religion were two separate realms of activity and that the state should not have control over religions other than to protect public order.¹² Katō Hiroyuki argued the same, showing that in European history, the union of politics and religion had brought disorder.¹³ Another Christian member of Meirokusha, Mori Arinori, published a short text entitled *Religious Freedom in Japan* (1872) in the US, quoting Emer Vattel and Robert Phillimore; Mori also proposed combining freedom of belief with state intervention to define the public status of religion.¹⁴ Aside from these intellectuals, some religious figures also supported the separation of state and religions. The case of Buddhist monk Shimaji Mokurai, for example, has recently been discussed (Yamaguchi 2013; Kramer 2014).

The word "secularism," coined in English by Georg Jacob Holyoake (1817–1906) in 1851, was also translated into Japanese in the Meiji period. It first appeared in books published by the democrats involved in the Freedom and People's Rights Movement (Jiyū minken undō), which gave rise to the first political parties and represented the main opposition to the imperial government between 1874 and 1890. I have found no mention of *sezokushugi* (secularization) before 1945, but the word *sezoku* for "temporal" is used in one translation of *Liberty, Equality, Fraternity* (1873) by James Fitzjames Stephen (1829–1894).¹⁵ The expression *seikyō bunri* may have been inspired by the expression *shinbutsu bunri* (separation between *kami* and buddhas), used in the early 1870s to justify the annihilation of Buddhism and the establishment of Shinto as the official religion of Japan (see *infra*). As far as I can tell from my research, the term *seikyō bunri* was first used in 1883 in *On Republic* (*Kyōwa seitairon*), a translation of a book which is almost certainly *La République radicale* (1873) by Alfred Naquet (Naquet, 1883).¹⁶ This book has a chapter about "separation of religion and state" (whereas in French it is separation between the church and state).

The only other example of the use of *seikyō bunri* in the 1880s can be found in a book by Nakayama Seiji, a rural journalist and complete unknown, who wrote a few books on women and was one of the first to defend an equal place for women

---

**12** Nishi Amane, "Kyōmon ron", Meiroku zasshi, 4, 5, 6, 8, 9, 12 in Yamamuro 2008, vol. 1. See Trent 2014: 105–107 for a more detailed discussion.
**13** Katō Hiroyuki, "Beikoku seikyō", Meiroku zasshi, 6, in Yamamuro 2008, vol. 1.
**14** Mori Arinori, "Shūkyō", Meiroku zasshi, 6, in Yamamuro 2008, vol. 1.
**15** For example in the translation of the chapter "the distinction of the temporal and spiritual power" in Steven 1882: 207–220.
**16** The Japanese transcription of the name of the author is *Nekkeru Furê* 納炭爾布礼ネッケルフレー, which is close to the name Alfred Naquet. Moreover, the structure of the book is entirely similar to the French book and the biography of the author clearly matches Naquet's. Okunomiya Kenji was member of the Freedom and People's Rights Movement and close to Nakae Chōmin.

in society (Nakayama 1887).[17] Nakayama, who appears to have been a Protestant, wrote a chapter on *seikyō bunri*, explaining its history in Europe and taking position in favor of freedom of belief and nonintervention of the state in religious and philosophical matters. He seemed very well informed and even quoted a speech given on January 8, 1873 by the liberal Protestant Edmond de Pressensé at the French National Assembly.

One important figure of the *Jiyū minken undō* deserves a particular mention here: Nakae Chōmin (1847–1901). Chōmin is well known for having introduced Jean-Jacques Rousseau, the father of the notion of "civil religion," to Japan, but his role in the process of secularization in Japan goes far beyond that. Chōmin did not concentrate exclusively on Rousseau but translated many texts from the French by the founding fathers of the French Third Republic and *laïcité*: Jules Barni, Jules Simon, Etienne Vacherot, Charles Renouvier, Eugène Véron, Alfred Naquet and Alfred Fouillée. The texts Chōmin translated were directly critical of religion and openly atheist (Dufourmont 2018). At the same time, he tried to combine Mencius and Rousseau to promote democracy, without paying attention to the notion of "civil religion." Chōmin was also the author of the first materialist and atheist essay with *One Year and A Half. A Sequel* (1901). He might also have been the first Japanese to be buried without a religious funeral. Immediately after his death, *One Year and A Half. A Sequel* became the target of the established Academy led by the main ideologue of the imperial regime, Inoue Tetsujirō, and his fellows (Dufourmont 2010: 71–90).

Chōmin's disciple Kōtoku Shūsui became one of the fathers of Japanese socialism and anarchism. He is well known for having kept the interest in Mencius Confucianism and Taoism alive. Yet while this interest does not appear to have disappeared among Japanese liberals after Kōtoku's death, Marxist thought became the reference. In the communist movement against religions in the Taishō period, there are no more references to Confucianism.[18] As for the word *seikyō bunri*, the few books that use it prior to 1945 can be divided in two groups: first, academic works (Onozuka 1908: 64–95; Hara 1915: 72–73; Kōno 1928, vol. 2) and official documents[19] related to France and, second, some books published by Christians or Buddhists, two groups very involved in advocating the separation of state and religion (Hasū 1921).

Thus, the idea of separation of state and religions appeared early in modern Japan, thanks to the Freedom and People's Rights Movement, inspired by secu-

---

[17] Some details exist on him in Kimura 1985: 153.
[18] See for example Asano 1932.
[19] Monbushō shūkyōkyoku 1923; Gaimushō ōbeikyoku 1930.

larist France. However, although the secularist movement endured after 1890 through the leftist movements, it diverged from its original French inspiration with the creation of an imperial civil religion.

## 3 The Renewal of "Closed Pluralism": Confucianism as Part of the Imperial Civil Religion (1868–1945)

### 3.1 The Invention of Shinto and Japanese Confucianism and its Role in the Establishment of Religious Policy (1868–1912)

The government formed in 1868 attached a great deal of importance to religions as it organized a huge wave of reforms to modernize the country. Confucianism featured quite late in the religious policy-making process compared to Shinto and Buddhism. The main reason for this is that the word "Confucianism" (*jukyō*) was a creation of the Meiji period, developed along with Shinto. Let us first outline the religious policy of the Meiji government in its early years.

The men who took power in 1868, the oligarchs, came from a political movement whose goal was to reestablish the eighth-century imperial regime and expel the Europeans and Americans from Japan (*sonnō jōi*). In the early years of the Meiji era, under pressure from the most radical wing, the oligarchs had to accept a return to "unity of religion and government" (*saisei icchi*), which meant no separation between politics and religions. The radical wing felt strong enough to launch a movement for the eradication of Buddhism ("separation of kami and buddhas," *shinbutsu bunri*), in view of making Shinto Japan's sole and official religion. Yet the oligarchs quickly understood that this goal was incompatible with their priority of institutional modernization; to establish a European-style nation-state, they had to recognize the existing religious diversity. The failure of the *shinbutsu bunri* movement, which was never popular, combined with pressure from the European and American powers to end the ban on Christianity in 1873, precipitated this change in government policy.

The defeat of the *shinbutsu bunri* movement led the government to begin drafting its own religious policy, which was initially very close to the policy of the Tokugawa period. In March 1872, the Department of Divinities merged with the Office of Shrines and Temples of the Ministry of Civil Affairs to become the Ministry of Religion (Kyōbushō). The ministry established an Institute of the Great Teaching (Daikyōin) in order to enlist monks and priests as public servants and to spread a morality of veneration for the kami and the country, moral teaching, and veneration of the emperor. This policy also came in response to the need for modernization and to European and American pressure to open up; in February 1873, the ban on Christianity was lifted and women were allowed to enter temples and shrines. The Kyōbushō was dismantled in January 1877 and replaced by an Office of Shrines and Temples (Shajikyoku) in the Home Ministry (Naimushō), which ignored Christianity, despite the end of the ban. The dismantlement of the Kyōbushō inscribed the "separation of rule and doctrine" (*seikyō bunri*) to complete the separation of rite and doctrine (*saikyō bunri*), which itself replaced the *saisei icchi* (Trent 2014: 136).

In the 1880s, the main contributor to the drafting of the 1889 constitution, Inoue Kowashi (1844–1895), devised a division of Shinto. Following Inoue's suggestion, the government separated the main shrines linked historically with the imperial family (such as the Ise shrine) from the other shrines and religious groups, defined as "Sect Shintō" (*shūha Shintō*). The main shrines became the body of "State Shintō" (*kokka Shintō*), which would be the civil religion of Japan and the expression of Japanese identity. Every Japanese was required to follow State Shinto regardless of his or her religious affiliation, precisely because, according to the government, State Shinto was a set of civil rituals and not a religion.

State Shinto was the product of efforts in the 1880s to combine moderate loyalty to the *sonnō jōi* ideal of a theocratic regime and the reality of a modern nation-state. It was first established by the 1889 constitution, in which the emperor was defined as the descendant of a divine and continuous dynasty (article 1), and a sacred figure (article 3), while freedom of belief was guaranteed (article 28). Shinto was the most obvious component of the imperial ideology but was, in fact, only half of it. Confucianism constituted the other half. The only way to compel the Japanese to believe in the emperor and his regime was to define the latter as a "State-family" (*kazoku kokka*) and draw on Confucianism for the appropriate moral values, as evidenced by the presence of loyalty (*chū*) and filial piety (*kō*) in the *Rescript on Education*, the main text of Imperial ideology. The emperor's tutor Motoda Nagazane is well known for having promoted Confucianism (Numata 2005) but he was not alone.

Inoue Kowashi himself showed a great interest in Confucianism and in French religious policy. The years he spent drafting the Japanese constitution coincided with the adoption of the first secular laws in France, and Inoue agreed with the idea of separating state and religion. The keywords of this time were "civilization and enlightenment" (*bunmei kaika*). This fostered Inoue's anti-religious and, especially, anti-Christian stance. He considered Confucianism a philosophy, and superior to Christianity because of its rationality. This interpretation of Confucianism derived in part from European translators such as James Legge and Guillaume Pauthier (1801–1873), and in part from the discourse of Inoue's fellow intellectuals and public officials Nishi Amane and Katō Hiroyuki, who defended the idea of Confucianism as equivalent to European philosophy (Saitō 2006: 31–52). Inoue read with interest the works of Emile Acollas, a French law professor and republican who taught Nakae Chōmin (Saitō 2006: 175).

Thus, Inoue aimed to use philosophy rather than religion as vehicle for patriotism. That is why he developed State Shinto as separate from Sect Shinto—the emperor would be only a moral symbol and State Shinto combined with Confucianism would form the civil religion of Japan. Inoue's project was typical of the first half the Meiji period because at that time, the main concern of the Japanese government and intellectuals was civilization. The government was supported by a group of intellectuals who were among the first to be trained in modern academic scholarship and were also public officials. As advocates of positivism and scientism, they were critical of religion. Watanabe Hiroshi even saw the intention of the Meiji political leaders to establish a religious policy as a "plot" (Watanabe 2005: 373–413).

Thus, the policy Inoue designed was possible because a secularist movement existed among the political leaders and the intellectuals close to them. Most of those who advocated keeping a place for Confucianism in imperial Japan did so by linking Confucianism with the imperial ideology, not necessarily as a heritage that should be preserved, but rather as part of a new ideology that should overcome religion to make the Japanese into good and loyal subjects of the emperor. Katō Hiroyuki introduced the materialist theories of Spencer and Haeckel, which led him to see religions as pure superstition. Tsuda Mamichi shared Katō's materialism. Nishimura Shigeki (1828–1902) proposed in *Dōtokuron* to create a new morality from a mix of reinterpreted Confucianism and Western philosophy. He established the Society for the Study of Moral Cultivation (Shūshin gakusha, later Society for the Expansion of the Imperial Way, Nihon Kōdōha).[20]

The main contributor to the establishment of imperial ideology was Inoue Tetsujirō (1856–1944), one of Japan's first philosophers educated according to European academic tradition. He also played a major role in the invention of Japanese Confucianism. The commentary Inoue wrote on the Rescript on Education

---

[20] Funayama. 1957: 172–242. Warren Smith indicates that some obscure organizations, such like the Daidōkan (Pavillon of the Great Unity), the Rongokai (Analects society), and the Kōshikyōkai (Society of the Teaching of Confucius), tried to promote Confucianism in the 1880s with little success (Smith 1959: 67–68).

(*Chokugo engi*, 1891) became quasi-official. Later he published historical works to show that Japanese Confucianism existed as a continuous school,[21] as well as books defending the imperial regime and bushido as a central part of Japanese identity.[22] In these books, Inoue did not seek simply to use the Confucian values of Zhu Xi's orthodoxy, but rather aimed to take elements from Confucianism and from other religions to make the imperial ideology into the civil religion of Japan, a new morality suited to contemporary times. Inoue developed this discourse in many books until his death in 1944, the best known of which is *Kokumin dōtoku gairon* (Outline of National Morality, 1912).

The intellectuals close to the government were not alone in using Confucianism as part of the imperial ideology. For example, Uchida Tadashi, a marginal and largely forgotten figure, developed interesting views on Confucianism as part of a necessary civil religion. For Uchida, the ideal of Confucianism was high morals and politics, not religion (Uchida 1909: 7). He saw religion as a system of superstition and fears that can be used to control people, without any consideration for the character (*jinkaku*) of the individual (Uchida 1909: 10). Christianity and Buddhism originated at a time when the state and society were not well organized and were therefore religion for "stupid people" (*gumin*). In contrast, Confucianism arose when the state and society were organized and was propagated by the elite classes, giving them a model of wisdom and instilling the ideal of service to the state. Buddhism was overly centered on the inner world and Christianity on the outer world, while Confucianism was concerned with both. Confucianism was scientific and practical, focused on this world and not, as religions are, on the afterworld (Uchida 1909: 25, 11). At a time when civilization was advancing but religious education was still poisoning minds, Confucianism represented the future. Uchida took French secularism (*seikyō bunri*) as an example. In his view, the goals of French *laïcité* and Confucianism were exactly the same (Uchida 1909: 18). Uchida seems to share a very similar position to Nakae Chōmin's but, like Inoue Kowashi, the inspiration he took from Republican France did not end in democratic demands. Uchida disliked individualism and wanted every Japanese

---

**21** These works are Nihon Yōmeigaku no tetsugaku (Philosophy of Japanese school of Wang Yangming, 1900), Nihon kogaku no tetsugaku (Philosophy of Japanese school of Ancient Studies, 1902), Nihon Shushi gakuha no tetsugaku (Philosophy of Japanese school of Zhu Xi, 1905).
**22** The most famous of these is An Outline of National Morality (*Kokumin dōtoku gairon*), published in 1912. Inoue repeated the ideas expressed in this book throughout his life, for example in Our National Essence and Our Morality (*Waga kokutai to kokumin dōtoku*, 1925) and The Essence of Japanese Spirit (*Nihon seishin no honshitsu*, 1934).

subject to serve the state. In Shinto he saw authoritarianism; in Buddhism and Christianity he saw individualism, globalism and socialism (Uchida 1909: 24).[23]

These few examples show that Confucianism defined as philosophy and not religion helped the government and its supporters to imagine the division of Shinto between State Shinto and Sect Shinto, with the former defined as the civil religion of Japan. After 1912, Confucianism became even more necessary to achieving this goal.

## 3.2 The Use of Confucianism in the State's Increasing Control of Religion (1912–1945)

The second part of the Imperial period saw an increasing use of religions by the state, which reached a climax during the fascist era. The Japanese government's religious policy between 1912 and 1945 was dominated by two topics: first, the need for a comprehensive law on religion and, second, the need to harness religions within the imperial ideology as a means to counter a growing attraction to socialism and communism among the Japanese. A Confucian lobby was formed in support of the official ideology, and Confucianism played an important role in renewing the imperial ideology, perhaps even more so than Shinto.

As Ogawara Masamichi has shown, behind the creation of the Office of Shrines and Temples in 1877 and the promulgation of the 1889 constitution was the state's constant difficulty in establishing a stable legal framework for religions until 1945 (Ogawara 2013). The first attempt to establish a comprehensive law in 1899 was unsuccessful. After two more failures, a law on religious organizations (*shūkyō dantaihō*) was finally promulgated in 1939. The first attempt failed because Buddhist organizations were loath to be equal in rank to their Christian counterparts. In fact, the government introduced the content of the 1899 bill into the Public Order and Police law of 1900 (*Chi.an keisatsu hō*) to provide a legal framework for controlling the activities of religious organizations—especially Christian ones. Even with freedom of belief guaranteed by the 1889 constitution, it was not until 1900 that the Home Ministry recognized Christianity as equal to Sect Shinto and Buddhism in the public sphere.[24] The same year, the

---

[23] This political stance is surprising, especially since in another text, Uchida saw common points between Confucianism and Kant, as did Chōmin (Uchida 1914: 13–17).
[24] Freedom of belief was guaranteed to foreigners living in Japan when trade treaties were signed with the United Kingdom in 1894 and with the other European and American countries the following years.

Office of Shrines and Temples was split in two: an office of shrines (Jinjakyoku) for State Shinto and an office of religions (Shūkyōkyoku) for religious Shinto and other religions.[25] Confucianism was not included in the "religion" category.

The Public Order Law of 1900 was also an instrument to combat the first leftist movements, which emerged at the same time; Kōtoku Shūsui, and Sakai Toshihiko created the first Socialist party in 1906. In 1912, the year following Kōtoku's execution, the home minister Tokonami Takejirō called on the leaders of Buddhist, Sect Shinto and Christian organizations (sankyō kaidō) for support against the growing socialist movement. In 1913, the Office of Religion was placed under the jurisdiction of the Ministry of Education, because the government's goal was to strengthen the link between education (kyōiku) and moral suasion (kyōka) (Suzuki 1979; Ogawara 2013). Indeed, this measure had the effect of heightening the implication of moral suasion movements, in which religious organizations collaborated energetically (see infra).

Fears for the future of the imperial regime increased with the end of World War I and the Treaty of Versailles. In 1919 in Korea, a huge demonstration for independence showed that the savage repression during the 1910s had not put to an end the resistance of the Korean people. In China, the May Fourth Movement turned into a manifestation of Chinese nationalism against Japan as well as Confucianism. At the same time in Japan, it was clear that the repression of the first socialists had failed because social conflicts continued to grow during the 1910s and beyond with the development of anarchism and communism. Of course, the success of the Bolshevik revolution in Russia in 1917 signified to the Japanese government that their most feared threat—socialism—might now find foreign support to overcome the imperial throne. Hence the Japanese government, even while dominated by political parties after 1918 due to a new wave of liberalism, kept up intense repression of communists throughout the 1920s (Dōkan kōkai 1933: 382–384). The annihilation of the left-wing movement and its anti-religious discourse in the 1930s was not really something new.

The nervousness of the political elite can be seen in the many attempts to promulgate a comprehensive law on religious organizations. The second attempt, in 1927, aimed to provide a legal framework for the participation of existing religious organizations in the kyōka movement (see below). It was also a response to the rise of "dangerous thought" (that is, socialism and communism) and of new sects such as Ōmotokyō, whose message was considered contradictory to ko-

---

[25] With the imperial decree on the public funding of sanctuaries, in 1906, a movement of fusion of sanctuaries (on the basis of one sanctuary per village) started and implicated the disappearing of 80% sanctuaries of the country.

*kutai*, the national essence symbolized by the imperial family. This attempt failed because the Shinto, Buddhist and Christian organizations protested against the possibility the bill gave the state to destroy religious organizations, without compensation, whenever it judged necessary. The third attempt came in 1929 and was led by the main opponent to the second, Andō Masamune. The goal was still to link religious organizations with the need for *kyōka* but with less ambition to control the organizations. The attempt failed because of the Tanaka cabinet's resignation following the murder of Chinese warlord Zhang Zuolin by an officer. The final attempt in 1939, during the fascist era, was successful because the law became part of the general mobilization for the "holy war" (*seisen*) launched by the army. An Institute of Divinities (Jingiin) was created as the restoration of the Jingikan in 1940, which was the year of the so-called 2,600$^{th}$ anniversary of the country's founding by the (fictitious) first emperor.

The use of Confucianism to renew the imperial civil religion increased after 1918. In that year, the government created an Extraordinary Council on Education (Rinji kyōiku kaigi) made up of high-ranking bureaucrats to develop the use of Chinese studies for the "defense of bushido and the Japanese spirit" against "dangerous thought" (i.e., communism). The council supported the sinologists Makino Kenjirō (1862–1937) and Matsudaira Yasukuni (1863–1945) in forming the Movement for the Promotion of Chinese Studies (Kangaku shinkō undō). As part of the promotion of Chinese studies, the Diet encouraged the creation of the Association of the Greater Eastern Culture (Daitō bunka kyōkai), which led to the establishment of Daitō Bunka Gakuin University in 1923. Inoue Tetsujirō and many other important political figures belonged to this association (Daitō bunka 1924: 180).

The Taishō period, also known as "Taishō democracy," saw a new wave of discourse and practices on Confucianism as part of the imperial civil religion. Inoue Tetsujirō continued to publish books on national morals but other authors began to follow suit. Among them was Inoue's son-in-law Yoshida Kumaji (1874–1964), who stressed the importance of Confucianism for the imperial ideology. In his view, although Confucianism in China never explicitly specified the concept of "national morals" and the moral teaching of Confucius was appropriate to Chinese antiquity, Confucianism had the potential to develop national morals because of its emphasis on daily life and its concern for the state and the family. The transfer of Confucian ideas to Japan was an opportunity to realize its potential as a civil religion (Yoshida 1918: 24–36).

The Japanese government also developed or encouraged new practices to promote the imperial ideology: the moral suasion campaigns (*kyōka undō*). These were run partly under direct governmental control and partly through civil organizations. *Kyōka* is a Confucian word meaning "moral education [of the people]." Sheldon Garon has conducted a detailed study of the moral suasion campaigns, which began in 1919 with the Campaign to Foster National Strength (minryoku kan.yō undō) focused on encouraging the public to worship at State Shinto shrines and suppressing the habits of luxury and self-indulgence. The campaign reached a climax in the aftermath of the Great Earthquake of Kantō in 1923, but its goal went far beyond the reconstruction of Japan. The aim was to promote work, austerity, and respect for Confucian familial values, under the slogan "rationalization of daily life" (*seikatsu no gōrika*). In 1928 the Ministry of the Imperial Household spearheaded the creation of a Central Federation of *Kyōka* Organizations (Chūō kyōka dantai rengōkai), which ran a moral suasion mobilization campaign (kyōka dōin undō) in 1929–1930 (Garon 1997).

Another manifestation of the growing Confucian lobby during this period was the Shibunkai (Society of Our Way), launched in 1919 by businessman Shibusawa Eiichi with the support of senior officials. An earlier attempt to reorganize Confucianism in Japan was the Academic Society of Our Way (Shibun Gakkai, 1880), which became quickly inactive. The Society for the Ceremony in Honor of Confucius (Kōshi Saitenkai), formed in 1907 by Miyake Yonekichi, Kanō Jigorō and other teachers from Tokyo Higher Normal School, immediately received official support from Inoue Tetsujirō, the Imperial household and officials (Shibunkai 1929: 305). Kōshi Saitenkai reinstituted the religious rite honoring Confucius (*sekiten*) the same year. The Society merged with other small organizations to establish Shibunkai as a recreation of the Shibun Gakkai.

The Shibunkai's official goal was the promotion of Confucianism. Its main activities included organizing Confucius festivals (Kōshi-sai), staging public conferences, and publishing a journal called *Shibun*. When the Great Kantō Earthquake of 1923 destroyed the Yushima Seidō, a Confucian temple built in the seventeenth century to house Hayashi Razan's (1583–1657) private academy, the Shibunkai launched a campaign to collect donations for its reconstruction, which was completed in 1935. In turn, the government entrusted the Shibunkai with managing the Yushima Seidō.

Behind this official goal, the texts published in *Shibun* when the Shibunkai was first formed clearly reveal the society's ideological role. The leaders of Shibunkai exalted the role of Confucianism in Japanese history and considered that "The holy meaning of the Rescript on Education should be clarified with the help of Confucianism." They added: "Our nation has made great progress and developed the facilities for daily life well, but the beliefs of the past have become superficial. To add to these signs of trouble, there are people who sometimes want to trouble the intellectual world with extremist ideas, loving the new and hating the old. This is what the scholars should be worried about." (Shibunkai 1919) As Warren Smith has shown, the Shibunkai also worked in the 1930s to legitimate the Japanese invasion of Manchuria and the creation of the Manzhuguo puppet state (Smith 1959: 184–199). In Korea too, the government encouraged Confucianism in order to steer Koreans away from communism and independence, with the support of the Shibunkai.

Another figure of the Confucian lobby was the Pan-Asianist Yasuoka Masahiro (1898–1983) (Dufourmont 2014). Yasuoka felt that the development of democracy and the appeal of communism in Japan, added to growing nationalism in China, were the signs of a crisis. He wanted to take action against the democrat Yoshino Sakuzō and the May Fourth Movement. Yasuoka developed a philosophy based on a mix of European personalism and Wang Yangming's Confucianism. With it, Yasuoka hoped both to propose an ethics for every Japanese individual and to make Confucianism a tool for *kyōka* and a "cultural weapon" (*bunbatsu*) for the "thought war" (*shisōsen*). Yasuoka developed a "Confucian personalism," a moral discourse for everyday life with a Confucian definition of values for every individual—values in accordance with the imperial and authoritarian ideology of the State-family.

Yasuoka's concern for the future of Confucianism was deeply linked to his worries for the future of the imperial throne. These worries, which arose following WWI, were compounded after 1945 by the popularity of the Communist Party. We use the word philosophy here but, in fact, Yasuoka made no real distinction between philosophy and religion. He used concepts of European philosophy to interpret Wang Yangming's Confucianism and, at the same time, he explained that Wang Yangming had drawn on the best of Taoism and Buddhism, which made his thought the essence of "Oriental philosophy." Yasuoka saw no contradiction in uniting Confucianism and Shinto and making them the two wings of the Japanese spirit. Employing Confucianism in the *kyōka* discourse was a way to make Confucianism the civil religion of Japan. Confucianism provided the ethical message that Yasuoka was unable to find in Shinto. In other words, Yasuoka contributed to the imperial civil religion that Inoue Tetsujirō had created by formulating his own blend of Confucianism and European philosophy.

After 1930, the imperial regime became increasingly intolerant and started repressing all opposition. Yasuoka himself led a group of bureaucrats who, when the prime minister was murdered in 1932, seized the opportunity to control the Saitō and Okada cabinets between 1932 and 1936. These cabinets stepped up the repression of leftists that had started in the late 1920s. The movement for the "clarification of national essence" (*kokutai meichō undō*) was started in 1935 to counter the liberal interpretation of the Meiji constitution. Thus, the years 1932–1936 saw the rise of fascism and the appearance of a "Confucian fascism" with the creation of the Association for the Propagation of Japanese Confucianism (Nihon jukyō sen.yō kai) in 1934. This organization's goal was to provide

Confucian arguments to justify Japanese expansionism and occupation of Asia (Paramore 2016 a: 157–158.).

This trend culminated with the drafting of *Kokutai no hongi* (The true meaning of national essence) by the Ministry of Education in March 1937, the first official text on the topic since the *Rescript on Education*. The book was widely circulated in schools and throughout society. In it, the authors (most of them scholars from the imperial universities) reformulated the imperial ideology by defining Japanese identity from the perspective of a philosophy of history. Confucianism had its place alongside Shinto and Buddhism in the "three teachings" (*sankyō*) that gave body to the "Japanese spirit." (Monbushō 1937: 48–52, 78, 123)

Thus, the role of Confucianism in the imperial civil religion increased dramatically due to the elites' fear of Marxism and, at the same time, the increasing numbers of people involved in promoting Confucianism to serve the regime. Therefore, the defeat of 1945 signified a double death for Japanese Confucianism: first, Confucianism lost its ideological role with the withdrawal of the *Rescript on Education* just as Shinto lost its role with the destruction of State Shinto. Second, the Japanese became free from any ethical model imposed from above with the decline of discourse on bushido and moral teaching in classes. Confucianism appeared more and more representative of the feudal past.

# 4 Conclusion: the Question of the Survival of Civil Religion in Postwar Japan

The imperial regime developed an ideology of the Family-State in order to justify its own existence and its control over society. State Shinto played a central role in this ideology, but Shinto alone was not enough to establish the civil religion its fathers had dreamed of in the 1880s, even when reframed as the indigenous religion of Japan. Confucianism was also necessary, precisely because Confucianism was perceived as a religion without God and churches, suited to the goal of civilization and close to the French model that inspired Inoue Kowashi. This alliance between Shinto and Confucianism existed until 1945 and even strengthened after 1918, since the government was increasingly afraid of Communism and any other opposition, both while political parties dominated and even more so during the domination by the army.

Thus, it is clear that modern Japan was dominated by a "closed pluralism," in which freedom of belief was recognized even as the civil religion made up of Confucianism and Shinto was imposed on every Japanese. Therefore, we can conclude that the theory of secularization developed by Jean Baubérot and Millot can be applied to Japan, with a transition to true pluralism in 1945 and not 1889 as they proposed. The process of secularization in Japan was undeniably a homegrown process in which the import of words was not a passive phenomenon. Secularization was interpreted early on as a separation (*bunri*). That is why the democratic state that was established with the constitution of 1947 clearly made a separation between the state and religions and not an association. Articles 20 and 89 recognize the freedom of conscience (contrary to 1889) and of religion, prohibit religious organizations from receiving money from the state and also forbid them any political activities. Despite this democratic turn, the civil religion of imperial Japan lasted a long time after 1945, since conservative governments, businessmen and associations (including people like Yasuoka Masahiro, active until his death in 1983) kept the need for *kyōka* on their agenda and tried successfully to recreate some of the symbols of State Shinto, for instance February 11 as National Foundation Day.

# References

Abe Yoshiya. 1989. *Seiyō bunri: Nihon to Amerika ni miru shūkyō no seijisei*. Saimaru shuppankai.
Ansart, Olivier. 2014. *L'Empire des rites, Une modernité indigène: Ruptures et innovations dans les théories politiques japonaises du XVIII$^e$ siècle*. Les Belles Lettres.
Asano Kenshin. 1932. *Mushinron to han shukyō undō*. Yuhikaku.
Asoya Masahiko. 1990. *Tennō no matsuri to seikyō bunri*. Tentensha.
Baubérot, Jean and Milot Micheline. 2011. *Laïcités sans frontières*. Seuil.
Bellah, Robert and Hammond Philipp. 1980. *Varieties of Civil Religion*. San Francisco, CA: Harper and Row.
Berthon, Jean-Pierre. 2010. "Une sécularité ancienne, une laïcité récente : l'exemple du Japon "., in Frank Laffaille (dir.), Laïcité(s), Paris : Éditions Mare et Martin, 2010, p. 13–51.
Bluntschli, Johann and Katō Hirokyuki, translators. 1874. *Kokuhō hanron*, Monbushō.
Dōkan kōkai. 1933. *Egi Kazuyuki ō keirekidan*.
Date Kiyonobu. 2015. "De la laïcité de séparation à la laïcité de reconnaissance au Japon ?" in Jean Baubérot, Micheline Milot, Philippe Portier, *Laïcité, laïcités. Reconfigurations et nouveaux défis*, pp. 169–188. Presses de la Maison des sciences de l'homme.
Dufourmont Eddy. 2018. *Rousseau au Japon. Nakae Chōmin et le républicanisme français (1874–1890)*. Presses Universitaires de Bordeaux, 2018.
Dufourmont Eddy. 2014. *Confucianisme et conservatisme. La trajectoire intellectuelle de Yasuoka Masahiro (1898–1983)*. Presses Universitaires de Bordeaux.
Dufourmont Eddy. 2011. "Une perspective historique sur le développement de la communauté musulmane du Japon, à l'aune du processus de laïcisation et de sécularisation". In Amin Elias, Augustin Jomier, Anaïs-Trissa Khatchadourian eds., *Laïcités et musulmans, débats et expériences (XIX–XX$^e$ siècles)*, pp. 161–181. Peter Lang.

Dufourmont Eddy. 2010. "Is Confucianism a philosophy? The answer of Nakae Chōmin and Inoue Tetsujirō". In Nakajima Takahiro, ed., *Whither Japanese Philosophy 2? Reflections through Other Eyes*, pp. 71–90. Tokyo, UTCP.

Elman, Benjamin, JohnDuncan, and Herman Ooms, eds. 2002. *Rethinking Confucianism: Past and Present in China, Japan, Korea and Vietnam*. University of California Press.

Ernils, Larsson. 2020. "Rituals of a Secular Nation: Shinto Normativity and the Separation of Religion and State in Postwar Japan". PHD thesis, University of Uppsala.

Espagne, Michel. 2013. "La notion de transfert culturel". *Revue Sciences/Lettres* 1 : 1–21.

Fitzerald, Timothy. 2003. "'Religion' and 'the Secular' in Japan. Problems in history, social anthropology, and the study of religion". *Electronic Journal of Contemporary Japanese studies*.

Fukuzawa Yukichi. [1866] 1958. Seiyō jijō in Keiō gijuku ed., *Fukuzawa Yukichi zenshū*. Iwanami shoten.

Funayama Shin.ichi. 1957. *Meiji tetsugaku shi*. Mineruba shobō.

*Gaimushō ōbeikyoku*. Tōhō shokoku, 1930.

Garon, Sheldon. 1997. *Molding Japanese Minds: The State in Everyday Life*. Princeton University Press.

Hara, Katsurō. 1915. *Ōbei saikinseshi jūkō*. Kōdōkan.

Hardacre, Helen. 1989. *Shintō and the State, 1868–1988*. Princeton University Press.

Hardacre, Helen. 2018. "The Formation of Secularism in Japan". In John Madeley, Mirjam Künkler, and Shylashri Shankar ed., *A Secular Age beyond the West: Religion, Law and the State in Asia, the Middle East and North Africa*, pp. 86–107. Cambridge, Cambridge University Press.

Hasū, Kanzen. 1921. *Shūkyō hō kenkyū*. Chūō bukkyōsha.

Hirano, Takeshi. 1995. *Seikyō bunri saiban to Kokka shintō*. Hōritsu bunkasha, 1995.

Hoshino Seiji. 2012. *Kindai Nihon no shūkyō gainen: shūkyōsha no kotoba to kindai*. Yūshisha Press.

Isomae, Jun.ichi. 2002. "Kindai ni okeru shūkyō gainen no keisei katei". In Komori Yōichi et alii eds., *Kindai chi no seiritsu*. Iwanami shoten.

Isomae, Jun.ichi. 2005. "Deconstructing 'Japanese Religion': A Historical Survey". *Japanese Journal of Religious Studies* 32 no. 2: 235–248.

Isomae, Jun.ichi. 2016. *Kindai Nihon no shūkyō gensetsu to sono keifu: shūkyō, kokka, shintō*. Iwanami shoten.

Jolyon, Baraka Thomas. 2019. *Faking Liberties: Religious Freedom in American-Occupied Japan*. University of Chicago Press.

Josephson, Jason Ananda. 2012. *The Invention of Religion in Japan*. University of Chicago Press.

Kimura Hiromi. 1985. "Iwamoto Yoshiharu no Joshi kyōiku shisō. Kindai teki katei teki hattatsu", *Shōhoku tankidaigaku* 52 no. 2: 153–162.

Kirigaya, Akira and Fujita, Hisanori ed. 2001. *Seikyō bunri to nichibei hikaku*, Daisanbunmeisha.

Kleine, Christoph. 2019. "Formations of Secularity in Ancient Japan? On Cultural Encounters, Critical Junctures, and Path-Dependent Processes". *Journal of Religion in Japan*.8 no.1–3: 9–45.

Kojima, Tsuyoshi. 2006, *Kindai Nihon no Yōmeigaku*. Tokyo: Kōdansha, 2006.

Kōno, Genzō. 1928. *Seiyō rekishi kōgi*. Konshi hōryūdō.

Krämer, Hans Martin. 2015. *Shimaji Mokurai and the Reconception of Religion and the Secular in Modern Japan*. Honolulu, HI: Hawai'i University Press.
Mill, John Stuart and Nakamura, Masanao translator. [1872] 1927. Jiyū no ri in Yoshino Sakuzō ed., *Meiji bunka zenshū*, vol.5 (jiyū minken hen). Nihon hyōronsha.
Monbushō. 1937. *Kokutai no hongi*. Monbushō.
Monbushō shūkyōkyoku. 1923. *Futsukoku seikyō bunri hō*. Monbushō shūkyōkyoku.
Mullins, Mark. 2012. "Secularization, deprivatization and the reappearance of 'public religion' in Japanese society". *Journal of Religion in Japan* 1: 61–82.
Nakayama, Seiji. 1887. *Nihon shūkyō iji kakuron*. Kushundō.
Naquet, Alfred and Okunomiya, Kenji translator. 1883. *Kyōwa seitairon*. Seiji shoin.
Numata, Tetsu. 2005. *Motoda Nagazane to Meiji kokka*. Meiji hoshushugi to Jukyō teki risōshugi, Yoshikawa kōbunkan.
Ogawara, Masamichi. 2013. "Seiji ni yoru shūkyō riyō, haijo. Kindai Nihon ni okeru shūkyō dantai no hūjinka wo megutte". *Nenpô seijigaku*, 1: 145–167.
Ogyū, Shigehiro. 2008. *Kindai, Ajia,*. Yōmeigaku, Perikansha.
Ōie, Shigeo ed. 1984. *Seikyō bunri: shinkyō no jiyū*. daiichi shobō.
Okuyama, Michiaki. 2012. "'Civil religion' in Japan? Rethinking the arguments and their implications". *Religious studies in Japan* 1: 61–67.
Okuyama, Michiaki. 2011. "'State Shintō' in Recent Japanese Scholarship". *Monumenta nipponica* 66 no. 1:123–146.
Onozuka, Kiheiji. 1908. *Ōshū gendai rikken seikyō ippan*. Hakubunkan.
Paramore, Kiri. 2012. "Political Modernity and Secularization: Thoughts from the Japanese Eighteenth and Nineteenth Centuries". *Journal of religious history*, 36 no. 1: 19–30.
Paramore, Kiri. 2016a. *Japanese Confucianism, a cultural history*, Cambridge University Press.
Paramore, Kiri. 2016b. "Religion, secularism and the Japanese Shaping of East Asian studies.". In Kiri Paramore, ed., *Religion and orientalism in Asian Studies*, pp. 129–143. Bloomsbury.
Reader, Ian. 1994. "Civil religion in contemporary Japan". *Copenhagen Journal of Asian Studies*, 9: 6–31.
Reader, Ian. 2012. "Secularization R.I.P? Nonsense! "The rush hour away from the Gods" and the decline of religion in contemporary Japan". *Journal of Religion in Japan* 1: 7–36.
Rocher, Alain. 2007. "Laïcisation et culture religieuse au Japon: les limites d'un concept". In Pierre Singaravelou dir., *Laïcité: enjeux et pratiques*, pp. 183–202. Pessac: Presses Universitaires de Bordeaux.
Rots, Aike and Mark Teuween, eds. 2017. "Formations of the Secular in Japan." *Japan Review* 30: 3–20.
Saitō, Tomoo. 2006. *Inoue Kowashi to shūkyō*. Meiji kokka keisei to sezokushugi, Kōbundō.
Sakamoto, Koremaru. 1994. *Kokka shintō keisei katei no kenkyū*. Iwanami shoten.
Shibunkai, "Shibunkai shuisho" (September 1918), *Shibun* 1 (February 1919): unnumbered page.
Shibunkai *Shibun rokujūnenshi*. 1929.
Shimazono, Susumu and Yoshio Tsuruoka. 2004. *Shūkyō saikō*. Perikansha.
Shimazono, Susumu. 2009. "La Laïcisation et la notion de religion au Japon." In Haneda Masahi ed., *Sécularizations et laïcités*, pp. 71–78. UTCP Booklet.
Shimazono, Susumu. 2010. *Kokka shintō to Nihonjin*. Iwanami shoten.

Shimazono, Susumu. 2016. "Religion and Public Space in Contemporary Japan: Re-activation of the Civilization of the Axial Age and the Manifestation of State Shintō and Buddhism". In Christoph Bochinger and Jörg Rüpke eds., *Dynamics of Religion*, pp. 31–46. Berlin: De Gruyter,.
Steven ? and Kobayashi Eiji trans. 1882. Jiyū byōdōron, Jiyū shuppan kaisha.
Sugihara, Seishirō. 2001. *Nihon no shintō, bukkyō to seikyō bunri*. Soshite shūkyō kyōiku, Bunka shobō hakubunsha.
Suzuki, Minako. 1979. "Kindai Nihon ni okeru shūkyō to kyōiku no kankei (jō)". *Ferisu jogakuin daigaku kiyō* 14: 27–60.
Suzuki, Norihisa. 1979. *Meiji shūkyō shichō no kenkyū*. Tōkyō daigaku shuppankai.
Tamakake, Hiroyuki and Minamoto, Ryōen ed. 1992. *Kokka to shūkyō, Nihon shisōshi ronshū*, Shibunkaku shuppan.
Teuween, Mark and John Breen. 2000. *Shinto in history: the way of the kamis*. Routledge.
Teuween, Mark and John Breen. 2010. *A New History of Shinto*. Wiley-Blackwell.
Trent, Maxey. 2014. The "Greatest Problem". *Religion and State Formation in Meiji Japan*. Harvard University Press.
Uchida, Tadashi. 1909. *Jukyō shingi*. Kōyūsha.
Uchida, Tadashi. 1914. *Jukyō risōgaku ninshikiron*. Iwanami shoten.
Unknown author. March 1924. "Daitō bunka kyōkai yakunin". *Daitō bunka*.
Wada, Mamoru, ed. 2014. *Nichibei ni okeru seikyō bunri to "ryōshin no jiyū"*. Mineruba shobō.
Warren Smith. 1959. *Confucianism in Modern Japan: A Study of Conservatism in Japanese Intellectual History*. Hokuseidō Press.
Watanabe, Hiroshi. 2005. "Kyō to inbō. Kokutai no kigen". In Watanabe Hiroshi, Park Chungseok, *Kankoku. Nihon. "Seiyō". Sono kōsaku to shisō hen.yō*, pp.373–413.Keiō gijuku daigaku shuppankai.
Yamaguchi, Teruomi. 2013. *Shimaji Mokurai. 'Seikyō bunri" wo motarashita sōryo*. Yamagawa shuppansha.
Yamamuro, Shin.ichi and Nakanome, Tōru eds. 2008. *Meiroku zasshi*. Iwanami shoten.
Yoshida, Kumaji. 1918. *Waga kokumin dōtoku*. Kōdōkan.

Ji Zhe
# Chinese Interpretations of French Secularism in the Early Twentieth Century

**Abstract:** This chapter draws attention to the fact that secularism seldom appears in legal discourse in China. At the beginning of the twentieth-century, Chinese intellectual circles appeared more interested in the state dominance in religious affairs embodied by French laïcité then the American ideas about religious freedom and political neutrality in relation to religions. The chapter looks at the reception by late Qing intellectuals and their translation into Chinese of the debates happening over the place of religion in society in France. It presents three of the issues that drew the reformers' attention during the transition period experienced by China: the significance of French laïcité in world history, the issue of Christian missionaries in China, and the future of Chinese religions.

## 1 Introduction

The concept of secularism is rarely mentioned in the official legal discourse in China. Among the ten or more constitutional texts drafted during the nineteenth and twentieth centuries, only the "General Principles of the Constitution of the Chinese Soviet Republic," which the Chinese Communist Party (CCP) adopted in November 1931, clearly stated the "implementation of the absolute principle of the separation of religion and politics (*zhengjiao fenli* 政教分离)." (He 2004: 103–107) None of the four Constitutions that the CCP has established since 1949 reintroduced the explicit statement of a separation between religion and politics. Similarly, the constitutional law of the Republic of China founded in 1912 endorsed the principle of freedom of religious belief, but without mentioning the separation of religion and politics. This does not mean, however, that the notion has had little impact on the Chinese world. Today, in both the PRC and in Taiwan, jurists and sociologists often consider the separation of religion and politics as an implicit constitutional principle.[1] The notion has also received in-

---

1 See for example Han 2005; Qu 2006.

**Ji Zhe** (Inalco)

https://doi.org/10.1515/9783110733068-010

creasing attention from religious and political actors since the start of the twenty-first century.[2]

The role of the separation of religion and politics in the modern history of Chinese ideas and institutions is extremely complex and cannot be dealt with exhaustively here. Rather, this chapter re-examines how French secularism (laïcité) was received in China. Although the first amendment clause of the United States' Constitution on the political-religion relationship was introduced in China as early as 1881 (Hu 2015: 95–103), American ideas about religious freedom and political neutrality in relation to religions were still far from the concerns of the Chinese elites. In fact, it seems that the separation of religion and politics only became a subject of debate in China after the adoption of the French law of 1904 prohibiting religious orders and congregations from teaching in public schools, and even more so after the famous law of 1905 on the separation of church and state. From then on, secularism, and its French version emphasizing the state's predominance in public affairs, attracted much interest in intellectual circles. In order to explore this process, we will examine articles published in the magazines *Wanguo Gongbao* (万国公报 The Globe Magazine), *Xinmin Congbao* (新民丛报 New Citizen) and *Dongfang Zazhi* (东方杂志 The Eastern Miscellany) between 1904 and 1907. These three periodicals had considerable influence on the development of modern China. The first (1868–1907), originally titled *Jiaohui xinbao* (教会新报 Church News) and renamed *Wanguo Gongbao* in 1874, was founded in Shanghai by Young John Allen (1836–1907), an American missionary of the Methodist Episcopal Church. In 1889, *Wanguo Gongbao* became in the official organ of *Guang Xue Hui* (广学会 The Christian Literature Society for China) and was published monthly thereafter. It was an important source of information for Chinese intellectuals who wanted to understand politics and society both in China and in the West.[3] *Xinmin congbao*, of which 96 issues were published in total, was founded by Liang Qichao 梁启超 (1873–1929) during his exile in Japan after the defeat of the Hundred Days' Reform. It was the main vehicle this reformist leader used to introduce Western politics, history and thought to the Chinese. The *Dongfang Zazhi* (1904–1948), launched and published by modern China's famous publishing house, The Commercial Press, was another important journal, and served as a political platform for reformers. It often republished comments from other Chinese newspapers that reflected differing points of view, which helps us get a picture of the general atmosphere during this period.

---

[2] On religion and politics in contemporary China, see Goossaert 2005; Ji 2015; Zhe and Goossaert 2017.
[3] On the important role of this journal in modern China, see Wang 2004.

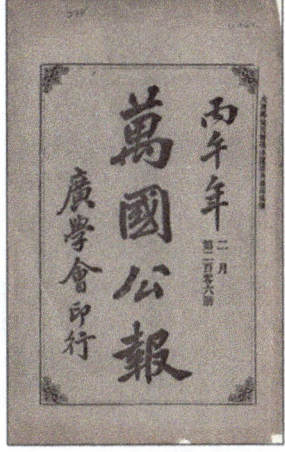

**Figure 1:** Wanguo Gongbao, Xinmin Gongbao, Dongfang Zazhi

By analyzing the texts on the separation of religion and politics in these three publications between 1904 and 1907, this chapter aims to clarify how Chinese intellectuals interpreted the French notion of the separation of religion and politics in both the Chinese and world contexts at the start of the twentieth century.

## 2 *Laïcité* or the Separation of Church and State: Translation and Transfer

In France, tension between politics and religion had existed long before the twentieth century. The Enlightenment thinkers already conceived of a republican regime and a form of civic morality on which religion would have no influence. One of the fundamental aims of the 1789 Revolution was precisely to oppose the political and economic prerogatives of the Catholic Church.[4] In 1789 and 1790, France abolished tithing, adopted the Civil Constitution of the Clergy, and voted for the nationalization of church property. The statement on freedom of opinion (and religion) in Article 10 of the Declaration of the Rights of Man and

---

4 On religion and the relationship between the state and Church during the French Revolution, see Tackett 1986; Vovelle 1988.

of the Citizen promulgated on August 26, 1789, can be seen as prefiguring the freedom of conscience that would constitute the main idea of French *laïcité*. Nevertheless, China would have to wait nearly a century for a full introduction to the French Revolution and the Declaration of the Rights of Man and the Citizen.

In nineteenth-century France, in spite of considerable political instability, conflict between the state and the Catholic Church was one of two constant issues of political debate, along with the "social question." Yet for a century, relations between the French state and the Church, and between France and the Holy See, were mainly based on the Concordat of 1801, signed by Napoleon Bonaparte (1769–1821), first Consul of the Republic, and Pope Pius VII (1742–1823). When the Third Republic was proclaimed in 1870, disagreements between the state and the Church reignited. It was precisely during this period that the codification of the separation of church and state began in France.[5] The key stages of this transition took place in 1904 and 1905, beginning with the field of education.

As a fundamental institution of socialization, education has always been the object of rivalry between religion and the modern state.[6] In 1902, the radical French Left came to power and began to strengthen the secular state's authority over public education. On July 5, 1904, the French Parliament adopted the law prohibiting religious congregations from teaching. In the months that followed, thousands of religious schools closed their doors. Diplomatic relations between France and the Vatican, already severely degraded due to anticlerical movements, were severed on July 30. On December 9, 1905, the French Senate officially promulgated the famous Law on the Separation of Church and State (also known as the "1905 law" or the "law of *laïcité*"), thereby laying the cornerstone for contemporary relations between religion and politics in France. The first chapter of the law, entitled "Principles," contains two articles. Article 1, which sets out the content of Article 10 of the Declaration of the Rights of Man and of the Citizen, states that the Republic guarantees freedom of conscience and the free exercise of religion provided that it does not harm public order; Article 2 stipulates that the Republic does not recognize or subsidize any religion, and that from January 1, 1906, it would eliminate any expenditure related to the exercise of religion from the state budgets. These two principles constitute the essence of the law and are still widely cited today. In addition, the law includes a series of detailed provisions on the management of religious property and the organization of religious activities.[7]

---

[5] For an in-depth study of this critical historical moment, see Portier 2016.
[6] For the role of educational reform in the separation of religion and politics in China, see Ji 2011.
[7] On the sociological and historical implications of *laïcité* in France, see Baubérot, 2004 and 2013.

At the time, the Manchu Empire in China was reeling from a succession of diplomatic, military and political defeats—the two Opium wars (1840–1842 and 1856–1860), the First Sino-Japanese War (1894), and the Hundred Days Reform (1898). Chinese intellectuals were seeking ways to pull the country out of this impasse, so they were extremely sensitive and receptive to political developments in the West. In this context, the laws of 1904 and 1905 relating to the separation of religion and politics were quickly translated into Chinese. *Dongfang Zazhi* reprinted a report by the newspaper *Waijiao Bao* (外交报 *Diplomatic Review*) devoted to the French laws (Dongfang Zazhi 1904a: 205–209), and published the Chinese translation of the full text of the 1904 law (Dongfang Zazhi 1905a: 159–161). It also published an article describing in detail the context of relations between state and church in France (Dongfang zazhi 1906: 165–170).

In 1907, *Dongfang Zazhi* published a Chinese translation of the 1905 law under the title "New French law on the differentiation between politics and religion" (Faguo zhengjiao fenli xin lü 法国政教分立新律). (Chen 1907: 176–187) The translator, Chen Lu 陈箓 (1877–1939), was studying law at the Sorbonne during this period. Chen offered a concise explanation of the origin and development of the 1905 law, described the context, and summarized the Concordat text of 1801 for comparison.

As Chen himself specified, he based his presentation and translation of the 1905 law on "the law and different views published in the newspapers about it." However, his translation diverges considerably from the French original. The text of the translation is condensed into 27 articles, which do not entirely correspond to the important points of the original French text with its six chapters and 44 articles. Only section 1 of the law is fully translated, but a certain interpretation has been added to the translation:

The democratic government perpetually guarantees that freedom of religious belief will be respected according to the law. With regard to the practice of worship by the churches, the government promulgates this law for the common good of the citizens (民主政府永守担保信教自由主义法典是遵，至教会实行祭祀，政府又当为国民公益计而颁是律).

(Original text: "La République assure la liberté de conscience. Elle garantit le libre exercice des cultes sous les seules restrictions édictées ci-après dans l'intérêt de l'ordre public.").

In my view, the most significant weakness of Chen's translation is that he translated the concept of "freedom of conscience" (*liangzhi ziyou* 良知自由, *liangxin ziyou* 良心自由 or *yishi ziyou* 意识自由) as "freedom of religious belief." In any case, this drastically abridged and re-edited version appears to have remained the most complete Chinese translation available. More regrettably still, when this law is discussed in the Chinese world a century on, the notion of "free-

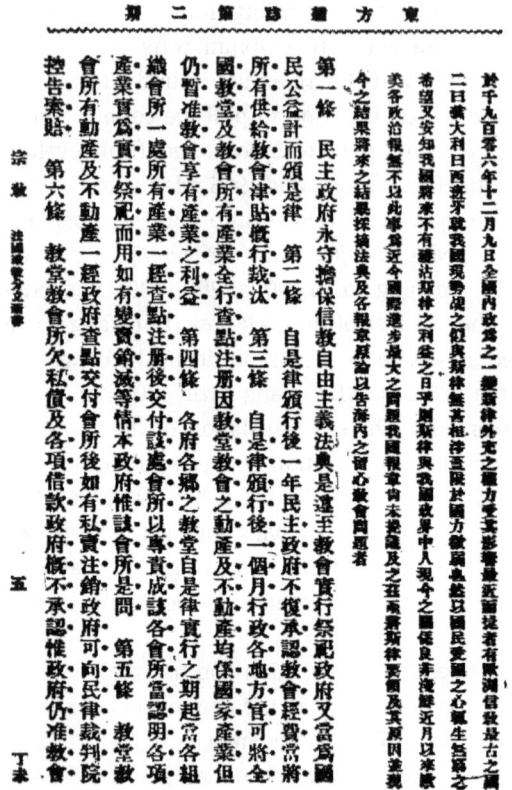

Figure 2: First page of the Chinese translation of the French "1905 law" on the Separation of Church and State

dom of conscience" is often still interpreted as "freedom of religion," "freedom of belief," or "freedom of religious belief."[8]

Like *Dongfang Zazhi*, Liang Qichao made it clear in the *Xinmin Congbao* that the "French Law on the Separation of Church and State" was one of the important events of 1905 and examined it separately from four angles: "the origin of the problem", "adoption of the proposal", "resolution," and "conclusion." (Liang 1906: 84–85) Meanwhile, *Wanguo Gongbao* published a report and a related commentary in 1906. We will analyze these interpretations later.

---

[8] For a rare example of research in Chinese that recognizes the importance of freedom of conscience in the 1905 law, see Wei 2017.

Between 1905 and 1907, "separation of church and state" was translated into Chinese in three different ways: separation of religion and politics (*zhengjiao fenli* 政教分离),[9] differentiation between politics and religion (*zhengjiao fenli* 政教分立),[10] and division of power between politics and religion (*zhengjiao fenquan* 政教分权).[11] At the time, the difference between these three translations attracted little attention. None of the texts published during this period mention it: it seems that there was no particular interest in these variants.

Yet gradually, the semantic value contained in each of these Chinese translations was highlighted and became a tool for constructing discourses. For instance, Taixu 太虚 (1890–1947), the most important reformist Buddhist leader in modern China, used all three expressions (Gong and Lai 2014: 121–122). In a petition he addressed to the Senate and the National Assembly, which was published in 1913 (Taixu 2006a), Taixu pointed out that since the founding of the Republic of China, some people had advocated both "differentiation and solidarity between politics and religion." This would be advantageous both for the state and for religion, because if there was no differentiation, whether politics dominated religion or religion dominated politics, either case would give rise to abuses and "solidarity" would be out of the question. But given the secular government's desire for control of Buddhist monasteries and the discrimination felt by some Buddhists, Taixu called on Parliament to recognize the "division of power between politics and religion." In speaking of "division of power," he was referring to the management of monasteries by a unified Buddhist association; other organizations, communities or private individuals should not interfere. Moreover, apart from their commitment to the Buddhist cause, Buddhist followers should not get involved in political life. Two years later, Taixu (2006) preferred to employ the term "separation of politics and religion." If he mentioned "separation," it is that aside from the purposes of "differentiation" and "solidarity" mentioned above, the political and religious domains differed in scope. Taixu considered that "politics is implemented within a nation, and religion is practiced on a world scale." Although they overlap, each pursues its own objective. Evidently, by using the term "separation of politics and religion," Taixu supported the idea that religion is superior to politics.

Today, *zhengjiao fenli* (政教分离 "separation of religion and politics") is a widely employed translation and has become an established concept in the Chinese world. Compared with *fenli* (分立) and *fenquan* (分权), there is greater se-

---

9 For example, Wanguo Gongbao 1906a; Liang 1906: 84.
10 For example, Dongfang Zazhi 1906: 88.
11 For example, Wanguo Gongbao 1906a: 14b–15b ; Wanguo Gongbao, 1906b: 28a.

mantic equivalence between the terms *fenli* (分离) and "separation". However, religious figures continue to stress the differences between *fenli* (分立), *fenquan* (分权), and *fenli* (分离) in order to assert their political demands.[12]

Yet all three ways of translating "church and state" converge in one respect that raises a central problem: "state" (国家 *guojia*) is translated as "politics" (政 *zheng*), and "church" (教会 *jiaohui*) as "religion" (教 *jiao*). In recent years, some have noted that the expression *zhengjiao fenli*—separation of politics and religion—corresponds in reality to the English expression separation of *state* and *church*. This has drawn much attention to the problem, and it is unnecessary to go into more detail here. Let us simply point out that this "erroneous translation" is due to the fact that the concept of the "church" does not exist in Chinese religion, and that the concept of "state" was not differentiated from "politics" in early twentieth-century China.

However, the choice of *zhengjiao* (政教) in the expression *zhengjiao fenli* does not only have the negative effect of obscuring the facts. In fact, *zhengjiao* is part of the traditional Chinese political vocabulary. It means "politics and instruction" and was still widely used at the end of the Qing Dynasty. As I mentioned in a previous study (Ji 2018: 61–85), politics, religion and education were interdependent in traditional China. In the term *zhengjiao*, *zheng* means "politics," while *jiao* refers to both "instruction" and "religion." Here, juxtaposed together, *zheng* and *jiao* come from a tautology: politics is religion, religion is politics, so the term reflects the idea of a unification of politics and religion. The emergence of the expression *zhengjiao fenli* at the start of the twentieth century made it necessary to treat *zheng* and *jiao* separately, which was in itself a real challenge to the original *zhengjiao* concept. In this respect, although "separation of religion and politics" is not as precise as "separation of church and state," the first translation probably sheds more light on the political-religious relationship in China, and even more fully reflects the nature of the issue of secularization in general.

# 3 The Fate of Religion: Interpretations in the International and National Context

The separation of religion and politics in France was heavily discussed in Chinese intellectual circles at the time. The debate was not limited to the legal relationship between state and church but dealt with the cultural and historical re-

---

12 For a recent example, see Guo 2017.

lations between "politics" and "religion" in a broad sense. To a certain degree, "*laïcisation*" as defined by French characteristics—centrality of the legal framework and regulation of the institutional limits of religion in public life—was interpreted by Chinese scholars as "secularization," namely an overall decline in religions in the evolution of modern civilization.[13] In 1904 and 1905, the debate in the Chinese world revolved around three aspects, to which we will now turn.

## 3.1 The Significance of the French Separation of Religion and Politics in World History

First, some Chinese intellectuals considered the separation of religion and politics in France as more than a merely local event, situating it in the *longue durée* of Western history, if not world history. Liang Qichao, for instance, stated in explicit terms in a commentary published in 1906 that the separation of religion and politics in France marked the culmination of the struggle between political and religious powers in Europe that had lasted five or six hundred years. "This event seems minor," Liang wrote, "but its denouement concerns the history of the whole world." (Liang 1906: 85). In other words, the "secularization" of the Western world had been definitively established.

**Figure 3:** Liang Qichao (1873–1929)

---

**13** On the distinctions and connections between *laïcisation* and secularization, see Baubérot, 2013.

The *Dongfang Zazhi* reprinted an article from the *Nanyang Riri Guanbao* (南洋日日官报 *Official Journal of Nanyang*) and analyzed in detail the history of religion in Western societies (Liang 1906: 165–170). The anonymous author seemed to adhere to the view of Auguste Comte (1798–1857), in that he split Western history into three periods: "superstition and theocracy" (fifth to fifteenth centuries), "ideal and deduction" (sixteenth and seventeenth centuries), and "science and experimentation" beginning in the nineteenth century. France, the country where Catholicism exerted most influence, had deprived the church of the right to teach because "religion is destined to decline." (Liang 1906: 166).

The author went so far as to assert that even if religion reorganized itself to adapt to modern civilization—"to eliminate the strange and absurd part in order to preserve its principle of astute purity"—it could not last "forever." In the light of progress in education and politics, "the future of religion is threatened!" The author perfectly mastered the modernist discourse on civilization, evolution, freedom, etc., and produced a comprehensive article on the theory of secularization.

Because of its Protestant background, the *Wanguo Gongbao* offered another interpretation. In 1906, it published a report and an article containing a lengthy analysis that denied the trend of religious decline and drew attention to religious diversity and "freedom of religion." (Wanguo Gongbao 1906b: 28a; Wanguo Gongbao 1906a: 64–68). The periodical argued that the separation of religion and politics in France targeted Catholicism first and foremost, and that the implementation of this policy was not symptomatic of the decline of religion in the twentieth century. Rather, it represented the starting point of the "freedom of belief in the Latin countries." This theory was certainly not without foundation. To a certain extent, Protestants and religious minorities were indeed in favor of and benefitted from French *laïcité*. However, this was by no means the majority point of view among Chinese scholars at the time.

## 3.2 A Timely Opportunity to Resolve the "Missionary Cases"?

Whereas in the context of their religious rivalry, Protestants welcomed the loss of Catholic influence, the two communities opposed the Chinese government by mutual agreement on the issue of freedom to preach. In contrast, Chinese scholars generally supported the Qing government. They sought to find a way out of the diplomatic crisis caused by the "missionary cases" (教案 *jiao'an*) the Qing court was facing at the time. After its defeat in the Second Opium War, the Qing government signed the Tianjin Treaty (1858) with the Western Powers, which gave special protection to missionaries and the Chinese Christian community. Soon afterwards, the Beijing Treaty of 1860 allowed Western missionaries to buy or rent land and build religious facilities in China. The expansion of Christianity had led to many clashes between Chinese and foreign missionaries, and between Chinese Christians and non-Christians.[14] Some had been extremely violent and caused losses on both sides, placing heavy diplomatic pressure on the Qing government. It is important to note that France's position on these conflicts was unique. As a great Catholic nation, France was protective of Catholicism in China, and its patronage had, to a certain extent, been recognized in Article 13 of the Tianjin Treaty. There was no direct diplomatic relationship between the Qing government and the Vatican—France had thwarted efforts to establish such a relationship. This allowed France to exert significant influence on the Chinese government to resolve the missionary cases, even those in which no French citizen was involved.[15]

In this context, the policy of separation between religion and politics in France encouraged the Chinese elite to rethink the resolution of the missionary cases. Some thought that the Qing government could take advantage of the antagonism between the French government and the Holy See and dissociate the missionary cases from diplomacy. A series of articles on the subject were published in *Waijiao Bao* (Yang 2001: 70). For example, an article reprinted by the *Dongfang Zazhi* in 1904 suggested seizing the opportunity represented by the breakdown of diplomatic relations between France and the Vatican to remove missionaries from French diplomatic protection (Dongfang Zazhi, 1904b: 49–51). In 1907, *Dongfang Zazhi* reprinted an article originally published in the newspaper *Nanfang Bao* (南方报 *Southern newspaper*) [16] which took the same point of view (Dongfang Zazhi 1907: 15–19). The author believed that Western countries had always taken advantage of religious proselytism to further their colonial policies. France resolved religious problems through diplomatic channels, and sometimes even with arms, which was in fact a "political fusion with religion." However, the "1905 law" promised the possibility henceforth of handling the missionary cases with the Pope rather than the French government.

In fact, some Qing officials had sought to escape French patronage and deal directly with the Pope in order to resolve the missionary cases. The 1905 law created more favorable conditions for this strategy. In January 1906, a French minister sent a diplomatic note to the Qing government's Ministry of Foreign Affairs stating that France would henceforth only provide protection for French Catho-

---

14 On the history of "missionary cases," Lü 1966; Zhang and Liu 1987; Chen Yinkun 1987.
15 On French diplomatic interventions in the "missionary cases," see Chen Zenghui 2000, included in the archives of the French Ministry of Foreign Affairs for the years 1894–1899.
16 *Nanfang Bao* was a newspaper published in Shanghai from 1905 to 1908.

lics and not for religious communities from other countries. Surprisingly, however, the proposal to resolve the missionary cases through the establishment of direct diplomatic relations with the Vatican did not receive the support of the Qing court. According to Yang Dachun 杨大春, this was because the Qing court had abandoned any effort to do so in 1896, following many failures. Another opinion prevailed among the authorities: it was only by abolishing the extraterritorial status of Western countries in China that religious conflicts could be resolved (Yang 2001: 70).

## 3.3 Chinese Religions and Their Future

The separation of religion and politics in France encouraged some scholars to reflect on the status of Chinese religions and their future. Their interpretations differed widely.

What first raised controversy was the position of Confucian teaching in the process of the separation of politics and religion. At the time, Protestantism was the biggest rival to Confucianism in China. Unsurprisingly, the *Wanguo Gongbao* stressed that the goal of the separation of politics and religion was "freedom of religion," and that therefore Confucian education should not have official support. In 1905, it reprinted an article from the *China West Daily* (中西日报 *Zhong-Xi Ribao*) by a Chinese Christian living in the United States, entitled "On the division of power between politics and religion" (Zhengjiao fenquan lun 政教分权论) (Huang 1905: 14b–15b). The author argued that in the West, state education did not discriminate between citizens on the grounds of their religion; it was different in China where government-controlled schools were forced to practice Confucian rituals, and reprimand and then expel students who failed to apply themselves at these ceremonies. The author concluded that the lack of separation between politics and religion was one of the biggest obstacles to progress in China.[17] Another commentary published in 1905 (Wanguo Gongbao 1906a: 68) maintained that the status of the Confucian school in China was equivalent to that of Catholicism in the West. These religions occupied a dominant position and had a monopoly on the education of citizens. Therefore, the author argued, China had a long way to go if it wanted to free itself from the domination of Confucianism and separate religion and politics as France had done.

---

**17** In fact, Chinese Protestants were probably the first who used the concept of "freedom of religion" in modern China to fight for their rights and interests. See Liu 2006.

Interestingly, non-Christian Chinese viewed the French separation of religion and politics as a legitimation of China's management of and restrictions on teaching by the Christian churches in China. Some Chinese went even further. For example, an editorial in *Dongfang zazhi*, "On the unification between politics and religion" (Zhengjiao heyi lun 政教合一论) (Ke 1904: p. 4–8), proposed a completely different viewpoint from the Christian one. The author considered that the origins of religions' social expression and political-religious relations were very different in China and the West. In Western countries, religions were institutional. At their inception, religions in the West were dissociated from politics, but they were later subject to a "forced adherence" to the state as part of the unification of state and church. In China, Confucianism and Taoism were diffuse religions, with no definitive form, which were originally associated with political life.[18] As time went on, "Religions that deceive the people instead of enlightening them must improve and progress"; the key to improvement and progress lies precisely in education, which had been a bone of contention during the separation of religion and politics in the West. Now, "the teaching of Confucius is instruction and not religion," "the greatest Chinese pedagogue is none other than Confucius," and "in order to put an end to the confusion due to today's religions we must begin with the fact that Confucius does not comment on our fate and does not speak of gods." For the editorialist, not only was Confucianism not an obstacle to secularism; it was a means of combating religious obscurantism. He therefore felt it necessary to keep a close eye on the future of political-religious relations in China, if separation or union were to take place.

Chinese intellectuals' interest was not limited to Confucianism. They also reflected on the future of Chinese religions in general. In 1905, *Dongfang Zazhi* reprinted a commentary from the *China and Foreign Daily* (中外日报 *Zhongwai Ribao*) containing a detailed classification and periodization of Chinese religions (Dongfang zazhi, 1905b). While the author initially admitted that scientific progress made the decline of religion inevitable, he pointed out that without religion, there would be nothing to inhibit the evolution of natural competition (天演之势, 浩然无所抵制 *tianyan zhi shi, haoran wu suo dizhi*), which was not a blessing for humanity. He divided the religions of the Chinese people into five religions: Taoism, Confucianism, Buddhism, Islam and Christianity, and then subdivided Confucianism into three periods which he characterized as follows: the era of re-

---

**18** Here I borrow the formulation of YANG Qingkun 杨庆堃 (C. K. Yang) who distinguish "institutional religion" (建制宗教 *jianzhi zongjiao*) from "diffuse religion" (弥散宗教 *misan zongjiao*) to translate "religion with definitive form" (*ding ming zongjiao* 定名宗教) and "religion without definitive form" (*wuding ming zongjiao* 无定名宗教). See Yang 1967.

ligious scholars (the Qin and Han dynasties), the era of famous scholars (from the period of the Three Kingdoms to the Sui dynasty), and the era of imperial examination candidates (from the Tang dynasty until the early twentieth century). The author considered that the era of imperial examination candidates had come to an end,[19] and that all other religions practiced in China had their problems. China must look for a new religion to settle the mind and appease the troubled political climate. Yet while the author asked, "What religion should China choose for the future?", he did not venture an answer. Similarly, an editorial by *Dongfang Zazhi* published shortly afterwards went straight to the point: (Mai 1906: 4–8) "Whatever the progress of the world, the influence of religion will not be weakened." This author made two arguments: that science cannot explain everything, so religion would always elucidate our understanding of the world; and that social development would lead to more inequality, and poor populations need to know that they will find comfort in the afterworld: the kingdom of heaven.

An article *Nanfang Bao* published before the translation of the "1905 law" and reprinted in *Dongfang Zazhi* systematically analyzed the misdeeds of Chinese religions (Dongfang zazhi 1907: 176–189). The author observed first of all that Europe freed itself early from the yoke of religion; that was why politics had been progressively "civilized." China, however, had been slow to liberate itself. People believed in superstition, and at the same time the political system was becoming more corrupt every day. The author warned that if China continued to remain faithful to "uncivilized" religions in a context where "communication and science are progressing day by day worldwide, superstitions have been eradicated on a planetary scale and the truth of freedom has been affirmed," the country ran the risk of losing its independence. Nevertheless, in determining what new religion would meet the needs of the time, as in the articles mentioned above, the author reserved his judgment. In addition, he remained ambiguous about the difference between "religion" and "superstition." An article in the *China and Foreign Daily* echoed by *Dongfang Zazhi* fulminated against "superstition and supernatural beings."[20] According to the author, the superstition that had taken hold of the lower-class people was one of the reasons for China's poverty and weakness, and "religions" and "erudition" were the prerogative of society's upper class alone. The cornerstone of the reform should therefore be to offer general education to the least favored social strata and children.

---

[19] The Qing government officially abolished the Mandarin exam system in 1905.
[20] Dongfang Zazhi, 1905, vol. 2, n° 4, p. 15–18.

In summary, Chinese scholars of the time generally considered that religion was facing a crisis in a multicultural society that benefited from scientific progress. They admitted the social function of religion, however, and began to take an interest in the reform of Chinese religions. In these debates, the opinion of the Chinese cultural elite of the twentieth century about some dominant positions on religion—for example the difference between Chinese and Western religions or the difference between religion and superstition—had already taken shape.

# 4 Conclusion

Around 1905, Chinese intellectuals quickly became interested in the process of separating religion and politics in France and took part in discussions on related topics. Scholars of this period already had a good general knowledge of Western history, and the modernist discourses profoundly influenced their thought and their expression. Their reflections involved a series of modern themes: politics, religion, education, science, progress, democracy, freedom, equality, etc. In this respect, French *laïcité* was a source of Chinese religious modernity.

Unfortunately, this Franco-Chinese ideological kinship was not developed further. From the data we have today, it seems that following the founding of the Republic of China in 1912, intellectual discussions and legal arguments relating to the political-religious relationship instead gave way to the question of "freedom of religion" dear to Protestantism. Even more regrettably, the Chinese scholars of the early twentieth century failed to fully comprehend the heart of French *laïcité:* "freedom of conscience," clearly stated in the first sentence of the first article of the 1905 law. The absence of "freedom of conscience" from modern Chinese secularism might be a key to understanding the troubled relationship between the state and religions in China during the twentieth century, and even today.

# References

Baubérot, Jean. 2004. *Laïcité 1905–2005: entre passion et raison*. Paris: Seuil.
Baubérot, Jean. 2013a. *Histoire de la laïcité en France*, 6th edition. Paris: PUF (Que sais-je?).
Baubérot, Jean. 2013b. "Sécularisation, laïcité, laïcisation," *Empan*, 2 (n° 90), p. 31–38.
Chen Lu 陈箓. 1907. "Faguo zhengjiao fenli xin lü 法国政教分立新律". *Dongfang zazhi* 4 no. 2: 176–187.
Chen Yinkun 陈银昆. 1987. *Min jiao chongtu de lianghua fenxi* 民教冲突的量化分析. Taipei: Shangwu yinshuguan.

Chen Zenghui 陈增辉,ed., translated by Geng Sheng 耿昇 and Yang Peichun 杨佩纯. 2000. *Qing mo jiao'an —— si: Fawen ziliao xuan yi* 清末教案——四：法文资料选译. Taipei: Zhonghua shuju.

*Dongfang Zazhi*. 1904a. "Shu Faguo jin yue jiaohui shihou 书法国禁约教会事后". vol. 1 no. 2: 205–209.

*Dongfang Zazhi*. 1904b. "Lun yong mi jiao'an zhengce 论永弭教案之政策". vol. 1 no. 10: 49–51.

*Dongfang Zazhi*. 1905a. "Faguo jinbi jiaohui xuetang xin li 法国禁闭教会学堂新例". vol. 2 no. 3: 159–161.

*Dongfang Zazhi* 1905b. "Lun Zhongguo qiantu dang yong hezhong zongjiao 论中国前途当用何种宗教". vol. 2 no. 5: 161–171.

*Dongfang zazhi*. 1906a. "Lun Faguo xianzhi jiaohui xuetang shi yin ji zongjiao guoqu weilai zhi zhuangkuang 论法国限制教会学堂事因及宗教过去未来之状况". vol. 2 no. 12: 165–170.

*Dongfang zazhi*. 1906b. "Faguo zhengjiao fenli wenti 法国政教分立问题". vol. 3–4: 88.

*Dongfang zazhi*. 1907. "Lun xiaoshi jiao'an de jihui 论消释教案之机会". vol. 4 no. 7: 15–19.

Gong Juan 龚隽 and Lai Yueshan 赖岳山. 2014. "Chonggu Taixu fashi (yin lun) —— yi 'Zhongguo di er lishi dang'anguan' suocang Minguo Jiaoyubu dang'an wei zhongxin 重估太虚法师（引论）——以"中国第二历史档案馆"所藏民国教育部档案为中心," *Hanyu Foxue pinglun* serie no. 4: 96–178.

Goossaert, Vincent. 2005. "Les fausses séparations de l'État et de la religion en Chine, 1898–2004". In Jean Baubérot and Michel Wieviorka, eds., *De la séparation des Églises et de l'État à l'avenir de la laïcité*, pp. 49–58. Paris: L'aube.

Guo Muyun 郭暮云. 2017. " 'Zhengjiao fenli' haishi 'zhengjiao fenli'? "政教分离"还是"政教分立"? http://www.pacilution.com/ShowArticle.asp?ArticleID=7755.

Han Dayuan 韩大元. 2005. "Shilun zhengjiao fenli yuanze de xianfa jiazhi 试论政教分离原则的宪法价值". *Faxue* no. 10: 3–8.

He Husheng 何虎生. 2004. "Lun Zhongguo Gongchandang zongjiao zhengce de chubu xingcheng 论中共产党宗教政策的初步形成". *Zongjiaoxue yanjiu*, no. 1: 103–107.

Hu Xiaojin 胡晓进. 2015. "Qing mo minchu meiguo xianfa zai Zhongguo de fanyi yu chuanbo 清末民初美国宪法在中国的翻译与传播." *Huadong zhengfa daxue xuebao*, n° 3, p. 95–103.

Huang Zicai 黄梓材. 1905. "Zhengjiao fenquan lun 政教分权论". *Wanguo gongbao* 196: 14b–15b.

Ji Zhe 汲喆. 2011. "Le jiao recomposé. L'éducation entre religion et politique dans la modernité chinoise". In *Religion, éducation et politique en Chine moderne (Extrême-Orient Extrême-Occident* 33: 5–34.

Ji Zhe. 2015. "Secularization without Secularism: The Political-Religious Configuration of Post-89 China". In Ngo, Tam and Justine Quijada, eds., *Atheist Secularism and its Discontents. A Comparative Study of Religion and Communism in Eurasia*, pp. 92–111. Basingstoke: Palgrave Macmillan, p. 92–111.

Ji Zhe and Vincent Goossaert. 2017. "Les politiques religieuses de la Chine postmaoïste". In Alain Dieckhoff and Philippe Portier, eds., *L'enjeu mondial: religion et politique*, pp.263–271. Paris: Presses de Sciences Po.

Ji Zhe. 2018. "The Origins of Secular Public Space: Religion, Education, and Politics in Modern China". In Mirjam Künkler, John Madeley and Shylashri Shankar, eds., *A Secular*

*Age beyond the West: Religion, Law and the State in Asia, the Middle East and North Africa*, pp. 61–85. Cambridge: Cambridge University Press.

Ke Quan 可权. 1904. "Zhengjiao heyi lun 政教合一论," *Dongfang zazhi* 1 no. 6: 4–8.

Liang Qichao 梁启超. 1906. "Guoqu yi nian shijie dashiji 过去一年世界大事记". *Xinmin congbao* fourth year, no. 2 (formerly no. 74):. 84–85.

Liu Yi. 2006. "Qing mo minchu sixiang yu zhengzhi sjijian zhong de xinjiao ziyou —— yi Jidu Jiaohui de huodong wei zhongxin 清末民初思想与政治实践中的信教自由——以基督教会的活动为中心 (1900–1917)". In Wu Ziming 吴梓明, Wu Xiaoxin 吴小新, eds., *Jidujiao yu Zhongguo shehui*, pp. 247–270. Hong Kong: Xianggang zhongwen daxue chong ji xueyuan zongjiao yu Zhongguo shehui yanjiu zhongxin

Lü Shiqiang 吕实强. 1966. *Zhongguo guanshen fan jiao de yuanyin 1860–1874* 中国官绅反教的原因 1860–1874. Taipei: Zhongyang yanjiuyuan jindaishi yanjiusuo.

Mai Zhao 麵照. 1906. "Zongjiao yang quan yin lun 宗教扬权引论". *Dongfang zazhi*, 1906. 3 no. 7: 4–8.

Qu Haiyuan 瞿海源. 2006. "Zongjiao xinyang ziyou de xianfa jichu 宗教信仰自由的宪法基础". In *Zongjiao、shushu yu shihui bianqian*, II 宗教、术数与社会变迁（二）, pp. 189–212. Taipei: Guiguan tushu chuban gongsi

Portier, Philippe. 2016. *L'État et les religions en France: Une sociologie historique de la laïcité*. Rennes: PUR.

Tackett, Timothy. 1986. *La Révolution, l'Église, la France, le serment de 1791*, translated by Alain Spiess. Paris: Cerf.

Taixu 太虚. 2006a. Shang cazong liangyuan qingyuanshu 上参众两院请愿书". In *Taixu dashi quanshu* 太虚大师全书, vol. 17, pp. 658–660. Taipei: Caituan faren yin shun wenjiao jijinhui.

Taixu 太虚. 2006b. "Zhengli sengqie zhidu lun 整理僧伽制度论". In Taixu dashi quanshu 太虚大师全书, vol. 17, pp. 1–185. Taipei: Caituan faren yin shun wenjiao jijinhui.

Vovelle, Michel. 1988. *1793, la Révolution contre l'Église: de la raison à l'Être suprême*. Bruxelles: Complexes.

Wang Lin 王林. 2004. *Xixue yu bianfa: "Wanguo gongbao" yanjiu* 西学与变法——〈万国公报〉研究. Jinan: Qi lu shushe.

Wanguo Gongbao. 1905a. *Faguo zhengjiao zhi fenquan* 法国政教之分权, vol. 204, p. 28a.

Wanguo Gongbao. 1905b. *Faguo zhengjiao fenli zhi yuanyin* 法国政教分离之原因, vol. 206, pp. 64–68.

Wei Wenyi 魏文一. 2017. *Gujia yu zuguo: Tuergan lun zhengzhi shehui de langge mianxiang* 国家与祖国:涂尔干论政治社会的两个面向, 社会 37 no. 6 : 134–164.

Yang Dachun 杨大春. 2001. "Wan Qing zhengfu yu Luoma Jiating de waijiao licheng 晚清政府与罗马教廷的外交历程" *Shixue yuekan*, no. 1: 67–71.

Yang Qingkun 杨庆堃. 1967. *Religion in Chinese Society*. Berkeley-Los Angeles: University of California Press.

Zhang Li 张力 and Liu Jiantang 刘鉴唐. 1987. *Zhongguo jiao'an shi* 中国教案史. Chengdu: Sichuan shehui kexueyuan chubanshe.

Bénédicte Brac de la Perrière
# 'Religion' as an Issue in Political Transition: Two Competing Secularities in Buddhist Burma (Myanmar)

**Abstract:** This chapter addresses Burma's confrontation with "modern" values in the context of the political reform since the adoption of the 2008 Constitution and its impact on "Buddhist secularity." It focuses in particular on the outburst of exclusivist Buddhist nationalism expressed in 2012 anti-Muslim violence and the formation in 2013 of a nationalist movement headed by monks (Mabatha) as reactions to the secularizing effect of political transition. In this regard, the political transition can be considered a replication of at least two previous historical confrontations, one at the time of the colonial encounter and the other when Burma gained independence. These confrontations fostered a similar discourse of "defense of Buddhism" and led the most extremist monks to religious activism embedded in electoral politics in 2015. The transitional process had the dual effect to push part of the Buddhist monastics into politics and to provoke a subsequent reaction from the newly elected democratic government to reassert its control over nationalist monks. It brought to the fore the ongoing debates on what is religious and what is political and on the place of monks in politics.

## 1 Introduction

"Can 'secularism' travel?" That was the question Charles Taylor asked in an afterword to *Beyond the Secular West* (Bilgrami 2016) as a comment on his monumental *A Secular Age*, published nine years earlier (2007). Akeel Bilgrami's purpose in editing *Beyond the Secular West* was to go beyond Taylor's formidable narrative about the category "secular" that began with the "axial age." It was to ask if

---

**Note:** The official name of Burma has been changed to Myanmar—an older and more literary version for the same word—by the military organ (SLORC) that took over in 1988. Both versions of the country name, the official and the historical, are found throughout academic literature, sometimes with political implications, sometimes according to the field of studies or the era covered. Burma is used throughout this chapter for convenience sake, except when quoting a specific expression.

**Bénédicte Brac de la Perrière** (Centre Asie du Sud-Est, CNRS)

the modern political doctrine of "secularism" that resulted from this long-term Western history was exportable to non-Christianized contexts. In other words, it was to question the thesis of secularization as a linear and teleological global process. It was also to extend the debate of alternative modernities with that of alternative secularities; the authors sought to move away from the teleological understandings of secularization and disenchantment that presume the reproducibility of the process from its Western template to non-European trajectories of the disentanglement of transcendence and the worldly. Indeed, some axial age transformations had been developing in parallel outside of Christendom, such as, for instance, the soteriological rather than ritual orientation of religious practice in the case of the Indian Buddhist primitive doctrine. Considering more recent moments of this long history, one also has to look at the complex interactions that occurred through colonization, decolonization, and globalization, in which secularism has, more or less explicitly, been an active model of the governance technologies involved.

As a political doctrine, "secularism"—i.e., the doctrine constituting religion as a domain of social life separate from those of politics and public life—was born in the West during the nineteenth century to substitute a democratic and liberal legitimation of modern state power for a religious one. It is the doctrine through which modern states regulate religions. As posited by Jean Bauberot in his introductory chapter, a sociological perspective on laicity (that he takes as an equivalent of secularism) would highlight socio-political relationships between state, religion and individuals. Fundamentally hegemonic, secularism is grounded in the conceptual binary of the secular versus the religious. The two categories are considered co-constitutive; they belong to a discourse that shapes religion and displaces it while clearing out a space for the secular state. The secular does not only emerge out of a socio-cosmological whole in opposition to religion; it also has an impact on religious beliefs and practices. As David McMahan stated in his recent "Buddhism and Global Secularisms," Buddhism thus provides its own illustrations of how particular configurations of the binary have been a significant factor in religious change (2017: 115).[1]

In this chapter, Myanmar's political transition and the ensuing outburst of strident Buddhist nationalism will be taken as a case in point of an unrecognized secularity that has affected religious dynamics and delineations. What is generally termed political "transition"—itself an expression of teleological premises in governance theories—describes the major top-down political reform that fol-

---

[1] About the secular and secularism see Talal Asad 2003, Danièle Hervieu-Léger 2010, Saba Mahmood 2016, Stanley Tambiah 1998 and Peter Van der Veer 2014.

lowed the adoption of a new parliamentary constitution in Burma through the 2008 referendum. A formal civilian government was invested in 2011 after the Union for Solidarity and Development Party (USDP, an offspring of previous military administrations) won the 2010 general elections. The 2015 general elections then brought the democratic opposition, (the National League for Democracy: NLD), to power through a landslide victory: this amounted to a political turnover. The NLD's popularity was confirmed by the party's still clearer victory in the November 2020 elections.

While the political reform of 2011 formally put an end to half a century of autocratic rule by the juntas, the constitution had been designed under military leadership to maintain the army in key power positions, allowing for the formation of a truly hybrid regime that proved to be a severe impediment to the democratization process.[2] The military felt vexed by the NLD's success in the 2020 polls; they resented the democratic landslide victory and the threat to lose their control over political reform. Because of this, they brandished the un-established claim that there were massive flaws in the electoral process, and spearheaded a military coup on February 1, 2021, thus suddenly interrupting the transitional experience.

The most harrowing example of the obstacles placed by the military establishment to democratic governance during the political transition is the dire repression campaign launched against the Muslim Rohingyas from Northern Arakan (Rakhine) that caused their massive exodus across the Bangladesh border, a tragic event that started acquiring international attention and making media headlines in September 2017. The roots of this tragedy are complex and entrenched. The Rohingya's progressive exclusion from the national Buddhist landscape, their electoral disenfranchisement due to the refusal to recognize them as a "national ethnic group" (*taingyintha*), and the failure of the 2015 elected civilian democratic government to prevent military exactions against them, all these contemporary developments resonate with the reinvigoration of an exclusively Buddhist national identity. The most instrumental player in promoting this exclusive national identity was the newly emergent Buddhist nationalist movement led by monks, known as Mabatha.[3] Nothing could bring the weaknesses

---

[2] By constitutional provision, members of the military are appointed to three main ministries, namely the Ministry of Home Affairs, Ministry of Defense, and Ministry of Border Affairs. 25 per cent of the Assembly seats are reserved for appointed members of the military who may use a veto in the case of a constitutional amendment.

[3] Mabatha is an acronym, often found as Ma Ba Tha in recent analyses on Burmese political transition and religious nationalism. Given that it has become ubiquitous in everyday language and in the literature, and in order to facilitate reading, I choose to normalize its transcription as

of the newly elected democratic government more starkly to international attention than the Rohingya tragedy, but this situation has also been sustained by the widely shared Burmese Buddhist opinion that the Rohingya do not belong to the Buddhist national identity that Mabatha has promoted. Founded in June 2013 under pressure from young activist monks who had just led a fierce campaign for the boycott of Muslim businesses all over Burma,[4] the movement called for broad participation from all strands of the monastic order and advocated for the "defense of the national religion," that is, Buddhism, whose teachings it perceived to be in need of revitalization, and under threat from Islamic pressure.

This kind of strident religious nationalism arising in a period of political transition is far from unique. Nationalism and religion are Western categories that have mutually enmeshed histories and have spread throughout the world, through colonial empires and then globalization, as two conflicting sociopolitical frameworks—namely, that of the secular nation-state and that of the religious identity of large-scale communities. Hannah Arendt once pointed out that the idea of the nation-state was in itself a perversion through which state protection of citizens became linked to the latter's nationality (1951). More recently, the diffusion of liberal ideology based on democratic secularist ideals has often elicited defensive reactions in liberalizing postcolonial countries that have brought together nationalism and religion in such a way as to make their coalescence seem unavoidable. Analysts of these contemporary phenomena have observed that the post-colonial societies where religious nationalisms have particularly taken hold are those where the idea of the nation-state was problematic and where secular nationalism was seen as a colonial importation.[5]

Somewhat ironically, these phenomena of religious nationalist reactions offer a perfect opportunity to look at secular formations specific to such societies, which were first marked by a colonial secular state and then caught up in secularizing tendencies inherent to the democratization process. The recent re-emergence of exclusivist Buddhist nationalism in contemporary Burma, also termed "ethnocentric Buddhism" or "chauvinistic Buddhism" (Fuller 2018), both reflects the resilience of religious tradition in politics and reveals the effect of the political transition in the religious field. In this mutual re-delineation, the Buddhist nationalist reaction expresses the secularizing effect of political transition, an effect that has not been considered in existing analyses of the situation.

---

a single word. For literature on these questions see Iselin Frydenlund 2017, Mikael Gravers 2012 & 2015, Juliane Schober 2017 and Matthew Walton 2014. For the analysis of the Mabatha's full title see Brac de la Perrière 2015a and below.

4 About this campaign known as 969, see below.

5 See particularly Mark Juergensmeyer 2010, Katarina Kinvall 2004.

This chapter addresses the Burmese confrontation with "modern" values in the context of the 2011–2021 political transition, and its impact on "Buddhist secularity." Through an analysis of Mabatha's formation, it seeks to uncover an ongoing and implicit debate on "Where should the Buddhist monk stand?" and "What is religious and what is political?" given that the delineation of these categories is both culturally specific and endlessly evolving. Political transition is taken as a particular moment in their genealogies. This moment can be considered a replication of at least two previous confrontations that led to a discourse of "defense of religion," occurring respectively at the time of the colonial encounter and of the newly independent Burma. First, the historical background is examined through a sketch of secularity in historical Theravadin polities, an outline of the emergence of "defense of religion" discourses in reaction to colonial secularist policies, and a brief depiction of the workings of secular political institutions and the governance of religion since Independence. The narrative then turns to Mabatha's formation and to the recent military coup as sites of secularization.

## 2 Theravadin Buddhist Formations as Bearers of a Form of Secularity

In a Theravadin society, the relationship between politics and religion is framed by the specific construction of Buddha's teachings as the prerogative of religious men, organized in the monastic order (the Sangha) according to the set of rules recorded in a part of the scriptures called the *Vinaya*.[6] These rules, supposedly set by Gotama during his lifetime, lay out the life of renunciation required of monks struggling on the path of salvation. Most important on the sociological level are the clauses barring monks from any productive work or business activity, making them dependent on their social environment for their maintenance; in Burma today, the daily alms-tour to collect food is integral to the religious way of life. Obedience to monastic rules allows monks to be merit-purveyors for the lay donors going their own way along the donation-path. This "symbiosis" between the religious order and society at large has been organized in Theravadin

---

6 About the *Vinaya*'s central role in the structures insuring the regulation of Theravadin monks and in the hybrid laws set up over time by the main Theravadin polities, see the recent special issue of *Buddhism, Law & Society* edited by Benjamin Schontal (2018).

societies in what has been called the Asokan model of kingship.⁷ It allows for the formation of two distinctive spheres of religious action, the merit-making path of people inhabiting the world (*lawki*) and the path of monks who ideally seek to escape the karmic cycle and get beyond the world (*lokuttara*). In this model, monks must stay out of worldly affairs to maintain their status as merit purveyors for people inhabiting the world. In Buddhist studies, the Pali word *upasaka*— meant to encapsulate the idea of Buddhist people as opposed to monks—is usually translated as "laypeople." *Upasaka* is rendered in Burmese as *lu*, literally meaning "human being."⁸

In this Asokan model, state and religious institutions were indeed "separate," as Mirjam Weiberg-Salzmann posited in her study on pre-colonial Sri Lanka (2014), so it looks as though a specific form of functional and ideological secularity was ingrained in Buddhist polity. However, the "lay" and "religious" fields were actually connected through their symbiosis in an all-encompassing Buddhist polity (*thathana-daw* in Burmese) formed as an area of Buddha's teachings (*thathana*, Pali *sâsana*)⁹ and distinguished through the adjunction of the qualifier for "royal" (*daw*). At the apex of this polity, the king was the prominent Sangha's patron. In this kind of polity, "hierarchy was about degrees of dependency" (Errington 2012: 22). It allowed for distinctive sets of religious observances, as Alexey Kirichenko (2009) has shown, and even a degree of religious pluralism. *Thathana*—often translated as "religion"—was really the all-encompassing Buddhicized social space (Brac de la Perrière 2017b).

## 3 "Defense of Religion" in Burmese Colonial History as Nationalist Politics

In Burma, however, this historical situation was critically disturbed by colonial conquest. Under British rule, and contrary to Burmese royal practice, non-inter-

---

7 This model of kingship is termed Asokan after the name of its mythic founder, the Buddhist Mauryan emperor, Asoka, who ruled over India from 273 to 232 BC. See in particular Robert Lingat 1989, and Stanley Tambiah 1976.
8 In Pali literature, Buddhist society is seen as constituted by four assemblies (monks, nuns, laymen and laywomen) according to two criteria: gender and religious status. This Buddhist framing of society still lays the groundwork for the conceptualization of a Buddhist civil society, independent of the state.
9 *Thathana* from the Pali *sâsana* has long been the main term for designating Buddhist teaching and its institutions in Burmese, a term that could be rendered as Buddhicized social space (Brac de la Perrière 2017b). See also Gustaaf Houtman 1990 and Alexey Kirichenko 2009.

ference in religious matters was official policy. To counter such "benign neglect," Burmese Buddhists were driven to engage in the safeguard of their "religion"—termed *thathana* (P. *sâsana*)—more directly than ever before. They expanded the donation-path by becoming involved in practices that were previously the prerogative of monastics, such as the study of Buddhist writings (*pariyatti*) and meditation (*patipatti*).[10] Alicia Turner writes that "the shared responsibility of preserving the *sâsana* produced a moral community that became a powerful source of identity, motivation and shared sentiment for Buddhists in colonial Burma" (2014:82). This movement to preserve Buddhist institutions (*thathana*, P. *sâsana*), she explains, was connected to earlier discourses on religious decline and reform, and later evolved into a proto-nationalist discourse. People's increased participation in the maintenance of Sangha and Buddhist teachings gave them a new sense of being Buddhists. The result was a social shift from the king-patronized Buddhist society to one patronized by "laypeople" (*lu*), building on pre-colonial symbiosis of Buddhist and state institutions. These developments can be seen as the first movement of "defense of *thathana*" by laypeople and a model for the contemporary reformulation of Buddhist nationalism.

The colonial situation caused the discourse of "defense of *thathana*" to evolve into a moral discourse of opposition to the institution in power, whether that be the colonial administration or, later on, the military. Members of the Sangha have voiced this moral discourse of opposition on several occasions, from the celebrated involvement of Ottama and Wisara in the nationalist cause in the 1920s to the no less celebrated "Saffron revolution" of September 2007. In all cases, the political authorities were liable to dismiss the monks' actions as an infringement of their state of renunciation. Both the colonial authorities and the military juntas effectively defrocked and jailed certain monks whom they qualified as "political," thus bringing their religious status into question. Although these authorities have been harshly criticized for their repression of monks, the "political" label applied to a monk has nevertheless acquired a very strong stigma.

---

[10] Interestingly, Houtman sees this shift as a "monasticization" of "laypeople," (1999) while it also could be seen as a product of secularization through which the responsibility for maintaining religious institutions shifted from the state to civil society.

## 4 The Category of *Lawki* and Religious Politics in the Burmese Independent State

Burma was established as an independent state in 1948. It inherited a secular framework from the colonial administration in which freedom of faith is constitutionally guaranteed, although Buddhism is recognized as the religion of the majority. Aung San, the founding father of the Burmese independent state—who was assassinated before its advent, in 1947—made use of the Buddhist concept of "this-worldly" (*lawki*) to articulate the secularist project of governance implied in the Constitution.[11] However, the phrase has not made its way into everyday language. Today, the locution that qualifies the state as "secular"—*lawki hsan de*—means "that which resembles the mundane." It is hardly known to common people in this usage, despite Aung San's using it while planning independence. To my knowledge, *lawki hsan de* is only discussed in specific constitutional discourse, or in new discourses derived from the opening up of a legal political field of action in Burma following the inception of political transition in 2011 after half a century of military rule. For instance, it was used in the *Journal of Human Rights and Democracy* of June 2014—a periodical published by nongovernmental organizations promoting democracy in Burma—in opposition to the outbreak of Buddhist nationalism linked to the anti-Muslim violence prevailing since 2012. Significantly, secularity is brandished in that publication as the antidote to religious extremist nationalism.

In fact, *lawki* is part of the Buddhist legacy in Burmese, and means "that which pertains to this world." It stands in contrast to *lokuttara*, which means "beyond this world" (Houtman 1999: 246). In this sense, it could perfectly fit the Western use of "secular," with which it would then share its original religious framing. However, *lawki* is rarely used to delineate a political or public sphere deliberately kept out of religious life, as revealed by the word *hsan de* "to resemble" being added to it in the phrase *lawki hsan de naingngan daw* to signify this specific use. *Lawki* instead brings to mind an alternative religious path to that of monks' renunciation, and thus a sphere in which monks should not enter if they are to maintain their state of renunciation. In other words, it has not lost its religious connotations, as in the case of the word "secular" in Western languages. Secularism—that is, the political discourse maintaining a dis-

---

[11] See Gustaaf Houtman 1999: 246. As also remarked by Matthew Walton, Aung San's choice of words reveals that "even those Buddhist Burmese political figures who have opposed the establishment of Buddhism as the national religion and advocated for separation of church and state still reason about politics from within a Theravada worldview." (Walton 2012: 75)

tance between politics/public life and religion—is not easily translated in common Burmese language, nor has it been readily adopted from its English form.

Religious issues repeatedly impacted state affairs in the newly independent Burma. Indeed, Buddhism was central to the building of national identity, as exemplified by the Kaba Aye 6$^{th}$ Theravadin Council that Prime Minister Nu sponsored in 1955.[12] While Nu promoted Buddhist nationalism as identity, his government was nevertheless under pressure from young monks who opposed his urban reformist Buddhism and religious policies.[13] In August 1961, amidst the disruption of the first parliamentary era, Nu moved to amend the constitution in order to make Buddhism the state religion, which was one of the opposing monks' demands. This move was one of the factors which caused the 1962 military coup. Ne Win, the strongman behind the coup, is known to have turned to a secular form of power to stop monks' interference in state affairs (Tin Maung Maung Than 1988). However, the new constitution adopted in 1974 (*The Burmese Way towards Socialism*) was explicitly designed as a Buddhist-inspired socialism, further demonstrating the importance of Buddhist ideals in Burmese political thinking.

In May 1980, Ne Win also implemented a religious reform to reassert the government's control over the Buddhist monastic order (the Sangha) by merging its various segments under a single administration, the *Sangha Maha Nayaka Ahpwe*.[14] This body of senior abbots was placed under the Department of Religious Affairs, which became an independent Ministry in 1992. This reform of the Sangha, drafted by an assembly of senior monks under state leadership, is still in effect today. It constitutes what Benjamin Schontal identifies as one of the hybrid law systems through which monastic governance has been implemented in South and Southeast Asian Theravadin countries (2018). However, while the Burmese scholar Tin Maung Maung Than praised the reform for its sec-

---

**12** On the role of this Council in the consolidation of the nascent nation, see in particular Chris Clark 2015.
**13** About this period, see Donald Smith 1965 and Hiroko Kawanami 2016.
**14** The merging of various segments of the Burmese Sangha under one single religious administration was conform to monastic rule that sanctions incitement to division with exclusion of the monastic order. However, disputes over religious discourses and practice were in fact intrinsic to the socio-religious dynamics of monastic orders in Theravadin polities and tendencies to segmentation—or "sectarianism" as put by Michael Mendelson—have marked religious history as shown by the number of historical branches composing the Burmese Sangha before the 1980 monastic reform (See M. Mendelson 1975). The overall merging in one single religious administration suffered but one exception, that of the Shwegyin branch, one of the latest and most elitist of the various segments that maintained its separate existence against Thudhamma, the main body of the Sangha.

ularism in 1988, parts of the Sangha have more recently raised harsh critiques, blaming it for having "yoked" monks to the government (Brac de la Perrière 2015a: 41; Keiko Tosa 2013) In fact, it appears that Ne Win's administration was truly concerned with restraining Buddhist monks' initiative by delineating their proper place according to monastic rule (*Vinaya*). Indeed, by forcing monks to stick to their religious role as it was defined in new regulations, Ne Win's reform of the Sangha had an enduring impact on religious politics in Burma.

Later on, the military's return to power after the 1988 events and the lost elections in 1990 signaled a restoration of the historical symbiosis between the state and Sangha—dating back to the times of Burmese monarchy—through a systematic policy of funding and supporting Buddhist institutions as an alternative source of state legitimation (Schober 2011). This renewed interdependency was only questioned by a few outstanding monastic figures, such as the abbot of Thamanya (Rozenberg 2010). However, it was strongly affected by the 2007 Saffron Revolution, which marked a return of monastics to the political arena as a force enjoying a certain degree of agency, as they experimented with new ways of fulfilling religious roles (Brac de la Perrière 2015b).

Even such a brief record of the relations between Buddhism and state administration since Independence shows that the secular frame of the state defined by the Burmese constitution has not prevented the pervasive presence of Buddhism in the public space and debate. As Niels Bubandt and Martjin van Beek wrote in their book *Varieties of Secularism in Asia* (2012), secularism is usually envisioned as having emerged in Asia with post-colonial questions of nationality. However, what has been observed in Burma since Independence looks more like tension between political institutions designed to be secular and a social life and national identity imbued with Buddhism.

## 5 Monks Intervening in "Defense of Buddhism"

The 2008 constitution guarantees freedom of faith to all citizens, "subject to public order, morality or health" through article I.34. It is further qualified in various articles of chapter VIII, particularly article 361 recognizing the special position of Buddhism as the faith professed by the great majority. Religious belonging is constitutive of citizens' identity and has to be mentioned on identity cards together with ethnicity. As for monks, they are separately registered as members of the Sangha under the Ministry of Religion. Not only does the monastic rule (*Vinaya*) prevent them from becoming involved in politics, considered worldly affairs, but, as is the case for Thai Buddhist monks, they are also constitutionally barred from doing so and even from casting their vote in political elections on the grounds of their renouncer status.¹⁵ With the advent of the political transition, the 2010 general elections and the subsequent opening up of a legal political field of action for civil society, some monks started to perceive their disenfranchisement as a severe disadvantage of their religious status.

It was in this context and amidst the outburst of dramatic anti-Muslim pogroms in central Burma that Mabatha was founded. The violence started in Arakan (Rakhine State) in June 2012 and was immediately followed by a massive campaign to boycott Muslim-run businesses all over Burma. This campaign, known as 969, was led by a network of already influential, relatively young and very active monks.¹⁶ Religious networks such as the *Theravada Dhamma Kumyet* (Theravada Doctrine Network) were launched in August 2012 for the express purpose of preaching the defense of Buddhism through the boycott of Muslim businesses and by praising the Buddhist Arakanese people as being Buddhist Burma's ultimate defense against the Muslim threat from the West.

The campaign's success came as a surprise. All of a sudden, in the winter of 2012–2013, 969 stickers were everywhere, stuck by Buddhist laypeople on all sorts of businesses, moto-taxis, betel stalls and more established shops. They displayed the 969 logo to assert that the businesses were run by Buddhists and thus eligible for transactions. Activist monks relied on the practice of mass preaching by night, at the invitation of lay collectivities, to distribute the stickers on masse. Such public preaching had all but disappeared during Ne Win era. But since the 1990s, the practice had slowly been revitalized with state encouragement, and since the Nargis cyclone it had grown exponentially. It was appropriated by a new generation of monks eager to gain some independence from the political and religious establishments while developing new ways to perform their religious role (Brac de la Perrière 2015b.). Indeed, 969 monks were able to secure access to a large audience through the renewed practice of public preaching and the wide circulation of sermons made possible by the loosening of censorship and the new media technologies available since the regime change.

---

**15** On the disenfranchisement of Buddhist monks in Theravadin societies, see Thomas Larsson 2015.
**16** The number 969 actually refers to the 9 virtues of the Buddha, the 6 ones of the Dhamma and the 9 ones of the Sangha, which together represent the whole Buddhist teachings. It was popularized by Moulmein monks as a didactic means to teach lay Buddhists and used in contradistinction with the number 786 that was then very generally signaling Muslim shops in Burma and was meant to be a numeral representation of Bismillah prayer.

Surprisingly, religious authorities, particularly the *Sangha Maha Nayaka Ahpwe*, which was the monastic central authority established by Ne Win administration, did nothing to check the often aggressively anti-Muslim speeches of 969 monks. Those ideas had spread so widely following the Rohingya issue that when I arrived in Burma for field research in March 2013, I heard rumors that because of this campaign, "religious war" (*batha taik bwe*) was about to break out. Indeed, two weeks later, anti-Muslims pogroms started to flare up in Central Burma.

However, on May 6, 2013, a general convention of monks was held in Yangon under the leadership of the abbot of Insein Ywama monastery, apparently to address the inter-confessional crisis. The context was very much one of criticism of the use of the Buddhist 969 symbol for an anti-Muslim campaign. What came out of this meeting was the formation of a new association that six months later would be dubbed "Mabatha." The main explicit objective of Mabatha was to defend Buddhism as the religion of the majority group in Burma. This expresses the tension inherent to the constitution's recognition of Theravada Buddhism as the majority group religion while also granting freedom of faith. It is worth taking a look at the conceptual framework of Mabatha's foundation in more detail, using two sources: the text that came out of the May 6 meeting, which is a sort of charter for Mabatha, and another text that was circulating in monasteries at the time, whose authors have requested anonymity.[17]

The name "Mabatha" stands for *amyo batha thathana saung shauk yay ahpwe*, which brings together three words qualifying different aspects of belonging in Burmese, all of which are difficult to translate. *Amyo* means familial group, ethnic group, nation or even race, according to the context; *batha* is 'religion' in the Western sense of individually professed denomination[18]; and *thathana*, as mentioned earlier, is the Pali *sâsana* and refers to the dispensation of the Buddha's teachings, that is, the institutions dedicated to the maintenance of Buddhism in Burma. These notions thus combined refer to Burmese national identity as exclusively Buddhist, as most Burmese conceive of it today. In this compound, *batha*—a concept introduced in the mid-nineteenth century to translate the Western concept of 'religion'—has become the main component of Bur-

---

**17** See my 2015 paper in French, "Ma Ba Tha, Les trois syllables du nationalisme birman," for a more detailed analysis.

**18** *Batha* is the Burmese rendering of the Indian *basha* meaning language. Its first meaning in Burmese is also language when used with the verb to speak (*pyaw*). When used with the verb to worship (*kokwe*), it refers to religion as an individually professed faith. In Mabatha's full name, the meaning 'religion' is inferred from the discourse of defense of religion that is the main objective advocated by the organization's leaders.

mese identity, while *thathana*, which had been the marker of the Burmese Buddhist polity and of the 1930s discourses of defense of Buddhism, is relegated to the background.[19] This conceptual shift is in itself telling of a relocation of religion in the socio-political configuration from an all-encompassing frame into a more individualized and private orientation defined as a faith, a process that traduces a degree of secularization.

The defense of the national religion is asserted in the Mabatha's founding charter as a common objective that religious and lay people alike must embrace, in other words, as the cement of national unity. By promoting national unity through the defense of Buddhism, monastics appropriate for themselves what had been the main prerogative of the army during the military regimes, and what a parliamentary regime accused of being "too divisive" could not achieve. By elevating the defense of Buddhism to a primary national "cause," monks appropriated national identity as their affair, a religious affair through which they act as surrogates of an army that had previously been the main guardian of the said identity. Thus, the initiative to form Mabatha has to be considered as emerging from the socio-political situation. It is a product of transitional Burma in which the army has to surrender a number of prerogatives, including the defense of national identity as Buddhist, while monks were left to look for their own role themselves.

Let us note that a general monks' convention outside of Mahana—as the central authority of the Sangha (the *Sangha Maha Nayaka Ahpwe*) came to be known after Mabatha's formation—was in itself a strong act of independence by monks behind the scenes, among whom 969 activist monks were prominent. Indeed, it could be taken as an act of secession that would be a major infringement of the Vinayic code. The matter was largely mitigated, however, by an explicit appeal to all the monks belonging to the Sangha to participate, on the grounds that the responsibility to preserve Buddhism was incumbent on all sorts of monks, whatever their practice or position. At first, the official and activist Buddhist organizations (Mahana and Mabatha) appeared partially to overlap. Mabatha's influence on Sangha was therefore not easy to assess if only because Mabatha monks were part of larger existing monastic networks.

---

**19** Houtman, 1990 and Kirichenko 2009. For the appropriation of the Western concept of 'religion' in Burma see Brac de la Perrière 2017b.

## 6 The *Discourse* of the "Political" Monks

I would like to consider another text, authored by monastics from circles that had previously opposed the juntas. This text was circulated into monasteries during Mabatha's formative period. The monks that gave it to me had been imprisoned under the previous administration and requested anonymity, so I can only use its headline to identify it: "Discourse addressed to the monastics to freely express their hidden wishes according to their religious karma" dated April 23, 2013 and signed by a monk who presents himself as an historian. The text is a strong critique of the status granted to the Sangha and monks in Burma since the 1980 monastic reform. While the overt opposition to the ecclesiastic authorities in this text is at odds with Mabatha's charter, its stance for the defense of "national religion" is, on the contrary, attuned to that of Mabatha.

The *Discourse* is a technical discussion of the various acts through which the monastic legal status and the Sangha institution have been run since Independence, according to the dialectics of "just rule" as compared to "rule of strength" (*dhamma sek/ana sek*). It is also a violent critique of the Sangha reform implemented under Ne Win's rule in 1980, which is said to have "yoked" the Sangha to the civilian order. Particularly disputed is the way religious men have been excluded from political action while, in their time, monks such as Ottama and Wisara, heroes of the anti-colonial fight, had taken on the responsibility of awakening lay people's patriotic spirit. Finally, the *Discourse* claims that political action is legitimate for monks, who should have the right to cast votes and to enter into a political contest.

In other words, the *Discourse* consists in a monastic view on the history of state-Sangha relations in independent Burma, opposing the way monks have been distanced from public leadership, in their view wrongly, whereas they were the true "fathers" of the nation. It expresses a strong opposition to military leadership and encourages the whole Sangha to take the opportunity offered by the democratic transition to recover political initiative in the name of the defense of religion. While there is no anti-Islamism in this text, what it has in common with Mabatha's charter is its insistence on reclaiming the monks' position as "nation" leaders, "nation" being understood as Buddhist.

What looking at the two texts together shows is that Mabatha emerged in 2013 in the midst of intense debate among the Sangha over what monks' role should be during political transition, a debate driven by the secularizing tendency of this process. However, the political dimension of Mabatha's program only became clear during the 2015 electoral campaign. Probably because political action is, as a rule, disregarded for monks in Burma, Mabatha monks had claimed no political role in their charter, whereas monks who once opposed the juntas — particularly those involved in 2007 "Saffron revolution"— called openly for such a role in their *Discourse*. Arguably, the reason for this is that, due to the ban on political action for monks and the unstated secularizing effect of political transition, no place had been carved out for monks.

As already noted, monks are deprived of the right to vote and of involvement in politics both in the new parliamentary constitution and from the monastic-rule point of view. However, what transpires most strikingly from Mabatha's charter and the *Discourse* is that, paradoxically, in the name of the defense of Buddhism, both texts claim the same position for monks as leaders of the "nation"— an exclusively Buddhist nation. Still, they both represent very different political positions that seem to continue the pre-transitional tension between "governmental monks" and junta-opposed "political monks".[20] In reality, these texts reveal a polarization of politically engaged parts of the Sangha, which probably consist only of minorities of the whole monastic body. In other words, the transitional process seems to have driven some monks to put their religious status under threat by involving themselves in worldly affairs rather than risk marginalization.

# 7 The Mabatha's Political Work

In the two years following its foundation, Mabatha took on more and more importance and became increasingly active on various fronts through a range of bodies that mushroomed according to needs. These include the *dhamma skuls* organization operating according to the Sri Lankan Sunday school template, the *Theravada dhamma* network facilitating monks' preaching activities, various monastic charity foundations (*parahita*), the Save the Shwedagon group, and all sorts of activities not directly linked to Mabatha but with objectives that tie in with its agenda and target its envisioned moral reform of Buddhist society. Most of these activities depend on renewed and growing religious donation networks, particularly through the incremental development of public preaching, which has become a new source of wealth for monastics. Meanwhile, the core of Mabatha organization's monks have been reacting to events, particularly by putting cases against what they consider "insults to (Buddhist) religion" (*thatha-*

---

[20] This enduring polarization of the engaged parts of the Sangha does not mean that individuals have not moved from one activist position to the other one as demonstrated by Wirathu's example, one of Mabatha leaders.

*na saw ka*) or moving against any public use of the designation Rohingya, which has become intolerable in the Buddhist ultra-nationalist worldview. Though not very numerous, maybe a few thousand, these monks have been supported by very dedicated lay followers and they have acted inside larger monastic networks. They could best be described as "religious activists" working through a nebulous network that has managed to boost the Buddhist nationalist discourse and made it all-pervasive on the public scene from 2012 to 2017, when the Mabatha organization was dismantled.

One important practical objective of Mabatha, already stated in the May 2013 charter, was to have laws preventing Buddhist women from marrying Muslim men. To quote the charter: "The most important thing to insure harmony between people of different faiths living together is to pass laws firmly protecting (Buddhist women); we believe it is the only way" (my translation). The argument supporting the proposal to legally require Muslim men who marry Buddhist women to convert to Buddhism is that Islam is a foreign religion and that Muslims are foreigners. The rhetoric of Buddhism as the religion of the Burmese nation actually blocks consideration of other religions in the national framework, regardless of the constitutional clause about freedom of conscience. Indeed, one of Mabatha's main achievements over its four years of existence has been the drafting and passing of a set of four inter-confessional laws regulating marriage, conversion, polygamy, and reproduction that are usually seen as targeting Muslim communities, although they are not expressed in this way.

Moreover, in the 2013 charter, religion is declared "of the utmost importance, being what shapes humanity." This declaration is to be read as a critique of democratic values, such as the individual freedom included in the Burmese translation of 'human rights' (*ahkwin ayay*). In Burmese, the expression evokes an overly relaxed attitude, which ultra-nationalist Buddhists contrast with the notion of 'human value' (*lu tanbo*). This is indirectly a political position, as the partisans of the decried human rights are identified as the democrats from the NLD. Moreover, the campaign to have inter-confessional laws passed in great hast, before the general elections of November 2015, was an indication that Mabatha's core people were aligned with the USDP (Union Solidarity and Development Party, the offshoot of the military administrations) during its mandate and that the USDP made use of the religious association for their political ends on this occasion. Meetings to promote the inter-confessional laws actually served as anti-NLD platforms during the electoral campaign, to the point where NLD complained to the electoral commission regarding the use of religion in politics, a bias expressly condemned in the electoral law.

However, the electoral commission's decision was to dismiss the NLD complaint because this was not a case of politicians misusing religion, but rather of religious men stepping into electoral politics, a situation that was not covered by electoral law. This shows the ubiquity of Mabatha, whose agency may be seen as political or religious depending on how one looks at it. Certainly, one argument that Mabatha monks recurrently used in their defense when criticized for infringing monastic rules was that their actions were not political, but merely performed in defense of the Buddhist religion, which is fully consistent with their role in the Sangha. This also shows that, in this case, the religious status of Mabatha monks encompassed that of politicians as it allowed them to get around electoral law. In any case, what was at stake was the place of monks in politics, questioning the inherent secularity of the political field.

Looking back, it seems that the inter-confessional laws must have been an object of trade between the governmental party, then USDP, and Mabatha, to have been passed in such a short lapse of time —less than two years. The question of the use of Mabatha as a political instrument surfaced during the 2015 general elections, only to be denied by the association's leaders, who reasserted that they were not linked to any party and were only acting for the benefit of Buddhism. In the end, Aung San Suu Kyi's NLD won the elections, suggesting that Burmese public at large considered it was not the place of monastics to interfere with politics. In this regard, the 2015 elections may be described as a performance of secularity by laypeople, in which they expressed disagreement with Mabatha's push to vote against NLD. However, this secularist performance only concerned the elections and was not followed by a decline of the Mabatha ideology, which sees Burmese identity as exclusively Buddhist.

This development did at least force the NLD and Aung San Suu Kyi to come out of their silence and overtly condemn Mabatha's political use of Buddhism. Aung San Suu Kyi had become a quasi-religious iconic figure due to representing the opposition to military rule for 25 years —most of this time under house of arrest —, and had appraised meditation and Buddhist values as powerful tools to resist the juntas' oppression. She was to distance herself from such a religious stance when she came to power. The new democratic government then made some moves against Mabatha. The first was to silence one of Mabatha's main leaders, Wirathu, whose extremism and anti-Muslim hate speech had made him infamous abroad, particularly through the film on "Evil" that Barbet Shroeder dedicated to this controversial character.[21] In 2016, Wirathu's Facebook page was closed and he was banned from public preaching for one year. Then, Mahana, the central monastic authority, declared Mabatha an illegal monastic organ-

---

21 *Le Vénérable W.* See also Brac de la Perrière 2017a.

ization; its label was outlawed in May 2017, as 969 had been in the summer of 2013.

Yet, this did not mean that religious-activist monks who had made the discourse of the 'defense of Buddhism' against the threat of Islam so strident over the past few years had disappeared or were less active.[22] On the contrary, some Mabatha monks then decided to act overtly on the political scene, planning to form a party of their own, though the right to do so has been denied to them. The ultra-nationalist rhetoric had become increasingly political, bluntly targeting the NLD governance for its supposed leniency towards foreign intrusions. In May 2019, Wirathu was put under an arrest warrant for sedition, after having publicly insulted Aung San Suu Kyi —which means that action against him had only been possible through a civil case. He then lived undercover amidst wild rumors until he suddenly decided to reappear and surrender to the police, just before the 2020 general elections. Though this last episode is puzzling, it is difficult to ignore its link with the coming polls, in preparation to which ultra-nationalist monks had campaigned for the military. Particularly, they had released at their Insein Ywama annual meeting, in June 2019, a much commented seven-point statement urging their followers to reject the acting government in the ballots.

The NLD government did not take any action against such political statements by ultra-nationalist monks, through electoral commission or Mahana, in spite of it going clearly against monastic rule, showing that in 2019 as in 2015, those monks' religious status and nationalist discourse allowed them to bypass political power. NLD politicians refused to comment on this issue, expressing their confidence that Buddhist laypeople already knew what to think about Insein Ywama's statement, thus pointing on Mabatha's loss of hegemony.[23] Indeed, the result of the 2020 polls was overwhelmingly in favor of Aung San Suu Kyi's NLD, to the dismay of the military establishment. This can also be seen as renewed evidence of the reluctance of the Burmese electorate to let monastics interfere with politics: as in 2015, the 2020 elections were a performance of secularity by laypeople.

---

**22** In May 2017, the group actually rebranded itself as the Buddha Dhamma Prahita Foundation shifting to a focus on charity activities (*parahita*) that had been recently upgraded as one possible way for monks to act in the world, and which had since become central to monastic fund raising.

**23** See for instance: Kyaw Phyo Tha, "Buddhist Nationalists Urge Voters to Shun NLD at Ballot Box" *The Irrawaddy*, 19.6.2019.

## 8 The Military Coup, the Resistance Movement and the Sangha

The 2020 NLD victory was soon contested by the USDP and military authorities, invoking massive flaws that have not been recognized by the electoral commission, driving Min Aung Hlaing, the chief of armies, to enforce a state of emergency and to take over power on February 1, 2021.[24] The coup from the military was not a surprise in itself: after all, far from having "returned to their barracks", the juntas had only gone for top-down political reforms as long as the constitution insured them control over the key power positions. The putsch's brutal occurrence 10 years after a political transition that had changed the people's quality of life and brought promises of a future for new generations was unbearable to most people in Burma. They massively turned to a protest movement that seems to prove resilient, in spite of harsh repression. The protesters first called for their votes to be respected, and for the liberation of the NLD leaders who had been arrested. A parallel government, the National Union Government (NUG) has now been formed, claiming legitimacy from the November 2020 polls. It is protected by a number of ethnic armies, which stand united against the Myanmar army (Tatmadaw). Now that the crisis is entrenched, and close to a civil war, there seems to be room for discussions on a new constitution, which would allow for more federalism and the eviction of the Tatmadaw.

It is impossible, on this day, to foresee what could come out of this radical confrontation between an entrenched military establishment and a resolute resistance movement emerging from civil society and ethnic and religious minorities, and led by a new generation advancing ideas about inclusive democracy. One point is striking concerning monks' involvement in the crisis, that is their remarkable avoidance of the scene: contrary to their role at the forefront of 2007 Saffron revolution, when they claimed to give a voice to the muted people against the military rule, and contrary to the hectic activism of ultra-nationalist monks since the beginning of the political transition, monks have been relatively discreet since the military coup. As stated by Susan Hayward: "It is not Buddhist monastics but young laypeople who are at the forefront".[25]

Only some groups of Mabatha monks have been part of the Buddhist ceremonies organized by military men to bless their renewed rule, and only some

---

[24] For an analysis of the 2020 elections and its narrative by the military, see Michael Lidauer's paper in Tea Circle (2021, May 17th).
[25] Susan Hayward, May 3, 2021, "Beyond the Coup in Myanmar. Don't Ignore the Religious Situation" *Just Security* blog.

young monks, particularly in Mandalay, the second city of the country known for its vibrant young monastic population, have marched along protesters of the military coup. This shows the continuing polarization between politically engaged parts of the Sangha which emerged from the political transition. However, the bulk of monastic people seem to have stayed at the rear of the resistance movement, although a number of them provide to lay activists their monasteries' shelter. A strikingly new phenomena appeared in February, when pictures of files of monks touring to give food to people involved in the huge strikes of civil servants were displayed, in a reversal of the normative religious donation relationship, conveying the idea of monks turning to "followers" of the civil disobedience movement (CDM) in these circumstances.

Logically, the bulk of monastic people seem to position themselves along with the majority of laypeople demanding the respect of their vote against the military rule, although they themselves are disenfranchised. As for the monastic establishment, Mahana and Shwegyin abbots called for the coup perpetrators to stop using violence. This can be seen as a rather mild position following the putsch, in the midst of the opinions voiced by the main actors of Burmese society. However, another statement was reportedly made by Mahana monks,[26] according to which they intended to halt their board activities in protest against the military rule, thus apparently joining the civil disobedience movement. Susan Hayward (*ibid.*) argued that, if this statement was confirmed, it would be the first time since 1980 that the monastic central administration would disentangle from the state. Until now, however, the monastics have been kept at the margins of decision making by the laypeople's resistance movement to military rule.

# 9 The Silent Work of Transition on Buddhist Secularity

During the political transition (2011–2021), public opinion has been divided in Burma on the question of how to consider the more extremist monks and whether their activism was acceptable given their monastic status. On the one hand, the religious ultra-nationalists seem to have succeeded in uniting Buddhist people around the exclusively Buddhist identity of the Burmese nation. On the other one, the specific form of secularity ingrained in Theravadin formations was still apparent in transitional Burma's reluctance to accept that monks may step into

---

**26** See also *Eleven News*, March 17, 2021.

world affairs and play an overt role in electoral politics. Moreover, the secularity of politics involved in the transitional process created new conditions for political action that formally excluded monks. Thus, some of them felt that the ongoing process of modernization threatened to deprive them of their central position of influence in the traditional all-encompassing Buddhist polity. In other words, two kinds of secularity were actually in conflict in the Burmese transitional situation: the Buddhist kind and the democratic kind.

As it is, the transitional process has had two interrelated effects in the religious field: first, to elicit the foundation of Mabatha in order to get around the containment of the Sangha in its religious role and for some monks to step into the political arena and take sides; second, to force the NLD to distance itself from Buddhist nationalist monks and to discipline Mabatha. In other words, it has the dual effect of pushing extremist parts of the religious body into politics and of provoking the reaction of the newly elected democratic government to reassert the governmental authorities' control over the monastic order. These movements are clear signals of an ongoing silent debate on where religion should be, caused by the opening up of the political field and of the inherent secularization process that goes with it. Yet these developments have not elicited an open debate concerning secularism and religious pluralism as matters of importance for democracy in Burma. It may be that the present crisis situation works as an eye-opener on the necessity for a more inclusive democracy in Burma. It should also signal the need to carve out a place of their own for Buddhist monks in an evolving socio-political configuration.

The transitional moment needs to be compared to that of the colonial encounter, when the British administration's neglect of religion led the Buddhist laypeople (*lu*) to assume the defense of Buddhist teachings (*thathana*) in the place of the kings, taking over religious actions that were previously the prerogative of monastics. Some monks formed Mabatha, an organization meant to supplement Mahana, the allegedly "impotent" central administration of the Sangha, and stepped into politics to "defend religion"—that is, Buddhism— as the national religion (*batha*). As a result, the moral discourse of "defense of religion" has moved from the traditional conceptual framework of religion as a Buddhicized social space (*thathana*) allowing for a relative religious pluralism, to the exclusivist notion of Buddhist faith as defining the national identity of the Burmese (*batha*). While the Buddhist laypeople defending *thathana* in the face of the colonial rule they resented had no agency left other than religious, the Mabatha monks felt compelled to enter the political and legislative arena to defend the Buddhist national identity and react to universal values of democracy. They thus seem to have undergone a sort of secularizing process.

# References

Arendt, Hannah. 1951. *L'impérialisme*, Gallimard.
Asad, Talal. 2003. *Formations of the Secular: Christianity, Islam, Modernity*. Stanford University Press, Stanford.
Bilgrami, Akeel, ed. 2016. *Beyond the Secular West*. Columbia University Press.
Brac de la Perrière, Bénédicte. 2015a. "Ma Ba Tha, les trois syllabes du nationalisme religieux birman". *Asie du Sud-Est 2015*, pp. 31–44. Bangkok, Irasec.
Brac de la Perrière, Bénédicte. 2015b. "A generation of monks in the democratic transition". In Egreteau, Renaud, and Robinne, Francois, eds., *Metamorphosis: Studies in Social and Political Change in Myanmar*, pp. 320–345. Singapore: NUS Press.
Brac de la Perrière, Bénédicte. 2017a. "Le Vénérable W., portrait d'une figure birmane de la provocation: Un troisième volet à la 'Trilogie du mal' de Barbet Schroeder". *Blog Terrain* Sept.
Brac de la Perrière, Bénédicte. 2017b. "About Buddhist Burma. *Thathana* or 'Religion' as Social Space". In M. Picard, ed. *The Appropriation of 'Religion' in Southeast Asia and Beyond*, pp. 39–66. Palgrave Macmillan.
Bubandt, Niels, and Martijnvan Beek, eds. 2012. *Varieties of Secularism in Asia. Anthropological explorations of religion, politics and the spiritual*. Routledge.
Clark, Chris. 2015. "The Sixth Buddhist Council: Its Purpose, Presentation, and Product." *The Journal of Burma Studies* 19 no. 1: 70–115.
Errington, Shelly. 2012. "The subject of power in Southeast Asia". In Lianna Chua, Joanna Cook, Nicholas Long and Lee Wilson, ed., *Southeast Asian Perspectives on Power*, pp. 16–36. London: Routledge.
Frydenlund, Iselin. 2017. "Religious Liberty for Whom? The Buddhist Politics of Religious Freedom during Myamar's Transition to Democracy". *Nordic Journal for Human Rights* 35 no. 1: 55–73.
Fuller, Paul. 2018. "The narratives of ethnocentric Buddhist identity". *Journal of the British Association for the Study of Religions* 20: 19–44.
Gravers, Mikael. 2012. "Monks, Morality and Military: The Struggle for moral power in Burma and the uneasy relation with lay power". *Contemporary Buddhism*, 13 no. 1: 1–33.
Gravers, Mikael. 2015. "Anti-Muslim Buddhist Nationalism in Burma and Sri Lanka: Religious Violence and Globalized Imaginaries of Endangered Identities." *Contemporary Buddhism*, 16 no. 1: 1–27.
Hervieu-Leger, Danièle. 2019. "Sécularisation". In *Dictionnaire des faits religieux*. Paris, PUF.
Houtman, Gustaaf. 1990. "How a Foreigner Invented Buddhendom in Burmese: from Tha-tha-na-to to Bok-da ba-tha". *Journal of the Royal Anthropological Society of Oxford* 21 no. 2: 113–128.
Houtman, Gustaaf. 1999. *Mental Culture in Burmese Crisis politics: Aung San Suu Kyi and the national League for Democracy*. Tokyo.
Juergensmeyer, Mark. 2010. "The Global Rise of Religious Nationalism". *Australian Journal of International Affairs*, 64 no. 3: 262–273.
Kawanami, Hiroko. 2016. "U Nu's Liberal Democracy and Buddhist Communalism in Modern Burma". In Kawanami, Hiroko, ed., *Buddhism and the Political Process*, pp. 31–55. Palgrave Macmillan.

Kinvall, Catarina. 2004. "Globalization and religious nationalism: Self, identity and the search for ontological security" *Political Psychology* 25 no. 5: 741–767.

Kirichenko, Alexey. 2009. "From Thathanadaw to Theravâda Buddhism: Constructions of Religion and Religious Identity in Nineteenth- and Early Twentieth-Century Myanmar" . In Thomas DuBois, ed. *Casting Faiths. Imperialism and the Transformation of Religion in East and Southeast Asia*, pp. 520–526. New York, Macmillan.

Larsson, Thomas. 2015. "Monkish Politics in Southeast Asia: Religious Disenfranchisement in Comparative and Theoretical Perspective". *Modern Asian Studies* 49 no. 1: 40–82.

Lidauer, Michael. 2021. "The Politics of Election Cancellations in Myanmar". *Tea Circle*, Oxford, May 2021, 17th.

Lingat, Robert. 1989. *Royautés bouddhiques. Asoka. La fonction royale à Ceylan*. Paris, EHESS.

Mac Mahan, David L. 2017. "Buddhism and Global Secularisms". *Journal of Global Buddhism* 18: 112–128.

Mahmood, Saba. 2016. *Religious Difference in a Secular Age. A Minority Report*. Princeton University Press.

Mendelson, Michael E. 1975. *Sangha and State in Burma: A Study of Monastic Sectarianism and Leadership*, edited by John P. Ferguson. Ithaca, NY: Cornell University Press.

Rozenberg, Guillaume. 2010. *Renunciation and Power: The Quest for Sainthood in Contemporary Burma*, transl. Jessica Hacket. New Haven, CT: Yale Southeast Asia Monograph Series.

Schober, Juliane. 2011. *Modern Buddhist Conjectures in Myanmar. Cultural Narratives, colonial legacies and civil society*. Honolulu, HI: Hawaii Press.

Schontal, Benjamin. 2018. "Buddhist Legal Pluralism? Looking Again at Monastic Governance in Modern South and Southeast Asia". *Buddhism, Law & Society Special Issue*.

Smith, Donald. 1965. *Religion and Politics in Burma*. Princeton, NJ: Princeton University Press.

Tambiah, Stanley. 1976. *World Conqueror, World Renouncer. A Study of Buddhism and Polity in Thailand against a Historical Background*. Cambridge University Press.

Tambiah, Stanley. 1998. "The Crisis of Secularism in India". In Rajeev Bhargava, ed. *Secularism and Its Critics*, pp. 418–453. New Delhi: Oxford University Press.

Taylor, Charles. 2007. *A Secular Age*. Harvard University Press.

Taylor, Charles. 2016. "Can secularism travel?" In Akeel Bilgrami, ed., *Beyond the Secular West*, pp. 1–27. New York: Columbia University Press.

Tin Maung Maung Than. 1988. "The Sangha and Sâsana in Socialist Burma". *Sojourn Journal of Social Issues in Southeast Asia* 3 no. 1 (February): 26–61.

Tosa, Keiko. 2013. "The Sangha and Political Acts: Secularization in a Theravadin Buddhist Society". *Internationales Asienforum* 44 no. 3–4: 271–297.

Turner Alicia. 2014. *Saving Buddhism. The Impermanence of Religion in Colonial Burma*. Honolulu, HI: The University of Hawaii Press.

Van der Veer, Peter. 2014. *The Modern Spirit of Asia. The Spiritual and the Secular in China and India*. Princeton, NJ: Princeton University Press.

Walton, Matthew J. 2012. *Politics in the Moral Universe. Burmese Buddhist Political Thought*. PhD Dissertation, University of Washington.

Walton, Matthew and S. Hayward. 2014. "Contesting Buddhist Narratives. Democratization, Nationalism, and Communal Violence in Myanmar". *Policy Studies* 71. Honolulu, HI: East-Waest Center.

Weiberg-Salzmann, Mirjam, 2014. "The Radicalization of Buddhism in the Twentieth and Twenty-first Centuries. The Buddhist Sangha in Sri Lanka". *Politics, Religion & Society* 15 no. 2: 283–307.

Marie-Dominique Even
# A Twisted Secularity. Anti-Religious Ideology *vs* Secularity and Secularization in Twentieth Century Mongolia

**Abstract:** Under Soviet tutelage from 1921 onwards, Mongolia was deeply transformed during the 70 year-long communist era, then embarked on another radical change of its political, social, and economic system in 1990 when the Soviet Union lost control of its satellite countries. Buddhism, the dominant religion since the seventeenth century, had been reduced to ashes through radical anti-religious policies and scientific atheism imposed as the new and only creed. Like in other post-communist countries, the collapse of communist regimes brought a sudden revitalization of religion, be it ancient beliefs or newly introduced ones. The rapid embrace of religiosity by a large part of the population, supposedly atheist, prompted in part the thesis of a de-secularization (Berger 1999). Conversely some East European sociologists expressed doubts on the degree of secularization in communist countries (Tomka 2002, Zrinščak 2004). The analysis of the religious situation in Mongolia during the twentieth century does not favor the thesis of de-secularization that implies that the society experienced previously a certain degree of secularization. If one follows Taylor's description of secularity as a situation opening a plurality of options in the stead of "unchallenged" God or faith (2007), Mongolia only experienced it after the end of the communist rule.

## 1 Introduction

While the concept of secularization helped to describe the undeniable decline of Christianity in the western world in sociological terms —decline, pluralization, rationalization or desacralization, privatization, institutional differentiation— rather than as a clerical problem of dechristianization, it tended to project the decline of religion at a global level with the progress of modernization. Early on, D. Martin (1969) criticized the extended use of the concept, in which he saw the imposition of a secular ideology rooted in the heterodox traditions of Christianity—the source, in S. Eisenstadt's analysis (2000), of European modernity. Asad (1993) in turn stressed the Christian basis of the concept of secularity and its consequences when translated in different worlds such as Islam. Martin

---
**Marie-Dominique Even,** Groupe Sociétés, Religions, Laïcités (CNRS, EPHE-PSL)

https://doi.org/10.1515/9783110733068-012

had also pointed to the wide variations between "religions" and the specific way they are perceived in different cultures, which prevented any unitary definition of what "religion" was and consequently made impossible to distinguish the religious and the secular. In the face of the persistent religiosity, of the social and political mobilization of religion (Casanova 1994), several criteria of the secularization paradigm were dropped. Progressively the paradigms of multiple modernities (Eisenstadt 1999), multiple differentiations (Casanova 2006) and secularities (Burchardt and Wohlrab-Sahr 2015) reframed the field of research. In this perspective, Soviet regimes that combined, in Casanova words, "extreme forms of philosophical-historical secularism and political secularism" (2019: 17) qualify as one secularity among others. However, such approach takes away some prerequisites of the original sociological concept (such as autonomy of the main social spheres and emancipation of individuals from a dominant religion or ideology) and leaves one concept to name opposite phenomena.

In particular, secularization does not equate to eradicating religion. For Charles Taylor (2007), autonomy best characterizes "our secular age", not the absence of religion but rather the plurality of options available to the individuals in a modern and secular regime. Traditional faiths are only some out of many possibilities that can be used to make sense of our lives. Here secularization is not analyzed as a loss, but as the opening of new possibilities in our experience of the world or in our frame of thought.

The concept "secularization" needs to be differentiated, as Jean Baubérot indicates in his introductory text, from political regulation of religions, the latter being better expressed by institutional arrangement ("laïcité", "secularism", "wall of separation", "neutrality of the state"). Baubérot and Millot (2011) proposed a model, an ideal-type of laïcité based mainly on criteria used in law studies to define a secular state, *i.e.* a state separated from religion and neutral towards religion, individuals enjoying freedom of conscience, and an access to citizenship independent from religion affiliation.

## 2 Post-Communism

If we look at the situation of post-communist countries, we observe that societies have been deeply modernized and transformed, politically, socially, and economically, and have experienced rapid industrialization and urbanization. The distinction made earlier by K. Dobbelaere (1981) and Steve Bruce (1982) seems at first sight relevant with regard to communist societies where "secularized" features at the societal level and individual religiosity (mostly hidden and re-emerging rapidly in the aftermath of the soviet collapse) coexisted. As for laicity or "secular state", elements appear to present at the institutional level. But were these societies as "secularized" and as "modern" and their states as "secular" as it appeared ? And what is the present secularization? Understanding the religious situation in post-communist Mongolia raises the question of the nature of the secularization process under communism and of the limits of its modernity in its philosophical meaning, and of a post-secularization process afterwards.

In communist regimes dominant religions have been violently expelled from their central position (when they held one, China providing a different context from Mongolia or Russia) and lost their influence as important political, social and economic actors. They stopped being the main provider of norms and ethical rules, all aspects that can be seen as marks of secularization. On the other hand, communist states have effectively expelled religious actors and organizations from the new society they aimed to build, if not eradicated them, and have substituted new dogmas (Marxism-Leninism, scientism, and atheism) to the former faiths providing a new and only system of norms and reference to the population. The utopian, even messianic dimension of the communist imaginary, the sacralization of the founding fathers and of the most authoritarian leaders, the mode of organization of its agents, the mobilization of the masses, should invite us to question the "secular" nature of these states, of the effective separation between religion and the state, and of the reality of the high degree of secularization process they have experienced. Their anti-religious and anti-clerical tenants, their valorization of sciences and call for modernization at all levels seem to correspond to the march towards the autonomy of communities and individuals from absolute, transcendental laws, but do they? Or should they be analyzed as failed avatars of universal religions? There is nothing new in seeing in these new ideologies lay, secular or civil religions (R. Aron, for example). The terminology does express the idea of a religious ideology, but it makes things more confused when one wishes to explore the question of secularity or secularization regarding communist societies.

In these apparently very "secularized" societies, however, populations have in a large part rapidly turned back to traditional beliefs or adopted new ones, as soon as the political circumstances allowed it. Although these societies share common features there is much variation in the revival patterns that can be observed, as underlined by Siniša Zrinščak (2004) being the most or the last religious country depends heavily on the sociocultural and political history of each country. Hungary or (East-) Germany differs from Russia or Poland, and from Mongolia, the three latter having gone through a stronger religious revival.

In Mongolia, a survey was conducted in 1994, *i.e.* four years after the peaceful transition to democracy and the instauration of a multi-party system in the Spring of 1990. In the survey, 71% declared themselves "believers", a striking contrast with the results of an earlier one carried in the middle of the 1980s, *i.e.* before the transition, when over 80% had declared that they had nothing to do with religion or were indifferent to it (Tsedendamba 2003: 13; 59–60). At the time, the old communist order was still in place, and atheism was perceived as a norm not to be transgressed. For Mongols today, the Russian and little used term "secularization" *(sekularizaciya)* is interpreted as "atheism", and if a few among the communist old guard still pride themselves as being "atheist" (Mong. *shashin-güi* "without religion"), the notion is perceived very negatively by most. After losing its Soviet mentor the Mongolia's People's revolutionary party had no other choice than shifting to social democracy to satisfy its new financial backers and maintain his loosened grip over Mongolia, winning the (first) free parliamentary elections staged in 1992. Yet very few of its members would declare themselves "atheist" or defend the communist purges, and indeed declared having been themselves personally victims of the anti-Buddhist purges. Young people were in general less uniformly "Buddhists", les interested in clinging to Mongolian Buddhism than their elders, and they were more susceptible to convert and become Christians.

# 3 Background

Before their exposure and eventual conversion to different established religions (Nestorian Christianism, Buddhism, Islam, or Taoism) from the twelfth century onwards and during they imperial rule in Asia, Mongol populations resorted to forms of ancestral worship and to shamanist practice which never fully disappeared, where a sociological distinction between the lay/secular, and "religion" as such was absent. This notion came in use with the adoption of Buddhism. The pre-Buddhist sources we have relate Chinggis Khan and his successors, and differentiate if anything between customs, beliefs *(yos)* which are common to a people to the rule of the king, his orders, and laws *(jasag)*.

Eventually a form of tantric Buddhism was chosen as an official religion by Khubilai Khan who completed the conquest of China. It is at that time that the notion of "Dual principle" *(khoyor yos)*, borrowed through Buddhism from ancient India (Ashoka, the third century BCE emperor who converted to Buddhism, gave rise to many Buddhist legends), was introduced in the political practice of the Mongols. It linked closely the temporal, civil power of the ruler, protector of the *Dharma* ("doctrine", i.e. Buddhism), with the spiritual protection of a spiritual master, all for the sake of the state and the people. This idealised model of alliance was implemented by Altan Khan, a powerful regional ruler in the late sixteenth century. It made a clear distinction between the Mongol ruler's secular, temporal rule, or law *(tör,* a term referring to the customary law, rule, or order in the language of the ancient Turks whose empire center was in present-day Mongolia, also found in medieval Mongolian and currently used today for "state") on the one hand, and, on the other, the religion (Mong. *shashin*, "religion", in absolute terms: *Burkhan shashin*, Buddhism) he adopted as national religion and supporting his rule. With the wider diffusion of Buddhism under various Mongol rulers in the 16–17th centuries a strong sociological distinction appeared between lay or "black" *(khar)* and religious or Buddhist (*shar,* litt. "yellow", a reference to the color of religious garments worn by the reformed Gelug order, while *ulaan*, "red", denote older currents of Tibetan Buddhism edged out by the Gelugpa); *khar khün* (a layman, litt. "black man"); *töriin khar khün* a civil servant, litt. "a black man of the state"; *khar bolox* "defrock, return to lay life"); *khariin dansa*, the "register of the laymen [the male population subject to military service]". The opposition black *vs* yellow differentiated the parallel lay (Chingissid) and clerical nobilities in the historiography of the Soviet period "black feudals" *vs* "yellow feudals".

The main word for "religion" (*shashin*, from Sanskrit *çâsana*) entered Mongolian lexicon probably before the fourteenth century through contacts between Mongols and other steppe people with the Sogdians and Buddhist Uighurs. Mongols used it in reference to Buddhism, often on it own as mentioned, and other world religions such as Islam (*laliin shashin*, the religion of Allah) and Christianity, in contrast to their own indigenous religious rites and cults devoid of creed or doctrinal teachings, of formal organizations and, one should add, of the notion of religious belief or faith *(süseg, süseg bishrel)* and its depreciated derivative "superstition" (*mukhar süseg,* litt. "truncated or blind faith") as opposed to the rationalized thinking deployed in the Buddhist monastic teaching and erudite writings. In other words, the concept of "religion" was familiar to the Mongols as was its pendant "lay, civil", expressed by *khar* "black" and, at the institutional level, by *tör*, the secular rule of the khan. These concepts were embedded in the local, strongly Buddhicized culture before the twentieth century modernization upheaval, and are of the same kind as the complementary opposition religious/clerical *vs* secular in the western Christian world.

The close alliance between secular and religious elites fully reinstated by Altan Khan in the late sixteenth century reached a peak in 1911, when after over two centuries of Manchu suzerainty, Khalkha Mongols enthroned as "Saint King" of Mongolia (Bogd Khan) their most prestigious reincarnated lama, the 8th Javzandamba khutagt (see below). The "Dual principle" inherited from Buddhist political concepts had an enduring legacy: it was reactivated after the 1990 transition within the Revolutionary Party by some members including the Prime minister Byambasüren, with the aim to develop a new political path in phase with Mongolia's traditions.

## 4 Modernization

Economic modernization started in 1911. As the Manchu empire was close to its end the main representatives of the Chinggisid nobility and the Buddhist high clergy organized the return to independence of the Mongols, and together established a form of theocratic regime (1911–1921/24). The country opened as much as the geopolitical situation would permit and new foreign resident from Russia, Europe, United States installed the first infrastructures (telegraph, banks, mines…). This economic modernization kept unchanged the old social order and its twin aristocracy, the Chinggisid secular nobility, and the clerical "yellow" aristocracy specific to Buddhism. The influence and prestige of Gelugpa Buddhism in Mongolia were indeed immense. Closely associated with the secular political nobility, Buddhism was able to secure a religious monopoly on the Mongols in the previous three centuries. This and the weakening of the Chinggisid nobility vassal of the Manchu emperors explained why it was the major religious figure, the Bogd Ghegheen ("Holy Enlightened One", the popular designation of the $8^{th}$ Jebstundamba, a lineage of reincarnated lamas coming in importance just after the ones of the Dalai lama and the Panchen lama) who was chosen as the new king, or Bogd Khan ("Holy King") of the restored Mongolian state, albeit being originally a Tibetan. At the time (1919) the number of monks was over 100 000, for a total population of about 650 000 people (in Northern or "Outer" Mongolia). Mongolia was what Taylor calls a society "religiously saturated" (2007: 816–817) where God or the spirits arose inevitably in all facets of life, still under its "ancient regime" form where, to use D. Hervieu-Léger's expression, "religion is everywhere".

Political modernization and reform only occurred after the so-called People's revolution of 1921, a fight for national independence which eventually turned into a Bolshevik regime, so as to gain Soviet support which came with Comintern's close guidance. The uprising was initially triggered by Mongolia's occupation (1919) by troops of Republican China, against a treaty signed in 1915 by Russia, China, and Mongolia. As Russia was in the turmoil of civil war, China who considered itself as the legitimate heir to the Manchu vast empire and vassal territories, sent troops to Mongolia.

## 5 Buddhism Faces Revolution

In the span of a few years a drastic rupture took place. The Mongols, who were playing the Russian card in order to escape Chinese occupation had no other choice but to shift from a feudal theocracy to a revolutionary government (1921) after a Soviet government replaced the tsarist regime in 1917. Since Communism was itself a by-product of Western modernity, Mongolia was to become a modern state, claiming separation of Church and state and advocating atheism under the close guidance of the Comintern. Nevertheless, most members of the Mongol " revolutionary " party and officials in the government were at the time declared Buddhists and had a very limited idea of Lenin's program.

Among lay Buddhists and monks, some trends could be identified: modern, nationalist, social. The modern one was represented by some high religious personalities like the Darva Bandida (who died in 1927), who were conscious of the need for religious as well as social and political reforms, and hence showed good-will for the on-going revolution. The idea of a reformed and purified Buddhism that would not conflict with communist ideals made its way in the minds of the reformers who tried to conciliate their religious views with the necessary modernization of their country. This "Pure Buddhism" or "Buddhist renewal" trend was new in Mongolia proper but was familiar to some educated Buryat Mongol nationalists living in nearby Buryatia (SU), who were in contact with Russian intellectual circles. These Buryat Mongols were to play an important role in the development of the new Mongolian state. People like Tseveen Jamtsarano had campaigned for a revitalized form of Buddhism based on simple primitive principles of the Buddha, freed from its popular superstitions and corrupted clergy, and presented as scientifically acceptable: he wrote that "what Buddhist faith and scriptures teach…corresponds perfectly with science" (Pürevjav et Dashjamts: 113; Bawden 1968, 284–285, 292). They would call it "Buddhism" instead of "religion of the Yellow (Gelugpa)" or "religion of the *burkhan* (bouddha)", as it was known among Mongols, or Lamaism. As a scientist and an influent political personality, Jamtsarano, with political Mongol politicians like Dambadorj, was instrumental in developing a nationalist rationale supportive of preserving Buddhism in Mongolia during the 1920s.

On the other side of the border (as the Mongols failed to be reunified), in Southern or "Inner" Mongolia, the contact with modernity was shaped not by Russian influence but by Chinese one and by China's own model for modernization, i.e. Japan. Contrary to Northern Mongolia, the intronization of a reincarnated lama had been badly perceived by progressist Southern Mongols, eager to modernize and reform their country and who resented the archaism and conservatism of the Bogd Khan's regime. And indeed later, during the troubled 1930s and the rising militarism of Japan, some Eastern Mongol leaders will choose to turn to a militarist but "modern" Japan as a better support of Inner Mongolian independence.)

- Nationalist trend. High clergy or "lamas", as Mongols indifferently call Buddhist monks in general, were not generally in favor of reforming Buddhism, but some were keen on developing a Mongolian form of Buddhism, the " religion of the Jebstundamba lama of the North ", downplaying its Tibetan aspect and the supremacy of the two main religious figures, the Dalai lama or the Panchen Lama, in favor of a Mongolian one [Bawden 1968: 286].

- Social trend. Ordinary clergy was on the other hand in favor of limiting privileges of the high clergy. In the nineteenth century critics were voiced more and more concerning the behavior of many within the monastic community. During the 1920s, the Mongol revolutionary party itself counted many lamas among its ranks and was encouraging class struggle inside the clergy. With some success: in 1925 and 1926, lower ranks of monks in Urga (present-day Ulan-Bator) violently opposed their hierarchy, demanding a more equal share in the income of the monasteries. They also proposed to use Mongolian language for religious teaching and not only Tibetan, the liturgical language: a little step towards religious modernization, although there has been a precedent: the use of Mongolian was more common in the early history of Mongolian Buddhism, and Mongolian liturgy was upheld in an important monastery in Southern (Inner) Mongolia.

# 6 A Forced "Secularization"

Eventually the political context hardened preventing any reform and "internal secularization" of Buddhism to occur (*Komintern* ...1996: see among other documents: n° 60, 7th July 1929 pp. 262 *sq.*, "notes from a meeting of the Secretaries for the Orient of the executive committee of the Comintern"; Pürevjav & Dashjamts 1965)

The new regime, closely guided by the Russian Bolsheviks and the Comintern, followed always closer on their steps. The initial policy aiming at restraining the monasteries' social and economic power, completed with anti-clerical propaganda, was succeeded by a radical atheist line and a direct interfering in religious affairs, culminating with political terror and mass killing in 1937–1939.

The government had forbidden in 1929 the search for the new reincarnation of the Jebtsundamba, delayed since its death five years earlier (1924), as well as of any other religious incarnation in the country. The same year (1929), at the 7th Congress, the more reformist Buddhists willing to conciliate the aims of the party and a "scientific" Buddhist faith were defeated and the project of a reformed Buddhism itself was definitively outlawed. The latter could have been in the long run more subversive for the regime than outright conservative Buddhism (indeed, according to P. Berger/1967, secularized churches in America managed to keep a central symbolic position "only by becoming highly secularized themselves.)

The anti-clericalist measures taken early on by the communist regime to weaken the influence of the Buddhist church had failed. When resistance against the revolutionary government broke out in the country in 1931–1932, local monasteries were at the forefront. The revolt spread quickly and could only be stopped with the help of Soviet military planes.

Eventually, failing to obtain from the Mongols themselves the eradication of this parallel power, what Stalin had called "a state within the state", the Soviets secured the matter in the hands of the Russian secret police (NKVD, People's Commissariat for Internal affairs). Under its direction, while the Great Terror was taking place in Russia, the Mongolian revolutionary ranks were purged, the monastery buildings (some 800) were destroyed but for a few temples, the ordinary monks forcibly secularized and many incorporated into the army while some 20 000 thousand others, among the most educated ones, were executed. By the end of 1939, Buddhism as an institution was officially eradicated. Freedom of religion was still recognized by the constitution, in conformity with the schizophrenic character of totalitarian regimes where discourse and facts are dissociated. After the war a handful of monks were reinstated in a partly preserved monastery to organize some religious service under close scrutiny from the party.

The relative normalization in the 1960s was less obvious in Mongolia than in Eastern Europe (brought up by political change in communist countries and Rome's new Eastern Policy following Vatican II).

In 1990, the collapse of Soviet Union brought in political and religious pluralism in the old satellite country. Mongol authorities started to apply Western models of political and economic governance. The period was marked by a strong religious revival characterized on the one hand by a return of local religions to many archaic features dating back to the stage when practice had to be suddenly abandoned at the time of persecution, and on the other hand by the arrival of dozens of foreign religions and religious movements, mainly protestant and often aggressively proselyte denominations. The latter situation led Mongolian political actors to make a distinction between the traditional religions, especially Buddhism, and the non-traditional or foreign religions that attracted mostly young people.

The 4th Constitution adopted in 1992 specifies (§ 9) that the state respect religions and that religions respect the state, and establishes a separation between church and state, corresponding this time to real life. An important change was brought regarding the wording. While the "fundamental laws" of the Soviet era mentioned "religion" (*shashin*), clearly targeting Buddhism but including Mongolian Khazaks' islam and shaman's rites, D. Tchoijamts, abbot of the Gandan monastery and member of the Parliament (Great Khural) and other religiously inclined members insisted on replacing religion (*shashin*) by church (*litt.* "monasteries", *süm khiid*). In the abbot's view, as he expressed many times, Buddhism is inseparable from Mongolia itself and in this perspective cannot be separated from the state of Mongolia. The idea of separation or independence of church and state is on the contrary well perceived by Buddhist authorities and clerics after decades of persecution by the state. The Constitution's provisions were detailed in the 1993 Law regulating relations between church and state (*tör*), in which § 4 underlines the privileged status of Buddhism: "Mongolia respect the preeminent position (*zonkhilox bair suuri*) of Buddhism on the ground of social peace and harmony (*ard tümnii ev negdel*) and of cultural history". If the new state and its representatives have sometimes appeared biased towards one religion by being supportive of Mongolian Buddhism and expressing publicly their worries about the latter's difficulty to adapt to today's population, and notably the Mongol youth, nevertheless the post-communist period can be considered as an era where a real secularization process appears to be actively engaged.

Analysing post-communist countries in terms of de-secularization should thus be questioned. As indicated by several authors, secularization should not be equated with the absence of religion or of religiosity in society. Looking from the Mongolian case, the possibility of political pluralism at the state level, and of freedom of conscience, religious or ideological, at the citizen level were important conditions for a secular state and a secularized society to take shape, for religions to go through their own internal secularization, and for individuals to opt for new choices.

To come to the point, can such a violent process, taking place in a totalitarian context, involving in practice (rights enshrined in the successive constitutions remained virtual) a non-neutral state, a non-separation of the two spheres of religion and state, and no freedom of conscience, be labelled a "secular state"? Would it fit the borderline case defined by Bauberot & Millot as "laïcité anti-religieuse/anti-religious secularism"?

Buddhism was being eradicated as an institution and as actors rather than opposed (the Buddhist showcase put in place at the Gandan monastery after WW2 with a handful of monks to prove the commitment of the new regime to religious freedom is not worth much more that the rights enshrined in the constitution), freedom of conscience was excluding not only religious freedom but any other views and hostile opinions, all with the assumed goal of replacing the former religion by another dominant ideology that would concern all aspects of life and society, in other words with the goal of establishing a new dominant faith. From such perspective, the communist regime has prevented rather than stimulated a secularizing process that was developing along local lines. If a secularizing process happened regarding the former dominant religion, the anticlerical action helping to pull the state and the society from the grip of the dominating Buddhist institution, it was immediately annihilated by the imposition of a new, ultra-dominant ideology. It stopped any possibility of a social process towards more autonomy from a dominant ideology, be it a former religion or a new dogma.

According to several sociologists (Dobbelaere, Wilson, Peter Berger, Yves Lambert sand Irena Borowik), patterns of social changes resulting in rising secularism in Eastern and Western Europe were similar, and again in the 1980s, when the opposite trend of religious revitalization emerged in central European countries. Some authors spoke of anti-secularization processes (anon. 1986, cited by Borowik 2006), implying that secularization took place.

Yves Lambert, in his 2004 article, identifies three similar trends in both Western and Eastern Europe: towards a decline of Christian faith, towards a Christian renewal, and a trend of the type "believing without belonging". To his eyes, the tendency towards "a sort of pluralist secularization", open to various religious expressions, constitutes a "radical de-secularization" in the post-communist countries.

Siniša Zrinščak (2004) notes that religious revival appeared strongest in post-communist countries where anti-clerical repression had been the more violent and had the strongest impact (Russia, Estonia, Ukraine, and we can add Mongolia). This last view is not entirely shared by Irena Borowik. She argues that religiosity in Russia and Orthodox countries after years of imposed atheism has many features in common with religiosity in western secular countries. She sees an external rather than a deep religiosity and considers—with reason—that it is a return to tradition, an attempt to reconstruct the continuity of historical experience that 1917 had interrupted, which plays a role in keeping national identities (2002: 504–505). Orthodoxy provides a sense of belonging as in Europe, even to the non-believers, the difference lying in the role devoted to religion and orthodoxy in the forming of the identities, whether individual, national, cultural and political" (2006: 275).

Concerning the modernization aspect, Zrinščak argues that it a partial and deviant one, it was restricted to an economical and political process but it failed to reach the core of the society, which makes it improper to speak of secularization about communist regimes. Tomka also commented in 2002 on "communist modernity" which is characterized by a systematic effort to hinder social regeneration and autonomy, was marked by institutionalized anomie and enforced individualism. In an earlier study (1991) he had suggested that the apparently secularist manifestations under communism came from the quick and violent destruction of the old social system and the social anomie that resulted from it. Tomka clearly refutes the reality of secularization under Communism: for this author religion was instead reinforced in its role of cultural memory and foundation for opposition. The role devoted to Buddhism by political representatives in contemporary Mongolia comforts this analysis. As a former president (N. Bagabandi) explained in 1998, during a conference devoted to the relations between the state and actors of the Mongolian (traditional) religions, Buddhism had a specific role in providing society with ethics and rule and a duty to reform itself and adapt to the needs of today's Mongols (anon. 1998). Despite the slow improvement by monasteries to train more and better educated monks and the low level of control and regulation of Buddhist bodies, not depending on a controlling center, this trend has not decreased. Worries are still regularly vented in the press by Mongols suspicious of the place religions are taking in the country. Some questioned the support provided by the state under the separation of church and state, evoked the risk of civil unrest that religious infighting might induce. In recent years appeared also fears of seeing China, a huge economic partner now but an aggressive neighbor in the past, manipulating influent monks to interfere with the recognition of the tenth Jebtsundamba, a very political issue. The ninth Jetsundamba, a Tibetan whom choice had been sanctioned by the Dalai lama, died in Mongolia ten years ago, a way of preparing his return this time in a Mongol child as no other option would be acceptable to most Mongols. Due to the high political charge of this figure, the issue proves to be very complex as well as dividing.

In the last few years, political authorities (namely the president Kh. Battulga and the then Prime minister U. Khürelsükh (he was elected president in 2021) belonging to the two main parties have both underlined the civilizational role expecting from Buddhism in shaping the country, reminding the clerics of the need for the state to the important experience of the monks and the Buddhist people in developing harmonious relations and reciprocal respect, in ruling the country according to the 'tradition of Dual Principle going back to Chinggis Khan' (sic), expressing publicly their faith (from Kh. Battulga's speech at the 9th Peace Conference of Asian Buddhists, on June 21, 2019). At the end of the same year, the Parliament adopted an amendment making the birth of the Buddha an official public holiday, the "Day of respecting ethics", following what is already done in several South-East Asian countries, and was officially celebrated in June 2020.

In addition to fellow Buddhist countries in Asia, with whom Mongolian Buddhist representatives had been encouraged to develop relations by the communist regime (in the interest of the international policy of the Soviet bloc), the United States' religious policy provides an inspiration to the Mongols. This view is exposed by N. Narantuyaa, a university professor, in an article on the need for improving ethics in Mongolian politics, impacted by corruption, published in *Sonin* (January 7, 2014) where she stresses that American democracy, science and technology do not imply atheism as the corresponding ethics, but go hand in hand with Christianity forming the basis of their national ethics. Following this path, she envisions a different, secularized approach to Buddhism that does not need to coincide with the traditional submission to religion or faith: Mongolian Buddhism offers many spiritual, ethical, and spiritual resource to the modern individual, as well as methods for his physical and mental well-being that can be included in the scholl curriculum. Mongols, she argues, can learn from the Americans the ways to make Buddhism the guide of state norms and ethics. Such views support Borowik and other East European researchers on the paradoxical effects of the program of atheization which once interrupted, has produced spontaneous process of secularization. As a concept, we can see that secularization has not lost its interpretative and comparative value.

# 7 Conclusion

In view of the Mongolian experience the reality of such secularization process is very debatable. Instead of limiting the preeminence of religion in society, the communist regime aimed at the concrete elimination of a religion that posed a threat to the total preeminence of its own ideology. Atheism was not freely chosen, not a consequence of social development but a part of the totalitarian rule, which came and stayed by violent means. Communism ideology was unchallenged. In obliterating religious traditions altogether, communism made impossible a laicization process which would imply the presence of a religious actor/a church on the one hand, and an effective separation from the state on the other hand, conditions which were formulated in the Constitutions of 1924, 1940 and 1960) but had no equivalent in real life. Buddhism became an object of knowledge for a few intellectuals in the academic field, but as a religion, it was left untouched for better times. Having had no possibility to go through the changes experienced by the main population, the Buddhist institution was no longer in phase with the Mongols when religious freedom reappeared in the 1990s.

Due to the radical purges at the time of the "Great Terror" (1938–1939) and the on-going anti-religious policy in the following decades, Mongolian Buddhism and its actors were crushed or extremely weakened: Buddhism was not in a position to become, as the Catholic church in Poland, a strong resource against communist alienation, nor could it accompany the struggle against the regime. But it remained symbolically significant. Freedom of religion was one of the pressing political demands in 1989.

Another consequence for the religious institutions in communist countries is that they were not able to undergo their own, internal secularization: religions emerged from communism little transformed on socio-cultural matters in comparison with their Western Europe counterparts. In a special issue of *Social Compass* dedicated to the religious restoration in Eastern Europe (49/4, 2002) several contributions showed that local churches lacked the necessary skills and information to cope with democracy. As summarized by M. Tomka in his introduction, Communist states hindered the development of adequate church organizations and promoted the strictly clerical character of these churches, leaving them structurally inapt for the challenges in post-communist countries (492–493). In Mongolia, once the one-party rule was dropped by the party in the spring 1990, Buddhism resumed its activity where it had brutally stopped, the feeble and distorted shadow of its old self. In comparison with mainstream religions in Eastern or Central Europe, it suffered a bigger blow, reduced to ashes and its huge monastic population either terminated or defrocked. Buddhism was thus eradicated, and its foundations had been shattered. The minimal Buddhist activity which was allowed to resume in 1944 has very little to do with even the reduced state of Buddhism in the mid-1930s. The tiny community of Buddhist monks, selected and controlled by the party, was never in a position to either challenge the regime or compromise it as did the Russian Orthodox church, nor in a position to train a reasonable number of monks that could overlook the revival of hundreds of temples in the aftermath of democracy. Rather, a form of anarchy prevailed allowing a few to take advantage of situation and act as lamas for the sake of money. Confronted with newly arrived foreign religious rivals that had gone through modernization and organizational secularization, Mongolian Buddhism found itself in a difficult situation and was slow to adapt. Buddhist monks did not enjoy much prestige and for years article in the press criticized or deplored the insufficiencies of the monks. Globalized Christianity was perceived in Mongolia in the 1990s as modern, in phase with the new generations, contrary to the Mongolian Buddhist institution (Even 2012). The latter shared three out of the four pressing problems faced by the Orthodox church listed by Borowik (2006): internal splits, lack of trained personnel and competition with other, very proselyte religions. (As for the fourth problem, "disagreements over property", it has not been raised: the said property has been almost entirely destroyed leaving almost no trace, and land property did not exist in Mongolian nomadic culture. Yet some religious authorities consider with envy the favorable treatment accorded to the Orthodox church by the Russian state). For the Mongol government, eager to maintain the recently recovered expression of national identity, one of the pressing tasks for Mongolian Buddhism was, and still is, to reform itself to fit the new needs of the country and to compete efficiently against the foreign religions, mainly Christian denominations, threatening the Mongolian cultural heritage.

If one follows Taylor's description of secularism as the opening of a plurality of options against pre-modern "unchallenged" God or unchallenged faith, communist practice (rather than discourse) falls within the unchallenged faith, or rather creed, not within secularism. S. Luerhrmann's rejects (2015) the religious metaphor for describing the communist system, arguing that its overlooks the difference in the object of faith and insisting on the human, not divine dimension of the communist ideology, and that equating communism and religion prevents our perception of the "dynamics of socialism". Yet ideological discourse and reality are dissociated in totalitarian regimes and create a schizophrenic environment. The divine nature of the sacralized figures of "Marx, Engels, Lenin, Stalin" may not be necessary to turn them in object of religious faith, as the human figures of the Christ and the Gautama Buddha show. Ideologues and secularized individual can have different perception of faith and religion from ordinary people, erudite monks and ordinary Tibetan or Mongolian Buddhists differ too. Fulfilling the same functions is not without consequences as it creates religious dispositions in people, as observed already after Lenin's death around its remains.

Considering the case of Mongolia, M. Tomka's earlier (2002: 549) remarks doubting the reality of a "de-secularization" appear more appropriate. In communist regimes coercion thwarted the functional differentiation induced by the modernization of the economy and eventually strengthened the function of religion as cultural memory, which became manifest after 1990: what was then observed could have been attempts, he suggested, to regenerate societies not yet secularized. Secularization is more of a future challenge for most post-communist societies.

# References

Anon. 1998. *Tör, süm khiidiin khariltsaa: orchin üye* [The relations of state and monasteries today]. Ulaanbaatar: Bembi-sang publishing house.
Vrcan, Srdan. 1986. "Omladina osamdesetih godina, religija i crkva [Youth in the 1980s, Religion and Church]". In F. Radin, ed., *Položaj, svest i ponašanje mlade generacije*

*Jugoslavije*, Zagreb, Beograd: CIDID i Institut za društvena istraživanja Sveučilišta u Zagrebu.

Asad, Talal. 1993. *Genealogies of Religion*. Baltimore: Johns Hopkins University.

Bagabandi, Natsagiin. 2001. *Shine tsag üye ba Mongoliin burkhanii shashinii ömnökh shine zorilt* [The new goals of Mongolian Buddhism in the new era]. Ulaanbaatar: Urlakh Erdem.

Bawden, Charles R. 1989 [1968]. *The History of Modern Mongolia*. London and New York: Kegan Paul International.

Borowik, Irina. 2002. "Between Orthodoxy and Eclecticism: On the Religious Transformation of Russia, Belarus and Ukraine". *Social Compass* 49 no. 4: 497–508.

Borowik, Irina. 2006. "Orthodoxy confronting the Collapse of Communism in Post-Soviet Countries". *Social Compass* 53 no. 2: 267–278.

Bruce, Steve. ed. 1992. *Religion and Modernization. Sociologists and Historians Debate the Secularization Thesis*. Oxford: Clarendon Press.

Casanova, Jose. 1994. *Public Religions in the Modern World*. Chicago: University of Chicago Press.

Casanova, Jose. 2019. *Global Religious and Secular Dynamics. The Modern System of Classification*. Leiden, Boston: Brill.

Dobbelaere, Karel. 1981. "Secularization: a multi-dimensional concept". *Current Sociology* 29 no. 2: 1–216 (reprinted 2002 in *Secularization: An analysis at three levels*)

Eisenstadt, Schmuel. 2000. "Multiple Modernities". *Daedalus* 129 : 1–29.

Even, Marie-Dominique. 2012. "Ritual efficacy or spiritual quest? Buddhism and modernity in post-communist Mongolia". In K. Buffetrille ed., *Revisiting Rituals in a Changing Tibetan World?* pp. 241–271. Leiden-Boston: Brill.

*Komintern ba Mongol: barimtiin emkhetgel*. [The Comintern and Mongolia: collection of documents]. 1996. National Mongolian Archives and Archives of Russia, Ulaanbaatar.

Lambert, Yves. 2004. "Des changements dans l'évolution religieuse de l'Europe et de la Russie". *Revue française de sociologie* 45 no. 2: 307–338.

Luerhmann, Sonja. 2015. "Was Soviet Society Secular? Undoing Equations between Communism and Religion". In Tam T.T. Ngo and J.B. Quijada, eds., *Atheist Secularism and its Discontents. A comparative Study of Religion and Communism in Eurasia*, pp. 134–151. Palgrave Macmillan.

Martin, David. 1969. *The Religious and the Secular. Studies in Secularization*. London: Routledge and Kegan.

Pürevjav, S., D. Dashjamts. 1965. *BNMAU-d süm khiid, lam nariin asuudliig shiidverlesen ni (1921 1940)* [The settling of the question of monasteries and monks in the People's Republic of Mongolia]. Ulaanbaatar: State Publishing Committee.

Taylor, Charles. 2007. *A Secular Age*. Cambridge Mss: Belknap Press of Harvard University Press.

Tomka, Miklós. 2002. "Tendances de la religiosité et de l'orientation vers les Eglises en Europe de l'Est ". *Social Compass* 49 no. 4: 537–552.

Tomka, Miklós. 2006. "Is conventional sociology on Religion able to deal with differences between Eastern and European developments?" *Social Compass* 53 no. 2: 251–265.

Tsedendamba, Samdangiin. 2003. *Mongol Uls dakhi shashinii nökhtsöl baidal* [The Religious situation in Mongolia]. Ulaanbaatar: State University.

Zrinščak. Siniša. 2004. "Generations and atheisms: Patterns of response to communist rule among different generations and countries". *Social Compass* 51 no. 2: 221–234.

# Index

*Adat* 97–105, 111
*Agama* 12, 72, 73, 80, 93–111
Agnosticism 152
Akbar (Emperor) 27, 33, 150
Aligarh 148
Anticlerical 52, 122f., 167, 190, 239
Anti-religious 15, 50, 53f., 119, 129, 131, 152, 174, 178, 229, 231, 238, 241
Apostasy 152
Arabic 16, 29, 85, 97, 152
Arakan (Rakhine State) 207, 215
Asad, Talal 25, 65, 116, 145, 149, 159f., 164, 206, 229
Atheism 15, 37, 79, 82, 117, 125, 128, 149, 152, 229, 231f., 235, 239, 241
Attatürk, Mustafa Kemal 75
Aung San Suu Kyi 221f.
Azad, Abul Kalam 147

Bali 12f., 93–96, 98–111
Bangladesh 27, 29, 35f., 53, 65, 207
Bhargava, Rajeev 4f., 21, 55, 146, 151, 157f., 160
BJP 27, 33
Blasphemy 31, 86f., 152
Brahmin 149
Brahmo Samaj 148
Burma (Myanmar) see Myanmar (Burma)

China (PRC) 9–11, 13f., 16, 21–23, 26–30, 36, 38, 53f., 61–65, 67, 117, 125, 181, 187, 198, 231f., 240
China (Republican) 6, 9, 11, 13f., 26–30, 37, 53f., 61–68, 75, 168, 178f., 187f., 190f., 193f., 197–201, 234f.
Chinese Communist Party 10, 37, 64, 187
Chondoism 36
Christendom 206
Civil society 34, 54, 118f., 132, 135, 153, 210f.,215, 223, 227
Communalism 147
Communist Party 10, 14, 37, 64, 82, 117, 129f., 181, 187

Confucius 55, 175, 179f., 199
Congress Party 147, 158

Daikyōin 174
Dalai lama 234, 236, 240
Dalit 154, 158
Darva Bandida 235
Democracy 8, 16, 21f., 37, 40, 46, 48f., 73, 75f., 79, 81, 84, 117, 141, 159, 172, 179, 181, 201, 207, 212, 223, 225f., 231f., 242
Desecularization 2, 59, 85, 115, 118f., 132f., 143
*Dharma* 13, 95–98, 101, 105–108, 110f., 150, 152, 232
*Đổi mới* 115, 117, 119, 130–134
Dutch 9, 12, 28, 72, 75f., 78, 97–101, 103–105

Egypt 73f.
Europe 5–8, 11–13, 20, 22–24, 38, 52, 54f., 57, 62f., 65–68, 78, 99, 132, 135, 163, 169, 172–175, 177, 181, 195, 200, 229, 234, 237, 239, 241f.

Falungong 10, 68
Freedom of conscience 14–16, 19–22, 28, 30–35, 37f., 43, 46–52, 79, 152f., 157, 166, 170, 183, 190–192, 201, 220, 230, 238f.

Gandhi, Mahatma 54, 62, 65, 68, 75, 150
Gelugpa 233–235
Gender 20, 155, 210
Germany 6, 66, 231
Gotama 209
Great Britain 6, 9, 11f., 27f., 35, 78, 145, 150f., 153, 160, 225

Hindu 9, 12f., 22f., 27, 33, 38, 53f., 65, 67f., 72, 75, 77f., 93, 95f., 99–101, 103–111, 146–151, 154–160
*Hindu Bali* 103–107, 110f.

Hizbut Tahrir 88
Hòa Hảo Buddhists 36, 128, 130
Holy See 190, 197

India 1, 4, 6, 8–13, 15f., 21–23, 27, 29, 33, 35, 37, 46, 48, 53, 55, 61–68, 96f., 101–103, 105–109, 145–160, 206, 210, 216, 232
Indonesia 92, 16, 28f., 37, 53, 71–89, 93–99, 104–111
Inoue Tetsujirō 172, 175, 179–181
Institutionalization 8, 12, 36, 123–125, 168

Jainism 147
Japan 2, 6, 9–14, 16, 21, 25–27, 33, 53, 55, 58, 66, 74, 121, 123, 133, 163–183, 188, 191, 235f.
Java 76–79, 85, 95f., 100–103, 108
Jinjakyoku 178
Jinnah, Muhammad Ali 35, 54, 62, 152
Jokowi 87f.
Judaism 8, 147

Katzenstein, Peter 30
*Kokutai* 176, 181f.,
Korea 6, 9f., 14, 22, 25f., 32f., 36f., 53f., 178, 181
Kshtriya 149
Kuomintang 65
Kyōbushō 173f.
*Kyōka* 178–181, 183

Lamaism 235
Latin America 7f., 23, 25, 31
Liang Qichao 188, 192, 195

Mabatha 205, 207–209, 215–225
Mahana 217, 221f., 224f.
Malay 8, 16, 19, 27–29, 31, 38, 72, 96f., 99, 101, 105
Malaysia 10, 28, 35f., 74, 78
Malraux, André 56
Manchu Empire 191, 234
Masyumi 73, 81
Meiji era 165, 170, 173
Missionaries (Christian) 8, 64, 77, 93f., 96f., 102, 104, 121f., 151, 187, 196f.

Modernity 2, 6, 8, 19–34, 36–38, 53, 63f., 66, 78, 89, 113, 116, 121f., 133, 167, 201, 229, 231, 235, 240
Modi, Narendra 62, 158
Mongolia 6, 9f., 12, 15f., 29f., 32f., 53, 229–243
*Moriscos* 168
Mughal 27, 33, 150f., 153
Muhammadiyah 83f.
Multiple modernities 6, 17, 19–41, 77, 89, 119, 126, 142, 230, 244
Myanmar (Burma) 9–11, 35f., 54, 65, 205–218, 223–225

Nahdlatul Ulama 73, 83f.
Nakae Chōmin 171f., 175–177
Nakamura Masanao 170
Nakayama Seiji 171
Ne Win 213–216, 218
Nepal 29, 32, 53
Nestorian Christianism 232
New religious movements/New religion 36, 84, 103, 117, 123, 200
Nishi Amane 170, 175
North Africa 8, 25

Oceania 23
Okuyama Michiaki 165
Opinion 48, 82, 94, 102, 108, 127, 132, 155, 189, 198, 201, 208, 224, 239
Opium wars 26, 191, 196
Orthodoxy/Heterodoxy 56, 87, 100, 112f., 152, 161, 176, 239, 244
Ottoman 29

Pakistan 6, 10, 27, 33, 35, 38, 53f., 62f., 65, 68, 73f., 147, 151f., 156
Pali 210, 216
Pancasila 12, 28, 37, 71–75, 77, 79–81, 83–89
Panchen lama 234, 236
Poland 231, 242
Postcolonial 4, 14, 63, 68, 119, 124f., 135, 142, 147f., 151, 158, 208
Pluralism 3, 15, 48, 56, 78, 88, 113, 115, 119, 123, 128f., 163, 166f., 169, 173, 182f., 210, 225, 227, 237f.

Public sphere/space  6, 38, 128, 130, 135, 153, 159, 168, 177, 186, 202, 212, 214

Rakhine  see Arakan (Rakhine State)
Religious policy  40, 71f., 83, 115, 117, 119f., 127, 129–131, 141, 143, 173–175, 177, 241
Reunification  117, 119, 129f., 142
Revolution  22, 38, 70, 123, 125, 127f., 131, 142f., 178, 189f., 203, 211, 214, 219, 223, 234f.
Rohingyas  207f., 216, 220
Rule of Law  15, 22, 40, 116, 133, 135
Russia  29, 178, 231f., 234–237, 239, 242f.

Sangha  28, 33, 132, 209–211, 213–219, 221, 223–225
Sanskrit  27, 72, 75, 77, 79, 94–97, 233
Saudi Arabia  74
Secularism  1–8, 15f., 21f., 33, 43, 45–50, 52, 55f., 58, 61, 63–65, 67–69, 72, 74, 83–86, 89, 95, 116–119, 121, 124–125, 127f., 131f., 139, 145–160, 163–169, 171, 176, 187f., 199, 201, 205f., 212, 214, 225, 230, 238f., 243
Secularity  2–5, 15, 61, 63, 95, 98, 115f., 118, 120, 122, 124, 131–133, 135, 150, 164, 166, 168, 205f., 209f., 212, 221f., 224f., 229–231
Secularization  1–6, 15, 43–48, 53–58, 64, 66, 72, 88, 93, 95, 97, 105, 111, 115–120, 124, 126f., 129, 132f., 135, 139, 145, 148, 160, 163–166, 169, 171f., 182f., 194–196, 206, 209, 211, 217, 225, 229–232, 236, 238–243
Shaiva  95
Shakta  95
Shamanism  9, 33, 232, 238
Shibunkai  180f.
Shinto  9, 13, 33, 66, 163–165, 167–171, 173–175, 177–183
Shūkyōkyoku  178
Sikhism  147
Sinitic  9, 14, 19f., 26–29, 31–34, 36f., 53
Soekarno  72, 74–82, 87

Soviet Union  24, 29, 123, 125, 229, 237
Sri Lanka  29, 35f., 54, 62, 65, 210, 219
Stalinism  23
State-church  59, 116, 127
Suharto  80–84, 88, 110
Sui dynasty  200
Sun Yat Sen  75
Superstition  10, 36, 61, 63–65, 69f., 94, 97, 103, 128, 130, 175f., 196, 200f., 233, 235

Taiping  26, 67
Taishō period  172, 179
Taiwan  9f., 14, 22, 26, 32f., 37, 53f., 187
Taixu  193
Tang dynasty  13, 200
Taoism  137, 168, 172, 181, 199, 232
Taylor, Charles  2, 5, 15, 77, 132, 205, 229f., 234, 243
Theravadin  209f., 213, 215, 224
Three Kingdoms  200
Tibetan  67, 233f., 236, 240, 243
Tokugawa dynasty  168, 173
Tominaga Nakamoto  168
Tôn giáo  26, 121, 128, 130, 132–134, 137–141
Turkey  1f., 5, 7, 21, 25, 29, 31, 43, 73–75

Uyghur  10, 67
United States  3, 5, 7, 17f., 22f., 31, 40, 49, 59, 116, 163, 188, 198, 234, 241

Vaishnava  95
Vietnam  6, 9–11, 14–16, 26, 36f., 53, 62–65, 67, 113, 116–119, 121–135
Vivekananda  150

Wohlrab-Sahr, Monika  3, 25

Xi Jinping  22, 62
Xinjiang  29, 67

Yasuoka Masahiro  181, 183
Yoshida Kumaji  179

Zhengjiao fenli  187, 191, 193f.

www.ingramcontent.com/pod-product-compliance
Lightning Source LLC
Chambersburg PA
CBHW050521170426
43201CB00013B/2043